MINIMUM CONTRACT JUSTICE

The collapse of the Rana Plaza in Bangladesh (2013) is one of many cases to invoke critical scrutiny and moral outrage regarding the conditions under which consumer goods sold on our markets are produced elsewhere. In spite of abiding moral concerns, these goods remain popular and consumers continue to buy them. Such transactions for goods made under deplorable production conditions are usually presumed to count as 'normal' market transactions, ie transactions that are recognized as valid consumer-contracts under the rules of contract law.

This book challenges this presumption of normality. It explores the question of how theories of justice bear on such consumer contracts; how should a society treat a transaction for a good made under deplorable conditions elsewhere? This book defends the position that a society that strives to be minimally just should not lend its power to enforce, support, or encourage transactions that are incompatible with the ability of others elsewhere to live decent human lives. As such, the book introduces a new perspective on the legal debate concerning deplorable production conditions that has settled around ideas of corporate responsibility, and the pursuit of international labour rights.

Minimum Contract Justice: A Capabilities Perspective on Sweatshops and Consumer Contracts

Lyn K L Tjon Soei Len

·HART·
PUBLISHING
OXFORD AND PORTLAND, OREGON
2017

Hart Publishing
An imprint of Bloomsbury Publishing Plc

Hart Publishing Ltd
Kemp House
Chawley Park
Cumnor Hill
Oxford OX2 9PH
UK

Bloomsbury Publishing Plc
50 Bedford Square
London
WC1B 3DP
UK

www.hartpub.co.uk
www.bloomsbury.com

Published in North America (US and Canada) by
Hart Publishing
c/o International Specialized Book Services
920 NE 58th Avenue, Suite 300
Portland, OR 97213-3786
USA

www.isbs.com

HART PUBLISHING, the Hart/Stag logo, BLOOMSBURY and the Diana logo are trademarks of Bloomsbury Publishing Plc

First published 2017

British Library Cataloguing-in-Publication Data
A catalogue record for this book is available from the British Library.

ISBN: HB: 978-1-78225-709-7
ePDF: 978-1-78225-711-0
ePub: 978-1-78225-710-3

Library of Congress Cataloging-in-Publication Data

Names: Tjon Soei Len, Lyn K.L. (Lyn Kim Lan), 1984–

Title: Minimum contract justice : a capabilities perspective on sweatshops and consumer contracts / Lyn K L Tjon Soei Len.

Description: Oxford ; Portland, Oregon : Hart Publishing, An imprint of Bloomsbury Publishing Plc, 2017. | Includes bibliographical references and index.

Identifiers: LCCN 2016054442 (print) | LCCN 2016055157 (ebook) | ISBN 9781782257097 (hardback : alk. paper) | ISBN 9781782257103 (Epub)

Subjects: LCSH: Foreign trade regulation—Moral and ethical aspects—Europe. | Offshore assembly industry—Law and legislation—Moral and ethical aspects—Europe. | Consumer goods—Law and legislation—Moral and ethical aspects—Europe. | Immoral contracts—Europe. | Law and globalization—Law and legislation—Moral and ethical aspects—Europe.

Classification: LCC KJC6791 .T58 2017 (print) | LCC KJC6791 (ebook) | DDC 343.408/7—dc23

LC record available at https://lccn.loc.gov/2016054442

Typeset by Compuscript Ltd, Shannon
Printed and bound in Great Britain by TJ International Ltd, Padstow, Cornwall

ACKNOWLEDGEMENTS

Very many people have helped to make this book possible. I owe a tremendous debt to all who have offered me their support, given me a sense of belonging and possibility, and a sense of home in academia and the world.

I would like to specially thank several people and institutions, while asking for the forgiveness of those I might unintentionally omit to acknowledge.

I like to thank Martijn Hesselink for his steadfast confidence in me, and for creating and inviting me to my first academic home. It is there that I met so many of the friends and colleagues who are the foundation of the academic community for which I am so grateful. I like to express my sincere gratitude to those who have given me advice, helpful comments, and excellent suggestions that have made this book better than it would have been otherwise: Chantal Mak, Hugh Collins, Aurelia Colombi Ciacchi, Aukje van Hoek, Anna Veneziano, Jeroen Kortmann, and Ton Hol. I am especially grateful to Aditi Bagchi for her friendship, dedication of time to read the manuscript, and insightful comments. Likewise, I am especially thankful to Hanoch Dagan for his kindness in reading and commenting on my work. I also like to thank Daniela Caruso, Franz Werro, and Muriel Fabre-Magnan for showing encouraging interest in my work and offering their academic support.

Alongside experiencing thoughtful exchanges with international scholars, I have received generous support from various institutions. In particular, I like to thank the following institutions and audiences: the Centre for the Study of European Contract Law, the Amsterdam Law School of the University of Amsterdam, the University of Chicago Law School, the Forum Scientiarum of the University of Tübingen, the Institute for Advanced Study in Nantes, Harvard Law School, and the University of New Hampshire.

I also like to thank Yvonne ter Horst for years of wonderful collaboration. Additionally, I wish to express my appreciation to both Bill Asquith, my editor at Hart Publishing, and Victoria Broom, for copyediting the manuscript. Also, I must thank my (former) colleagues at the Amsterdam Law School, particularly Anniek de Ruijter, Stephan Hollenberg, Joasia Luzak, Jaap Baaij, Dewi Hamwijk, and Jaap Barneveld for their friendship. And my sincere gratitude is owed to my colleagues at the University of New Hampshire. Of these, a particular note of thanks is due to Marla Brettschneider and Julia Pond, without whom I could not have finished this work.

Finally, I am grateful for the love and support of my family: Liesbeth Bergman; Robert and Lian Tjon Soei Len; Taco, May Li, and Qilan Houwert; Astrid Helstone; and Laurel, Winston A., and Lauren Thompson. I am thankful for the same from my friends Kim Meertins and Eva van Steijn.

Most importantly, I want to thank Winston Charles Thompson for his unrivalled virtues, and ability to love. And Elliot Oliver Thompson, who is the greatest joy in our lives; his arrival and existence has shifted the world of my values and provides a renewed sense of perspective in my endeavours.

CONTENTS

LIST OF CASES

Netherlands

Germany

France

England

Introduction

Our lives are connected to the lives of others through globally sourced consumer goods. As consumers, we encounter the products of others' work all around us. While this is no new phenomenon, details about the lives of other people elsewhere and the conditions under which they produce goods that are sold on our markets are more readily available than ever. Notably, in recent years there have been numerous occasions that raised public awareness about deplorable production conditions. On 11 January 2012, mainstream media reported on the threat of mass suicide by Chinese assembly line workers at a factory that produces popular consumer goods.[1] Reports varied regarding the number of workers (ranging from 80 to 300) who threatened to end their lives and the news regenerated concern regarding actual suicides at the same location a few years earlier, allegedly caused by poor working conditions.[2] On 24 April 2013, the Rana Plaza in Bangladesh collapsed, killing more than 1100 people.[3] The majority of those who lost their lives were factory workers, predominantly women, who laboured in one of the garment factories that were housed in the Rana Plaza. The Foxconn suicides in China (2010–2012) and the collapse of the Rana Plaza in Bangladesh are just two of many cases reported by mainstream media to invoke critical scrutiny regarding the conditions under which popular consumer goods sold on our markets are produced elsewhere.[4]

[1] See: M Rundle, 'Microsoft Investigating Mass Suicide Threat By Chinese Workers At Foxconn Xbox Plant' www.huffingtonpost.co.uk/2012/01/11/microsoft-investigating-mass-suicide-at-foxconn-plant_n_1198860.html, accessed 15 September 2015; A Chakrabortty, 'The Woman who Nearly Died Making your Ipad' *The Guardian*, www.theguardian.com/commentisfree/2013/aug/05/woman-nearly-died-making-ipad, accessed 15 September 2015.

[2] 'Taiwan iPhone-Maker Foxconn Suffers another Death' *The BBC, Online*, www.bbc.co.uk/news/10169595, accessed 15 September 2015; D Barboza, 'String of Suicides Continues at Electronics Supplier in China' *The New York Times*, Online Edition http://www.nytimes.com/2010/05/26/technology/26suicide.html, accessed 15 September 2015.

[3] JA Manik, 'Western Firms Feel Pressure as Toll Rises in Bangladesh' *The New York Times* www.nytimes.com/2013/04/26/world/asia/bangladeshi-collapse-kills-many-garment-workers.html, accessed 15 September 2015.

[4] See for instance: M Bunting, 'Sweatshops are Still Supplying High Street Brands' *The Guardian*, Online Edition www.guardian.co.uk/global-development/poverty-matters/2011/apr/28/sweatshops-supplying-high-street-brands, accessed 15 September 2015. With regard to environmental damage, see: 'Shell dringt affakkelen gas in Nigeria terug' *Het NRC Handelsblad*, Online Edition http://vorige.nrc.nl//economie/article2547901.ece/Shell_dringt_affakkelen_gas_in_Nigeria_terug, accessed 15 September 2015. With regard to modern forms of slavery see: 'Pact to End African "chocolate slavery"' *The BBC, Online* http://news.bbc.co.uk/2/hi/africa/1963617.stm, accessed 15 September 2015.

These goods figure as intimate elements in our lives: we exchange money to eat these goods, to wear them, and use them to communicate and write books, which makes the association between these goods and the deplorable production conditions under which they are produced unsettling. Although we are often physically removed from the locations where, and the ways in which the goods we buy are made, our knowledge thereof is often not so remote. As a topic of debate, cases involving deplorable production conditions have proven to be structural and persistent over time, receiving media, political and academic attention, raising broad moral concern.

Arguably, these moral concerns arise in part because these cases entail market activities that are perceived as imposing unacceptable costs on others who are already disadvantaged. The production of goods under deplorable conditions, externalises costs that are associated with producing goods under decent conditions.[5] The market transactions between consumers and corporations for sweatshop goods do not reflect the costs of decent production. Instead, these costs are externalised to and borne by those who are affected by deplorable conditions, but who lack the ability to adjust their conduct accordingly in response to these market activities.

In spite of moral outrage regarding the conditions under which popular brands produce their goods, these goods are still offered on our markets and consumers continue to buy them. Those transactions are usually presumed to count as 'normal' market transactions, ie, transactions that are recognised as valid consumer-contracts under the rules of contract law. This book challenges the presumption of normality and asks whether these transactions should be considered as 'normal' or acceptable at all.

Considered as cases of cost externalisation, consumer contracts for sweatshop goods raise a particular concern in the current global setting. Although the globalisation of economic and social cooperation is praised for the potential to contribute to economic growth and human welfare, the current distribution of advantages and disadvantages thereof is heavily criticised as unjust. Those who are already the most vulnerable and who have the least power, bear a disproportionate share of the disadvantages of global cooperation.[6] In this context, imposing costs of market activities on others who are disadvantaged elsewhere exacerbates global

[5] See: Van Dam, C, *Onderneming & Mensenrechten* (Boom Juridische Uitgevers, 2008) 17–18; Mattei, U, 'Hard Code Now!' (2002) 2 *Global Jurist Frontiers* 1–26, 25; Lipschutz, RDR and James, K, *Globalization, Governmentality and Global Politics* (Routledge, 2005)28; Johnston, A, 'Facing Up to Social Cost' (2011) 20 *Griffith Law Review* 221–44.

[6] The literature on questions of distributive global justice and inequality is vast. For different approaches to questions of global justice, see: De Greiff, P and C Cronin (eds), *Global Justice and Transnational Politics: Essays on the Moral and Political Challenges of Globalization* (Studies in Contemporary German Social Thought, MIT Press, 2002); Nussbaum, MC, *Frontiers of Justice* (Harvard University Press, 2006); Pogge, T, *World Poverty and Human Rights* (Polity Press, 2002); Rawls, J, *The Law of Peoples*, 4th edn (Harvard University Press, 2002); Sen, A, *Development as Freedom* (Oxford University Press, 1999); Singer, P, 'Famine, Affluence, and Morality' (1972) 1 *Philosophy and Public Affairs* 229–43.

inequality. The inability of those already disadvantaged to make different choices and pursue alternative options in response to the market activities of others may reflect an inability to function in a way that is thought to be of central importance for human beings. The latter raises a deep concern from a capabilities perspective on minimum justice. Minimum justice, as envisaged from a capabilities perspective, requires that all human beings have a basic set of abilities to function in valuable ways, and a decently just society should be structured in a way that promotes and secures these basic capabilities to all individuals.[7]

As a normative frame, a capabilities perspective offers an illustration of what minimum justice requires of the basic structure of society, which includes the fundamental legal structures underlying market transactions. This book explores a capabilities perspective on minimum justice, and extends it to the realm of contract law, in particular, to the legal rules that deal with consumer transactions that impose costs on others elsewhere.

This book evaluates contract law's norms from a capabilities perspective on minimum justice. Central to the current inquiry is the specific normative question: *should mutually beneficial contracts that impair the basic capabilities of others elsewhere be invalid under a regime of contract law?* The capabilities perspective on minimum justice informs a standard of minimum contract justice. Minimum contract justice is the framework within which the following questions are discussed: How is a regime of contract law to deal with transactions on a market that impair the basic capabilities of others elsewhere? As a model for just market conduct, should contract law take account of the costs imposed by market transactions on others elsewhere? Asked differently, should the state support such transactions through a contractual regime?

The central normative question is raised in tandem with a question of positive law, namely: *are mutually beneficial transactions that impair the basic capabilities of others elsewhere, immoral and on that ground invalid under current rules of contract law in Europe?* This question seeks to examine if such transactions are compatible with the fundamental values reflected in minimum standards for contractual behaviour. Within the book's overall investigation, consumer contracts for sweatshop produced goods serve as a case illustration. In relation to that case, the normative question, and the inquiry into positive law, can be rephrased as: how should society deal with consumer contracts for sweatshop goods, and how do, or would, various legal regimes assess consumer contracts for sweatshop goods?

These questions can be read as a continuation and exploration of current moral concerns that people have about goods sold on the market, which have been produced under deplorable production conditions elsewhere. In the context of this book, however, these questions are raised in tandem, first and foremost, as part

[7] Nussbaum, MC, *Women and Human Development: The Capabilities Approach* (Cambridge University Press, 2000); Nussbaum (2006) ibid; Nussbaum, MC, *Creating Capabilities* (The Belknap Press of Harvard University Press, 2011).

of a larger topic of debate concerning social justice and contract law. This book approaches the negative implications of contracts on others elsewhere as an issue of minimum contract justice, and takes a specific case thereof to illustrate the implications of a capabilities perspective on minimum justice. Hence, this book not only contributes to general normative private law theory, but also aims to contribute to the current debate on social justice and contract law by addressing a topic and a perspective that deserve additional consideration. Before turning to the discussion on minimum contract justice, let me end with three clarifying statements that explain the project's overall goals.

First, a central task for private law theory is to evaluate and to make normative sense of contract law's norms in their particular context. This book understands contract law to represent a model for just market conduct.[8] As such, it considers contract law to represent a fundamental legal structure underlying market transactions: it contains normative standards that reveal how transacting parties should behave towards each other, others and society as a whole when engaging in market activities, if they wish to have state power available for the enforcement of their transactions. Contract law reflects a society's fundamental values and a contemporary vision of a way of life through minimum standards for contractual behaviour.[9] In this light, the presumption that consumer transactions for products made under deplorable production conditions are 'normal' can be questioned: how ought a decently just society deal with exchanges of money for goods that are made under deplorable production conditions?

Second, the debate on social justice and contract law, in particular in Europe, encompasses several large questions, including the contentious and general issue within private law theory whether or not contract law should pursue social justice aims.[10] This book, starts from the assertion that contract justice is, in part, a matter of social justice, and that the central question is what notion of social justice should be reflected by contract law. This book does not purport to give a comprehensive answer to this larger question, nor does it suggest that the answer should be sought exclusively through legal academic research. Instead, this book aims to engage in the normative debate that this question generates. It aims to make a contribution by putting forward a novel standard of minimum contract justice that is informed by a capabilities perspective and illustrated by its application

[8] See similarly: Hesselink, MW, 'The Case for a Common European Sales Law in an Age of Rising Nationalism' (2012) 8 *European Review of Contract Law*, 342–66, 359–62; Collins, H, *The Law of Contract*, 4th edn (Cambridge University Press, 2003) Chapter 1.

[9] This perspective on contract law is also reflected by the Study Group on Social Justice in European Private Law, 'Social Justice in European Contract Law: A Manifesto' (2004) 10 *European Law Journal* 653–674; Singer, JW, 'Things that We Would Like to Take for Granted: Minimum Standards for the Legal Framework of a Free and Democratic Society' (2008) 2 *Harvard Law & Policy Review* 139–59.

[10] In theories of private law, the question regarding the relationship, or absence thereof, between social justice and private law (or contract law in particular) is foundational. For a negative answer to the question of whether or not social justice is a legitimate aim of private law, see: Weinrib, EJ, *The Idea of Private Law* (Harvard University Press, 1995) and Weinrib, EJ, *Corrective Justice* (Oxford University Press, 2012); see also Gordley, J, *Foundations of Private Law* (Oxford University Press, 2007).

to the particular case of contracts that have impairing implications for the basic capabilities of others elsewhere. The book does not argue that this perspective on minimum contract justice exhausts the answers we may give to questions regarding the relationship between contract law and social justice. Instead, this book offers a capabilities perspective on minimum contract justice as an illustration of what minimum justice may require of our society and our contract laws, generally.

Third, the role of contract law in actually bringing about just outcomes in the world should not be inflated. Contract law is not the most effective or efficient instrument particularly in relation to the specific case discussed in this book. The objective is thus *not* to search for an instrument to improve directly or contribute to solving the problem of deplorable production conditions globally, ie, this book does not propose contract law as a problem-solving instrument. The purpose of raising contract law questions with regard to mutually beneficial transactions for goods made under deplorable conditions elsewhere, is to reflect on the normative standards of contract law, and on the underlying narrative of, for instance, European initiatives and developments in the area of contract law. This exploration asserts the underlying idea that whether or not a market order can be considered just depends, in part, on its contract law.

1

Minimum Contract Justice: Context and Outline

This chapter provides a broader context for the idea of minimum contract justice, as explored in the subsequent chapters. The following sections will show how this book's approach differs from the way in which the issue of deplorable production conditions elsewhere is usually discussed and approached in various scholarly discourses, and in particular in legal scholarship. It will detail the connections and contributions that this book can make between, and to, those endeavours, respectively. The chapter will also reveal the scope and limits of the current inquiry and offer an outline of the subsequent chapters.

I. The Questions in a Broader Context

The deplorable production conditions elsewhere of goods sold on the market receive much attention in civil society, politics and academia. Particularly, those concerned with corporate social responsibility are acutely aware of the issues involved in global supply chains and often address sweatshops and other deplorable production conditions primarily as matters of private, corporate responsibility. Similarly, efforts to create international non-binding normative frameworks, notably codes of conduct, address and call for socially responsible private conduct by corporations. At the core of these inquiries, is the idea that deplorable production conditions are a matter of irresponsible private conduct for which we need to develop a better form of transnational private regulation.

Without negating the relevance and importance of such efforts, this book departs from this focus on private responsibility, and offers a complementary focus on the idea that a society sets minimum standards for private conduct. When thinking of private market conduct, our attention should be directed at the normative standards that a society adheres to when asking what transactions and private behaviour it will support through its contract law, ie, through state power. Addressing the issue of deplorable production conditions within the realm of contract law, emphasises the importance of the underlying normative standards that inform how a society judges the legal permissibility of certain contracts and contractual terms. Private parties may consent to a range of contracts and terms, but they have no ultimate authority in deciding whether the state ought to make its power available for their pursuits. The distinction between legally acceptable and unacceptable market transactions is not a matter for private parties to decide.

In the area of private law and particularly the realm of contract law, the issue of deplorable production conditions has also been viewed and addressed, primarily as issues pertaining to corporate conduct.[1] In the area of tort law questions are raised, for instance, regarding the liability of corporations involved in practices that cause harm to others, either directly or through the activities of supply chain partners.[2] For instance, can an injured party claim damages from the corporation or its shareholders? In the area of contract law, deplorable production conditions have raised questions regarding the non-conformity of the good delivered to the consumer. Can a consumer rescind a sales contract, if the good does not meet her reasonable expectation, ie, the expectation that a good is produced under decent conditions?[3] Another issue is the potential relevance of publicly expressed corporate commitments to responsible conduct, for instance as part of a traditionally non-binding normative framework, ie, a code of conduct, for the interpretation of legal standards.[4]

[1] See for instance: Eijsbouts, AJAJ *et al*, *Maatschappelijk verantwoord ondernemen* (Handelingen Nederlandse Juristen-Vereniging, Kluwer, 2010; Van Dam, C, *Onderneming & Mensenrechten* (Boom Juridische Uitgevers, 2008); Castermans, AG, *De burger in het burgerlijk recht. Of de eigenschappen van perensap* (Boom Juridische Uitgevers, 2009); Tjong Tjin Tai, TFE, *Over de grenzen van het privaatrecht* (Tilburg University, 2011).

[2] See for instance: Gatto, A, *Multinational Enterprises and Human Rights* (Edward Elgar Publishing Ld, 2011); Betlem, G, 'Transnational Litigation against Multinational Corporations before Dutch Civil Courts' and Nollkaemper, A, 'Public International Law in Transnational Litigation against Multinational Corporations: Prospects and Problems in the Courts of the Netherlands' both contributions in: Kamminga, M and S Zia-Zarifi (eds), *Liability of Multinational Corporations under International Law* (Kluwer International Law, 2000); Castermans, AG and JA van der Weide, 'The Legal Liability of Dutch Parent Companies for Subsidiaries' Involvement in Violations of Fundamental, Internationally Recognized Rights' (Commissioned by the Ministry of Economic Affairs, 2009). See also: Crowe, J, 'Does Control Make a Difference? The Moral Foundations of Shareholder Liability for Corporate Wrongs' (2012) 75 *Modern Law Review*.

[3] This question is raised in legal scholarship, though not (yet) in practice. See: Wilhelmsson, T, 'Varieties of Welfarism in European Contract Law' (2004) 10 *European Law Journal* 712–33. This question was also raised by Hugh Collins at the Conference on 'Public policy and Social justice in European Contract Law' hosted by the Groningen Centre for Law and Governance at the University of Groningen, October 2012.

[4] See for instance: Vytopil, AL, Contractual Control in the Supply Chain (Boom Juridische Uitgevers, 2015).

The most pertinent issues are whether or not publicly expressed commitments can be understood as 'firm' rather than aspirational. In the former sense they can constitute misleading commercial practices under Article 6 section 2(b) of Directive 2005/29/EC of the European Parliament and of the Council of 11 May 2005 concerning unfair business-to-consumer commercial practices in the internal market and amending Council Directive 84/450/EEC, Directives 97/7/EC, 98/27/EC and 2002/65/EC of the European Parliament and of the Council and Regulation (EC) No 2006/2004 of the European Parliament and of the Council [2005] OJ L149/22. Another pertinent question is whether or not production conditions are to be understood as 'qualities' of the good with regard to which the consumer had reasonable expectations. If buying and selling 'goods' is understood as buying and selling 'brands' then production conditions may be essential qualities of the good. Namely, if the most salient aspects of goods are how they relate to image or identity, as opposed to physical characteristics, then production

In raising the question of the permissibility of contracts for sweatshop goods, this book departs from the dominant framing in law, in which issues relating to contracts for sweatshop goods are discussed under the heading of corporate social responsibility.[5] In doing so, it also provides an alternative narrative that underlies the discussion of corporate social responsibility. Particularly in the context of private law, legal inquiries into corporate social responsibility bring to the fore a narrative in which we find both a 'usual suspect' and 'victim'. Namely, when considering transactions for sweatshop goods, these inquiries perceive corporate actors as suspect transgressors of legal and social norms. In the context of consumer transactions in particular, corporate parties are considered powerful and capable of taking advantage of weaker, vulnerable consumers. Viewed from this perspective, consumers are perceived as weak and vulnerable, and as parties in need of legal protection when transacting with corporate actors for goods made under deplorable production conditions.[6]

It is no surprise then, that to the extent that contract scholars have addressed the issue, they have largely focused on consumer protection as the focal point for questions regarding the deplorable production conditions of goods sold on the market. The most prominent explanation for this focus is found in the foundations of contract law and its understanding among contract scholars. The descriptive starting point for contract law is, by and large, the principle of freedom of contract, often referred to in the same sentence with the binding nature of contract and the relativity (or: privity) of contract, representing different expressions or sides of the concept of party autonomy.[7] The principle of freedom of contract states that parties should be free to decide whether or not to contract, with whom and on what terms.[8] The principle of relativity of contract refers to the idea that contracts are generally only binding between the contracting parties, that is to say, they only confer rights to and impose obligations on those persons who are

conditions may constitute or contribute to its image/identity, for instance whether a good can be regarded as 'green' or 'responsible'. See: Klein, N, *No Logo* (Macmillan, 2003). See on the relation between publicly expressed commitments and liability for instance Van Dam (n 1) nr 16.

[5] Beyond questions of private law one can also think of issues pertaining to criminal liability. See for instance the contribution by Kristen, FGH, 'Maatschappelijk verantwoord ondernemen en strafrecht' in Eijsbouts, AJAJ *et al*, *Maatschappelijk verantwoord ondernemen* (Handelingen Nederlandse Juristen-Vereniging, Kluwer, 2010) or Clapham, A, 'The Question of Jurisdiction Under International Criminal Law Over Legal Persons: Lessons from the Rome Conference on an International Criminal Court' in M Kamminga and S Zia-Zarifi (eds), *Liability of Multinational Corporations under International Law* (Kluwer International Law, 2000).

[6] See for a different view Tjong Tjin Tai (n 1) 11 who also raises the question regarding liability of consumers.

[7] Du Perron, E, 'Contract and Third Parties' in Hartkamp, A *et al* (eds), *Towards a European Civil Code*, 2nd edn (Kluwer Law International, 1998) 314.

[8] As articulated for instance in: The Study Group on a European Civil Code and Research Group on EC Private Law (ed), *Draft Common Frame of Reference* (Sellier, 2009) Article II.1:102(1) and 62; and Lando, O and H Beale (eds), *The Principles of European Contract Law Parts I and II* (Kluwer Law International, 1999) Article 1:102.

parties to the contract.[9] In other words, contract law focuses on the legal positions of contracting parties, their autonomy, and freedom to engage in market transactions. The salient justice issues for contract law and the corresponding questions are found primarily in those instances where the autonomy of contracting parties is at stake. A prime example concerns inequality of power between parties, raising questions regarding legal protections for weaker parties. Power inequality may be brought to the fore as a justification for the manifest involvement of a society in setting mandatory contract rules, ie, rules from which private parties cannot deviate.[10] In this context, the consumer is the model example of a weaker party and consumer protection rules are the model of justified mandatory rules.

As stated, this book departs from the use of this common frame for the issue of consumer contracts for sweatshop goods. *Minimum contract justice* does not presume that these contracts are the result of power inequality that gives opportunity for corporate actors to mislead or exploit consumers. It does not presume that consumers either prefer not to buy sweatshop-made goods, or that they must have been misinformed at the time of purchase. Either case would offer obvious justificatory bases for offering consumers legal protection. Instead, this book takes an alternative starting point. Whilst the autonomy of the contracting parties is fundamental to contract law, contract law also takes account of the interests of third parties and society as a whole. Private parties—whether as businesses or consumers—are able to make decisions, which the state does not wish to endorse and support. The starting point for further inquiry is thus the idea that the state determines the permissibility of private market conduct and contractual terms, and the book starts with the question as to how a society is to deal with mutually beneficial transactions for goods made under deplorable production conditions. This book considers it to be plausible that consumers and businesses need not have been deceived, otherwise misinformed or uninformed when they engage in such transactions.[11] As transacting parties, they may be indifferent to the conditions under which their goods are made in light of their potential preferences; for instance preferences for lower costs or higher profits.[12] This image draws attention to the fact that, in some cases, the interests of third parties or society as a whole may take

[9] Cahen, JLP, *Overeenkomst en derden*, 2nd edn (Monografieën Nieuw BW B-57, Kluwer, 2004); Du Perron, CE, *Overeenkomst en derden* (Kluwer Rechtswetenschappelijke Publicaties, 1999); Du Perron (n 7).

[10] Loth, MA, *Dwingend en aanvullend recht* (Monografieën Nieuw BW A-19, Kluwer, 2009).

[11] Available information with regard to the deplorable conditions under which products are made can potentially undermine claims of non-conformity (see above). Namely, if information is provided regarding the product's production conditions, a consumer can no longer reasonably expect other conditions. See for instance: Article 2 of Directive 1999/44/EC of the European Parliament and of the Council of 25 May 1999 on certain aspects of the sale of consumer goods and associated guarantees [1999] OJ L171/12.

[12] Empirical research in the area of consumer behaviour, and particularly on the topic of avoidance mechanisms, suggests that:

1. consumers may generally express preferences for ethically certified products and a willingness to pay a premium, but there is no evidence that they seek out those products when actually

priority over the interests of contracting parties.[13] Legal systems impose, through contract law, a minimum standard of decency applicable to all contracts and the ways in which contracts may affect others and society as a whole.[14] A society does not support all individual preferences through contract law, regardless of what those preferences are. And, where the interests of others are weighed in against the interests of contracting parties, the question arises: which interests count and how are these interests balanced against the interests of contracting parties?

II. Tracing Developments in European Contract Law

The connections between contract law, the market and pursuit of justice have important social significance in any society, but the pivotal leverage points that exist between them bear a distinctive strain within the context of globalisation and trans-nationalisation. Within this book, the EU functions as a paradigmatic example of the challenges in building a just society through contract law and the market within a pluralistic, global setting.

Until recently, the answers to questions of contract law were exclusively dependent on rules of contract law of national origin in Europe. However, changes have taken place in the last decades. Besides the introduction of legal instruments on an international level, the discussion of which lies outside the scope of this book,[15] dynamic developments in the context of European integration have brought and continue to bring definite change in the area of contract law.[16] In this context, 'contract law in Europe' (also: European contract law (ECL)) now refers to the

engaging in market transactions: Hiscox, MJ et al, 'Consumer Demand for Fair Trade: New Evidence from a Field Experiment Using eBay Auctions of Fresh Roasted Coffee' https://papers.ssrn.com/sol3/papers.cfm?abstract_id=1811783, accessed 15 September 2015; and

2. Consumers are reluctant to ask for information regarding ethical product 'attributes', particularly if they care about the underlying ethical issue. Ehrich, KR and JR Irwin, 'Willful Ignorance in the Request for Product Attribute Information' (2005) 42 *Journal of Marketing Research* 266–77. Individuals avoid learning about 'inconvenient' facts, see for instance: Van der Weele, JJ, 'When Ignorance Is Innocence: On Information Avoidance in Moral Dilemmas' https://papers.ssrn.com/sol3/papers.cfm?abstract_id=1844702, accessed 15 September 2015.

[13] For an integrated approach to the relation between freedom of contract and society, see Sieburgh, C, *Tertium datur: de niet uitgesloten derde in het burgerlijk recht* (Kluwer, 2004).

[14] Kötz, H and A Flessner, *European Contract Law. Volume One: Formation, Validity, and Content of Contracts. Contract and Third Parties* (Clarendon Press, 1997).

[15] United Nations Convention on Contracts for the International Sale of Goods (CISG) 1980.

[16] A recent example of European legislation in this area is the Consumer Rights Directive 2011/83/EU of the European Parliament and of the Council of 25 October 2011 on consumer rights, amending Council Directive 93/13/EEC (Unfair Terms) and Directive 1999/44/EC (Consumer Sales) of the European Parliament and of the Council and repealing Council Directive 85/577/EEC (Doorstep Selling) and Directive 97/7/EC (Distance Selling) of the European Parliament and of the Council [2011] OJ L304/64.

rules that originate from a structure of multi-level law-making that includes rules of national and European origin.[17]

In the context of European integration, contract law is used by the European legislator as a tool for the enhancement of the functioning of the internal market and the digital market in particular. The growth of cross-border market exchange (especially e-commerce) is one of the primary aims pursued by the European Union. In this context, the divergence between different national regimes of contract law in Europe, is perceived and presumed to be an obstacle to enhanced market functioning. This outlook, communicated by the European Commission since 2001, started to emerge in earlier academic initiatives on European contract law in the 1980s.[18] The European Commission injected political energy into the exploration of a more coherent and common contract law in Europe by means of changing existing laws and introducing new EU legislation, and by developing common frameworks for European contract law.[19] The European Commission put forward 'An Action Plan' in 2003, in which the articulation of a political view and position towards contract law in Europe took further shape.[20] The Action Plan and the publication of 'The Way Forward' in 2004 placed several concrete action points on the agenda, including the development of a Common Frame of Reference (CFR) and the consideration of an optional instrument of European contract law.[21] Currently, neither the CFR nor an optional instrument is fully established, but they have developed from action points into an academic Draft Common Frame of Reference (DCFR) and a proposal for a Common European Sales Law (CESL) respectively.

The outline edition of a DCFR was published in 2009, the result of an academic undertaking and collaboration primarily between the Study Group on a European Civil Code and the Research Group on EC Private Law (Acquis Group).[22] The DCFR was presented as an important preparatory work for the development of a political CFR. In 2010, the European Commission set up an Expert Group to

[17] Joerges, C, 'The Impact of European Integration on Private Law: Reductionist Perceptions, True Conflicts and a New Constitutional Perspective' (1997) 3 *European Law Journal* 378–406; Joerges, C, 'European Challenges to Private Law: On False Dichotomies, True Conflicts and the Need for a Constitutional Perspective' (1998) 18 *Legal Studies* 146–66. See also: Hesselink, MW, 'A European Legal Method? On European Private Law and Scientific Method' (2008) 15 *European Law Journal* 20–45.

[18] An important first initiative that firmly established the ongoing study of European contract law was the Commission on European Contract Law. This academic Commission, also known as the Lando-Commission, embarked on the development of Principles of European Contract Law (PECL) in 1980. See: PECL (I-II), (1999) and Lando, O et al (eds), *Principles of European Contract Law, Part III* (Kluwer Law International, 2003). The formulation of principles of European contract law, aimed to formulate principles, which would be favourable for trade on the internal market of Europe and explicitly reflected what the Lando-Commission believed the law should be, given this aim.

[19] European Commission, *On European Contract Law* (2001) COM (2001) 398 Final.

[20] European Commission, *A More Coherent European Contract Law, An Action Plan* (2003) COM (2003) 68 Final.

[21] European Commission, *European Contract Law and the Revision of the Acquis: The Way Forward* (2004) COM (2004) 651 Final.

[22] DCFR (2009).

give advice on the development of a politically endorsed instrument of European contract law to stimulate economic activity and increase efficiency in the internal market by offering a 'user-friendly and legally certain' contractual regime.[23] The work of the Expert Group was published in May 2011 as the 'Feasibility Study'.[24] In October 2011, the Commission presented the political output of a decade of developments: a proposal for a CESL.[25] The proposed CESL represents the latest effort to enhance the functioning of the internal market through a comprehensive set of rules, ie, a common contract law.[26] It was proposed as an instrument of contract law, to be shared between all Member States, as a second optional national regime of contract law for contracting parties which engage in cross-border sale transactions on the internal market, with the possibility for Member States to extend the instrument to internal transactions as well.[27] In December 2014, the Commission announced that the CESL would be modified to serve the Digital Single Market Strategy and enhance online consumer sales in the internal market, and thus, that it would no longer be pursued as a comprehensive instrument.[28]

While the scope and content of the CESL-based proposal for online sales is limited, its development remains based on the justificatory language of market efficiency. From the onset, the developments of contract law in Europe, and in particular the initiatives of the European Commission towards a European contract law instrument, have been predominantly embedded in the language of market efficiency and have aimed at enhanced market functioning. This language is, for instance, reflected by the Commission's emphasis on a commitment to the principle of freedom of contract, which 'should be one of the guiding principles of such a contract law instrument'.[29] The Commission has referred to mandatory rules as restrictions on contractual freedom, only justified for 'good reasons'.

[23] European Commission, *On Policy Options for Progress Towards a European Contract Law for Consumers and Businesses* COM (2010) 348 Final. Various forms for such an instrument were suggested, among which both the 'toolbox' option as originally connected to an idea of a CFR, as well as a Regulation, which would set up an optional instrument as a second regime of contract law in all Member States.

[24] The Expert Group on European Contract Law, *Feasibility Study on a European Contract Law for Consumers and Businesses* (2011) http://ec.europa.eu/justice/contract/files/feasibility_study_final.pdf, assessed 13 October 2016.

[25] European Commission, *Proposal for a Regulation of the European Parliament and of the Council on a Common European Sales Law* COM (2011a) 635 Final. Also: European Commission, *Communication on a Common European Sales Law to Facilitate Cross-Border Transactions in the Single Market* COM (2011b) 636 Final.

[26] European Commission (2011a) ibid, Article 1.

[27] The CESL is proposed with limited scope, primarily focused on cross-border sales between consumers and traders (B2C contracts). See Art 4–7 CESL.

[28] See Annex 2 to the Commission Work Programme 2015, COM (2014) 910 final, 12 nr 60. In shifting to a Digital Single Market Strategy, the European Commission now focuses its efforts on the growth of online sales. The resulting proposed legal instruments target e-commerce only, and no longer propose a comprehensive instrument of common European sales law. See: the recent proposal by the European Commission for a Directive on certain aspects concerning contracts for the online and other distance sales of goods, COM (2015) 635 Final, which has subsumed parts of the original proposal for a Common European Sales Law.

[29] European Commission (n 21) 18. European Commission (n 20) 23.

In this context, the Commission has emphasised the main goal of pursuing common European rules of contract law: the smooth functioning of the internal market.[30] As such, 'good reasons' for restrictions on contractual freedom in the form of mandatory rules (eg, in the area of consumer protection) are to be found in the economic importance of consumption for the internal market, that is, in their contribution to market efficiency.[31] The language of market efficiency is similarly used in support of the proposed CESL as an instrument intended to promote and increase cross-border buying and selling.[32]

A. A Maturing European Model of Just Market Conduct

For a future contract law instrument in Europe to fulfil the aims of the European legislator, it will have to be influential in setting normative guidelines as to how private parties are to behave towards each other, others and society as a whole, when engaging in (internal) market activities. As such, those contract law instruments would reflect the stages of a maturing European model for just market conduct.[33] And in this context, the language in which these developments are embedded has special meaning.

From the outset, the project of developing rules of general contract law on a European level focuses on market functioning. It has been criticised for being presented as a 'technical' project, while nevertheless involving normative choices that are politically contentious.[34] Notably, taking into consideration the fact that the European legislator articulates rules of contract law,[35] a group of legal scholars (further: Social Justice Group) argued that the development thereof should be accompanied by a larger, democratic debate on the notion of social justice reflected in (an instrument of) European contract law. The Social Justice Group emphasised the political dimensions of the development of contract law in Europe in its Manifesto.[36]

30 European Commission (n 21) 20.

31 European Commission (n 21) 20.

32 For instance: Reding, V, 'The Common European Sales Law—Breaking the Mould to Help Businesses and Customers Realising the European Single Market' (Vice-President of the European Commission, EU Justice Commissioner) SPEECH/12/164 Forum Europe Brussels *Press release*; and the European Commission, 'The European Commission Proposes an Optional Common European Sales Law to Boost Trade and Expand Consumer Choice' IP/11/1175 *Press release*. This language is also present in the Digital Single Market Strategy.

33 Both the DCFR and the CESL can be addressed as potential European models of just market conduct. See also: Hesselink, MW, 'The Politics of a European Civil Code' (2004) 10 *European Law Journal* 675–97.

34 Hesselink, ibid; Study Group on Social Justice in European Private Law, 'Social Justice in European Contract Law: A Manifesto' (2004) 10 *European Law Journal* 653–74.

35 The Europeanisation and harmonisation of rules of contract law in Europe itself is also subject to critical scrutiny, see for instance: Legrand, P, 'Against a European Civil Code' (1997) 60 *The Modern Law Review* 44–63.

36 Study Group on Social Justice (n 34).

The Social Justice Group argued that contract law expressed the contemporary ideals of social justice in a market society because the market plays a pivotal role for the satisfaction of individual basic needs (increased by privatisation of central realms of life relating to, for instance, education and health), and contract law provides the basic guidelines for just conduct on the market.[37] The argument is based on the recognition that the market functions as a prominent mechanism through which an order of wealth and power is established in a society.[38] Contract law's normative stance on the transactions that are or are not, permissible on the market, has predictable distributive outcomes. A particular set of rules governing the market order, thus patterns a predictable distribution of advantages and disadvantages from market activities. As such, the Social Justice Group argued, questions of contract law in Europe should be answered in consideration of an articulate notion of social justice.

The view put forward by the Social Justice Group is supported by developments observed in national legal systems in Europe during the twentieth century, the associated collapse between a principled distinction between private law and public law; and the corresponding arguments put forward by the Critical Legal Studies (CLS) movement, which builds on legal realism. This *principled* distinction between public and private law, refers to the idea that public law should be concerned with public and social aims such as social justice, whereas private law should be free from public and social aims and only pattern corrective justice, ie justice between the contracting parties.[39]

The arguments from CLS challenge the idea that this distinction makes sense, viewing every legal rule essentially as a form of state regulation that reflects a particular set of beliefs.[40] From this perspective, private law (and contract law), does not form a politically or value neutral autonomous discipline, but rather a discipline permeated by its political function. In the context of contract law in Europe, moreover, the distinction is thought to have collapsed, firstly, in view of the fact that national legal systems in the twentieth century increasingly countered market outcomes considered unfavourable or incompatible with national notions of social justice.[41] The national rules of contract law increasingly reflected protection

[37] Study Group on Social Justice (n 34) 655 and 667.

[38] Study Group on Social Justice (n 34) 665; Collins, H, *The Law of Contract*, 4th edn (Cambridge University Press, 2003) Chapter 1; Kronman, AT, 'Contract Law and Distributive Justice' (1980) 89 *The Yale Law Journal* 472–511.

[39] Prominently argued in Weinrib, EJ, *The Idea of Private Law* (Harvard University Press, 1995) and Weinrib, EJ, *Corrective Justice* (Oxford University Press, 2012).

[40] For instance: Schwartz, LB, 'With Gun and Camera through Darkest CLS-Land' (1984) 36 *Stanford Law Review* 413–64; Rose, N, 'Beyond the Public Private Distinction—Law, Power and the Family' (1987) 14 *Journal of Law and Society* 61–76; Horwitz, MJ, 'The History of the Public Private Distinction' (1982) 130 *University of Pennsylvania Law Review* 1423–28.

[41] For an elaborate discussion on how social (distributive) concerns settled in the realm of contract law: Collins, H, *Regulating Contracts* (Oxford University Press, 1999) chapters 3–4; Collins (n 38) chapters 1–2. See also: Hesselink (n 17); Deakin, S, '"Capacitas"': Contract Law and the Institutional Preconditions of a Market Economy' (2006) 2 *European Review of Private Law* 317–41; Van Schaick, AC, *Contractsvrijheid en Nietigheid* (WEJ Tjeenk Willink, 1994); Wilhelmsson (n 3).

for certain categories of persons, in order to provide them with more advantages, or less disadvantages, than they would have received otherwise (eg, consumers, tenants, employees). Secondly, the principled distinction has given way to a dominant instrumental view of contract law in Europe, reflected in the language of market efficiency.[42] Provided that the European legislator conceives of contract law as an instrument of governance to pursue the public aim of the enhanced functioning of the market, other public aims cannot be ruled out from questions of contract law on the basis of its principled distinction from public law. Questions of minimum contract justice therefore seem appropriately posed in relation to the ongoing developments of trans-nationalisation of contract law in Europe.

B. Private Law Constitutionalisation

Although consumer protection is positioned as a central instrument to the enhanced functioning of the internal market,[43] consumer identity has also been meaningful for questions of social justice in contract law. In that context consumers represent a category of weaker contracting parties (other examples include tenants and employees) who are in need of legal protection. In the area of weaker party protection in private law, the influence of constitutional, fundamental rights cannot be overlooked. Private law constitutionalisation is an important development in European contract law that traces the impact of constitutional, fundamental values and rights on private legal relationships. In many Member States of the European Union, fundamental rights (ensconced in national constitutions or European sources, eg, European Convention on Human Rights) have been given effect in private legal relationships by the courts. The horizontal effect of fundamental rights has taken shape through plural approaches, including the recognition of direct effect and indirect effect of fundamental rights.[44] While direct effect indicates that private parties can directly invoke fundamental rights as a source for private law claims against counter parties, indirect effect refers to the interpretation of private law norms through a fundamental rights perspective. For the questions discussed in this book, the indirect effect of fundamental rights is particularly pertinent.

The indirect effect of fundamental rights takes place through the judicial interpretation of general clauses and open norms, such as norms regarding contractual

[42] Schmid, CU, 'The Instrumentalist Conception of the Acquis Communautaire in Consumer Law and its Implications on a European Contract Law Code' (2005) 2 *European Review of Contract Law* 211–27.

[43] See for instance, European Commission (2011a and 2011b) (n 25), in which consumer protection is understood as an instrument to boost consumer confidence and enhance cross-border sales.

[44] Mak, C, *Fundamental Rights in European Contract Law* (Kluwer Law International, 2008); Cherednychenko, O, *Fundamental Rights, Contract Law and the Protection of Weaker Party* (Sellier, 2007); Brüggemeier, G, A Colombi Ciacchi, and G Comandé (eds), *Fundamental Rights and Private Law in the European Union* (Cambridge University Press 2010) Volume I and II; Micklitz, H (ed), *Constitutionalization of European Private Law* (Oxford University Press 2014).

immorality. Social justice outcomes are often achieved through constitutionalisation of contract law in this way. Contract law's normative guidelines as to how private parties are to behave towards each other, others and society as a whole, can thus be influenced by the effects given to fundamental rights within the context of private relationships. While this normative effect is observable when it comes to the fundamental rights of (weaker) contracting parties, fundamental rights argumentation is not established in relation to contractual relations that infringe on the fundamental rights of others elsewhere. Hence, minimum contract justice can provide a normative basis for extending contract law constitutionalisation in this direction. The book's normative framework provides an independent justification of what minimum contract justice, as a matter of justice in our society generally, requires of us. Constitutionalisation of contract law has served social justice aims in relation to the positions of weaker contracting parties through the interpretation of open norms, such as contractual immorality. Minimum contract justice can be read as an evaluative and guiding frame for further development in European contract law, including the extension of contract law constitutionalisation to questions that relate to others elsewhere, as a matter of social justice. It can therefore be read to resonate and explore further the observation that

> If at least one of the aims of European contract law is to contribute to social justice through enhancing substantive freedom it is inconceivable that the concern for justice will be only limited to those who are already the most privileged on our planet.[45]

III. Market Conduct in Europe in a Global Setting

The answers to the central questions of minimum contract justice provide an insight into our way of life in terms of the transactions we engage in and the transactions that our society supports through contract law. Our model of just market conduct and its developments on national and European levels should be informed by our understanding of global interdependence and interconnectedness. The market is a prominent mechanism through which private parties engage in cooperative activities with one another globally. Today's world is commonly described with reference to globalisation, a term used in relation to a wide range of dimensions—including economic, social, governance, culture, and information –, to indicate an increasing interconnection and interdependence across national borders.[46] Globalisation has accelerated in the last four decades particularly in the

[45] Hesselink, MW, 'Capacity and Capability in European Contract Law' (2005) 13 *European Review of Private Law* 491–507, 505.

[46] Giddens, A, *The Consequences of Modernity* (Stanford University Press, 1990) 70 et seq; Beck, U, *What is Globalization?* (Wiley, 2000) 11–13; see also UNDP Human Development Report, 'Globalization with a Human Face' (1999).

dimensions of consumption and production.[47] The goods bought and sold on the European market are produced in many countries and information is increasingly available to European citizens through the development of new technology.[48] Provided that market activities are increasingly globalised, and information is increasingly available, modern regimes of contract law are confronted with the challenge of how to govern market transactions in this setting. The patterns of welfare distribution to which a market order contributes globally are becoming increasingly predictable. A modern regime of contract law in Europe thus answers the question of which interests count globally and how these interests are to be balanced with the interests of contracting parties.

It is clear that globalisation influences the lives of individuals throughout the world in complex ways. The globalisation of economic and social cooperative structures is normatively ambiguous. On the one hand, globalisation is praised for stimulating economic growth, but on the other hand, also fiercely criticised for its negative impact on the social dimensions of life and the exacerbation of global inequality.[49] The conduct of corporate actors engaged in cross border activities is of central concern in those critical reflections. In the context of pervasive global inequality, multinational corporations are able to increase profits and offer lower prices to consumers, while those who produce the goods (or who live close to production facilities) work under deplorable conditions and are exposed to devaluation of their living environment through, for instance, environmental damage.[50] In this narrative, current consumption patterns too are associated with the perpetuation and exacerbation of global inequality. Notably, consumption decisions are associated with disposal and production processes that negatively impact the lives of others elsewhere.[51] In this context of global inequality consumption decisions have been framed as '(…) decisions about the levels of wealth inequality (…) that

[47] These topics were also central in the UNDP Human Development Report (1999) ibid and the UNDP Human Development Report, 'The Real Wealth of Nations' (2010).

[48] Although globalisation is not new, there are new aspects of globalisation, such as global consumer markets with global brands, new actors such as multinational corporations that have shifted centres of influence, and new tools of communication and technology. UNDP Report (n 46); UNDP Report (2010) ibid, Chapter 4.

[49] The criticism regarding exacerbation of inequality does not merely pertain to economic wealth, see for instance in: UNDP Report (n 46); but also to social and environmental factors that influences the lives individuals are able to live. Some critical perspectives are presented in De Greiff, P and C Cronin (eds), *Global Justice and Transnational Politics: Essays on the Moral and Political Challenges of Globalization* (Studies in contemporary German social thought, MIT Press, 2002), see for instance the contributions by A Sen, M Nussbaum and T Pogge.

[50] The race to the bottom is commonly referred to as an illustration of the way in which current global structures maintain and exacerbate global inequality by securing disproportionate advantage for those who are already advantaged and imposing disproportionate disadvantage on those who are already disadvantaged. The race to the bottom hypothesises that globalisation of profit making by powerful corporations pressures regulatory regimes of poor countries towards lower environmental standards, labour standards and tax regimes. See for instance: Van Dam (n 1), sections 2 and 3.

[51] UNDP Human Development Report, 'Consumption for Human Development' (1998) Chapter 3. 'Because consumption is now a principle vehicle by which individuals are connected to a globalized world that includes social injustice and ecological fragility, it is also through consumption that those

individuals believe are appropriate (…)',[52] namely, 'because consumption is now a principal vehicle by which individuals are connected to a globalized world that includes social injustice (…) it is also through consumption that those individuals' hesitancies and objections are becoming most apparent'.[53] Although this analysis is contentious,[54] it illustrates the underlying view regarding the potential incompatibility between consumption decisions for goods made under deplorable production conditions and notions of social justice in a global setting of inequality.

The other-regarding global aspects that this book connects to the analysis of contract law, ties in with a growing global orientation throughout legal scholarship. There is great awareness that local activities and law-making have global implications that are increasingly observable, measurable, and foreseeable. This awareness has resulted in normative explorations of the question: ought, and if so, how can we take into account the implications and consequences of our activities for others with whom we do not share a national jurisdiction or political community? Globally oriented legal scholarship is vast, with leading examples in the area of international law where advocates of global constitutionalism, or other-regarding obligations of sovereigns, pursue varying venues to serve aims of global justice.[55] In these inquiries, public law responses to 'justice-sensitive negative externalities' are of central concern.[56] Yet, issues of social justice are also appropriately considered within the realm of contract law, and its normative stance with regard to the negative implications of transactions elsewhere is significant within a context of predictable substantive outcomes globally. If a society is concerned with issues of global justice, and their place in a setting of global inequality, questions that engage these concerns in the realm of contract law deserve our attention.

IV. Outline

After reading the previous sections, readers will see that the book's discussion of how a decently just society ought to deal with exchanges of money for goods that

individuals' hesitancies and objections are becoming most apparent', Kysar, DA, 'Preferences for Processes: The Process/Product Distinction and the Regulation of Consumer Choice' (2004) 118 *Harvard Law Review* 636. That consumers' preferences increasingly reflect awareness and importance placed on responsible (eg, ecologically and morally) methods of production. See Kysar ibid.

[52] Kysar ibid 526–642, 636 fn 478.

[53] Kysar ibid 636.

[54] As Kysar discusses, this view goes against the dominant view that individuals express 'public-regarding values' when acting as citizens as opposed to acting as consumers on the market. Ibid 531–33, 636.

[55] See for instance on the former Kumm, M, 'The Cosmopolitan Turn in Constitutionalism: An Integrated Conception of Public Law' (2013) 20 *Indiana Journal of Global Legal Studies* 605–28 and on the latter Benvenisti, E, 'Sovereigns as Trustees of Humanity: On the Accountability of States to Foreign Stakeholders' (2013) 107 *The American Journal of International Law* 295–333.

[56] Kumm ibid.

are made under deplorable production conditions, could start from and be motivated by various concerns and interests. Some may be interested in this question via a concern for the problem of deplorable production conditions and a quest for a resolution. For those seeking legal recourse, the book's discussion of contractual invalidity on the basis of immorality can be interpreted as a supplement to the current legal landscape that has already been explored. Most approaches have viewed corporate actors as suspect transgressors of social and legal norms and, consequently, have focused on the ways in which legal instruments can contribute to holding corporate actors accountable (eg, through questions of liability). From this dominant viewpoint the contractual question of invalidity and immorality is easily overlooked. The issue of contractual invalidity can offer an additional legal strategy to advance corporate responsibility and potential activist agendas that combat exploitative labour conditions. For those who pursue change in these areas, this book offers the doctrinal arguments and the underlying moral justification in support of those goals. However, projects that aim to solve the issue of deplorable production conditions should always take the effectiveness and efficiency of a proposed instrument into account. In these terms, the role that contract law could play should not be inflated. In fact, within the context of this book, contract law is not proposed as a problem-solving instrument.

The question of contractual invalidity attracts, and is deserving of, our attention when we wonder how a decently just society ought to deal with exchanges of money for goods that are made under deplorable production conditions. From this perspective, the sweatshop case simply functions as one example of an instance that raises this question. The case is an appealing example because it is topical and attracts moral scrutiny in political and public arenas. Yet, it is not the only example that could prompt this inquiry. Other cases that spark similar public debates, or may do so in the future, can equally illustrate the question of contractual invalidity (eg, cases that fall within the definition of modern slavery, cases that involve the structural occurrence of animal cruelty or, cases of environmental damage). To the extent that those practices are morally contested or deemed morally unacceptable in our society, they can function as test cases to explore, examine, and illustrate the current bounds of legal invalidity on the basis of immorality. More importantly, they can detail the implications of a capabilities based view on minimum contract justice that may provide normative justification for a suggested alteration of current legal practices.

This book presents the problem of global exploitative production conditions first and foremost to contract law theorists and contract law scholars: how ought our contract laws deal with transactions for goods made in sweatshops elsewhere? The deplorable production conditions of goods bought and sold on our markets functions as a centre for the doctrinal and comparative legal approach of this book, as well as for its more theoretical and normative discussions. For those engaged in normative private law theory, the book's contribution will mostly be found in the capabilities perspective on minimum contract justice, which produces evaluative criteria for the defining structure of contractual relations. In this context, the sweatshop example illustrates the implications of minimum contract justice and can be read as a particular illustration of what justice requires of our contract laws. This suggestion may be of particular interest to those who follow closely the developments of contract law in Europe. Although the relation between social justice and contract law is contested, debate on this topic has matured under the influence of the Europeanisation of private law. For those who seek to advance that debate, the book's integrated approach—bringing together the socially relevant and topical sweatshop case with a capabilities perspective on minimum justice and the rules of contract law in various legal systems—can be read as a way of continuing that debate in a manner that is accessible to a wider audience than usually invited in contract law discourse. Although each part of the book makes its own independent contributions, which are more or less appealing to various readers, I hope to show the value of discussing them together. This book situates our shared minimum standards for contractual behaviour in direct relation to the decency and justice to which a society may strive. The transactions we engage in and that our society supports through contract law, provides insight into and an opportunity to reflect on the way we live.

This book employs several methods that correspond to the interdisciplinary character of the underlying study. The structure of the book follows a methodological division between a normative and positive approach, which are connected by a concrete example, ie, the example of consumer contracts for sweatshop goods. Each book part sheds light on the relationship, between consumer transactions and the deplorable production conditions of the goods that are exchanged, from a different perspective. These perspectives are brought together in the present section. The thesis that this book aims to defend is, briefly stated, that mutually beneficial market transactions that impair the basic capabilities of others elsewhere should not be considered as 'normal' market transactions, ie, transactions that are recognised as valid consumer-contracts under the rules of contract law. As an illustrative example, this book argues that the knowing consumption and sale of sweatshop-produced goods should not be regarded as acceptable conduct on our market. Instead, contractual regimes should withhold their endorsement and support of such activities. The following sections provide an outline to the book chapters, starting with the normative approach underlying the central thesis.

A. A Capabilities Approach to Minimum Contract Justice

The central question in this book—should mutually beneficial contracts that impair the basic capabilities of others elsewhere be invalid under a regime of contract law—is a normative one. To avoid an idiosyncratic treatment, this question is answered within a normative framework rooted in the capabilities approach as developed by Martha Nussbaum (Chapter 2). This book presents this capabilities perspective on minimum justice as one view on what justice may require of our society, and extends its application to the realm of contract law. Minimum contract justice offers a normative account of how our contract laws should treat contracts for goods made in sweatshops in a society that strives towards minimum justice.

Nussbaum's capabilities approach is part of a broader development of capabilities based frameworks. The capability concept was developed initially by Amartya Sen for the purpose of evaluating 'individual advantage' in the area of welfare economics. It has become increasingly influential in the area of human development, for instance, shaping the Human Development Index (HDI) used by the United Nations to rank nations in the Human Development Reports. Capabilities frameworks have also advanced in the legal discipline, for instance in the area of constitutional law,[57] but also as a basis for private legal theories and concepts. Notably, in the area of private law, the capabilities concept has been employed to develop 1) an empowering consumer concept that advances the abilities of consumers to engage in market transactions;[58] 2) an understanding of contractual capacity and an interpretation of rules of contract law as capability enhancing;[59] and 3) a property law theory that seeks to advance the basic capabilities necessary for human flourishing by imposing an obligation on owners to share surplus private property and an obligation for the state to enforce social sharing.[60] While the former two applications in contract law employ Sen's capability concept, the latter application in property theory utilises Nussbaum's capabilities approach. This approach represents a partial theory of social justice in which she identifies central human capabilities that each human being is entitled to. As a minimum benchmark for justice, Nussbaum's capabilities approach functions to evaluate whether or not a human society can be considered minimally decent and just. This book explores the implications of this minimum standard of decency and justice within the realm of contract law, specifically, for the question as to whether or not mutually beneficial contracts that impair the basic capabilities of others elsewhere should be invalid. This book argues that the answer to this question is affirmative, in light of the political function of contract law in shaping a market order that has predictable consequences for the lives that people are able to live. Contract law reflects the normative guidelines and the basic structure for just market conduct, ie, for just social and economic cooperation. Structuring a market order in such a way as to endorse and support transactions that have adverse effects on the central capabilities of others elsewhere is incompatible with the account of minimum contract justice that this book develops on the basis of Nussbaum's capabilities approach.

[57] See: Nussbaum, MC, 'The Supreme Court 2006 Term Foreword: Constitutions and Capabilities: "Perception" against Lofty Formalism' (2007) 121 *Harvard Law Review* 4–97.

[58] See: Benöhr, I, *EU Consumer Law and Human Rights* (Oxford University Press, 2013).

[59] See: Deakin, S, '"Capacitas": Contract Law and the Institutional Preconditions of a Market Economy' (2006) 2 *European Review of Private Law* 317–41.

[60] Alexander, G, 'The Social-Obligation Norm in American Property Law' (2009) 94 *Cornell Law Review* 745.

B. Sweatshops as an Example

The positive approach to the question of contractual immorality and invalidity under rules of contract law in Europe (chapters 4–5) will be illustrated by the specific example of sweatshops in the supply chains of clothes bought and sold on the market in Europe. Chapter 3 provides the background for this type of case. It describes the term 'sweatshop' on the basis of the literature, commonly referred to as a combination of deplorable working conditions that includes low pay and long working days, unhealthy and unsafe conditions, and a regime entailing elements of force and degradation. The chapter also provides an overview of the main arguments brought to the fore in the debate on the objectionable status of sweatshops predominantly characterised by an economic case for sweatshops, and an ethical case against sweatshops. As such, the overview on this debate illustrates why transactions for goods made by others in sweatshops elsewhere raise questions of contract invalidity on the basis of immorality. Moreover, the debate illustrates the relevance of the normative language used to justify the existence of contractual rules and outcomes. Namely, to examine the question whether or not a contract should be held immoral and invalid because of the cost imposed on others (ie, a negative externality), much depends on the underlying language that determines what is to be understood as unacceptable cost externalisation. Overall, this chapter speaks to the way in which consumer contract terms for sweatshop goods can be linked to sweatshop conditions and it details the context and market dynamics in which sweatshop conditions are necessary implications of those consumer-transactions.

C. Contractual Immorality in Europe: A Sweatshop Test Case

The following chapters discuss the positive legal question of whether or not mutually beneficial contracts that impair the basic capabilities of others elsewhere are invalid under current rules of contract law in Europe (Chapter 4). The development of contract law in Europe functions as a paradigmatic example of the challenges related to transnationalisation, and pursuits of justice through the legal institutions underlying the market in a global setting. Chapter 4 details a case study that entails a mutually beneficial contract for clothes made in a sweatshop elsewhere and the contracting parties are presumed to be aware of that fact. Chapter 4 also discusses several objections to the hypothesis that the contract in the case study would be held immoral and on that ground invalid under several legal systems, including Dutch, German, French and English law, as well as proposed European instruments of contract law. These objections include the fact that the sweatshop is too remote from the transaction and that the potential objectionable aspect of the transaction does not affect the contracting parties' interests. Chapter 5 shows, however, that these facts are not, on principle grounds, beyond consideration in any of the legal systems within this book's inquiry. However, the rules of contract law in different legal systems in Europe do yield diverging approaches to the question of contractual immorality and consequent invalidity. There are some general differences in the approach, for example, the fact that the contract would be invalid if the sweatshop conditions would be considered immoral foreseeable consequences under Dutch law, whereas this would depend on the question whether or not the sweatshop production conditions of the clothes would render the contract's comprehensive character as immoral under German law. Specific differences can be noted, for instance, regarding the knowledge requirements that the legal systems apply concerning the fact that clothes are made in sweatshops. Notably, some proposed European instruments of contract law suggest that parties' knowledge should be irrelevant, but under national systems this knowledge is relevant, either if at least one party was, or both parties were, aware of the sweatshop production conditions. Overall, the divergences lead to varying degrees of the likelihood that the case study contract will be held invalid under the various legal systems.

D. The Frontiers of Minimum Contract Justice

The final chapter brings together the capabilities perspective on minimum contract justice with the resulting assessment regarding the contractual immorality and invalidity of transactions for clothes made in sweatshops. From a capabilities perspective on minimum contract justice, a decently just society should not endorse contracts that impair the basic capabilities of others elsewhere. That is to say, if a society aims to construct a just market order it should consider such market conduct as unacceptable. This capabilities perspective forms the basis of this book's proposed standard of minimum contract justice and offers a normative view of how contract laws should treat consumer contracts for sweatshop goods. Minimum contract justice thus favours the outcomes of certain legal systems over others, corresponding to the varying degrees of likelihood with which legal systems will hold the case study contract as immoral and on that ground invalid. The book's normative claim regarding the immorality and invalidity of mutually beneficial contracts that impair the basic capabilities of others elsewhere offers a critical view regarding the frontiers of minimum contract justice, as well as evaluative guidance for further developments in contract law in Europe.

2

Minimum Contract Justice: A Capabilities Approach

This chapter discusses a capabilities based approach to minimum justice (part 1) and details its normative implications for contract law, specifically, the rules on contractual invalidity and immorality (part 2). This depiction of contract law's role from a capabilities perspective informs what this book puts forward as a standard of 'minimum contract justice', illustrated by the rules that distinguish acceptable from unacceptable private transactions. I will refer to these rules as outlining the defining structure of contractual relations: they determine under what conditions state power is available for the enforcement of an agreement between private parties. The standard of minimum contract justice forms the normative framework for further discussion of the test case of consumer contracts for sweatshop goods in following chapters. This test case is used to examine whether the legal systems, part of the comparative analysis in this book, are to be regarded as minimally just. This chapter shows that the leading question for that inquiry is whether or not a legal system provides support to and enforces contracts that have foreseeable adverse implications for the basic capabilities of others elsewhere.

I develop the relationship between a capabilities based approach to minimum justice and contract law, and the resulting standard of minimum contract justice, through the following questions: should we view (parts of) contract law as responsible for supporting and advancing a society's pursuit of minimum justice? If so, what are the implications, if any, of the requirements of minimum justice for questions concerning the validity of contracts, or in other words, for the availability of state power for the enforcement of agreements between individuals? And consequently, how do minimum contract justice requirements bear on rules regarding contractual immorality? Before turning to the central question of contract law's role in the pursuit of minimum justice, this chapter starts with a brief description of 1) the development of the capabilities concept and 2) some of the basic arguments that support a capabilities approach to justice vis-à-vis alternative theories of justice. This description will allow me to explain why a capabilities approach to minimum justice functions as the basis for the normative framework developed in this book, specifically, why it grounds minimum contract justice in Nussbaum's capabilities approach.

I. The Development of the Capabilities Concept and Capabilities Perspectives on Justice

The capabilities (or capability) concept has gained increasing impetus in areas of human development, welfare economics and political philosophy over some decades.[1] It represents the core concept within a theoretical paradigm that focuses on individual freedoms, understood in terms of individuals' real abilities to be and do valuable things, as the basis for evaluative assessments of quality of life and well-being. Initially developed by Amartya Sen, the capabilities concept serves to evaluate 'individual advantage': if we want to know how well people are doing, we have to look at what people are really able to be and do in their lives.[2] Sen coined these abilities, or substantive individual freedoms, ie, *capabilities*, countering dominant approaches that focused on what people collectively (eg, national GDP) or individually (eg, GDP per capita, primary goods) have.[3] Divergences among human beings, Sen argued, lead to salient differences between what people are able to be and accomplish with the means at their disposal. The normative significance of this argument propelled the capabilities concept as an important basis for evaluative judgements about justice.

A. Capabilities and Alternative Approaches to Justice

The capabilities literature offers various approaches that provide elements of a theory of justice, though none establish a fully-fledged capabilities theory of justice that specifies the requirements of full justice.[4] In this respect, Nussbaum offers the most advanced version of a partial theory of justice that details the requirements of minimum justice in terms of capabilities.[5] This version of the capabilities

[1] Notably, since 1990, the United Nations Development Program (UNDP) publishes the Human Development Reports, which are based on a capabilities-inspired index, ie, the Human Development Index (HDI). On the basis of the HDI, the UN ranks nations in terms of their success regarding the quality of human lives, measured in the areas of education, health, and living standards. For an overview of the developments and applications of capabilities based frameworks and other introductory readings, see: Robeyns, I, 'The Capability Approach: A Theoretical Survey' (2005) 6 *Journal of Human Development* 93–114; Nussbaum, MC, *Creating Capabilities* (The Belknap Press of Harvard University Press, 2011). For more applied forms, see: Deneulin, S and L Shahani (eds), *An Introduction to the Human Development and Capability Approach* (Earthscan, 2009).

[2] See: Sen, A, 'Equality of What?' in S McMurrin (ed), *Tanner Lectures on Human Values* (Cambridge University Press, 1982); Sen, A, *Inequality Reexamined* (Oxford University Press, 1992); Sen, A, *Commodities and Capabilities* (Oxford University Press, 1999a); Sen, A, *Development as Freedom* (Oxford University Press, 1999b); Sen, A, *The Idea of Justice* (Allen Lane, 2009).

[3] For instance, utilitarian approaches that focus on aggregate measures such as GDP, or Rawlsian frameworks that focus on primary goods. See: Sen (1992) ibid, Chapter 5; Sen (1999b) ibid, Chapter 3.

[4] See for instance: Sen (2009) (n 2); Nussbaum, MC, *Frontiers of Justice* (Harvard University Press, 2006); Anderson, E, 'What is the Point of Equality?' (1999) 109 *Ethics* 287–337.

[5] The articulation of a list of capabilities for political purposes represents a major divergence between Nussbaum's approach and Sen's capability approach. For a discussion on their differences,

approach, as did the capabilities concept itself, developed in conversation with and opposition to alternative, dominant strands of justice, such as utilitarian approaches and Rawls' theory of justice. The approach offers a distinct capabilities critique of some of the elements that are at the core of the normative evaluations offered by these alternative accounts of justice.

The basic, capabilities informed critique of (most) utilitarian approaches to justice includes two claims.[6] First, it suggests that utility concepts mistakenly capture incommensurable plural goods within a homogenous measure. For instance, a utility concept may count individual well-being achieved from having good health, from the ability to be free from assault, or from the freedom to exchange property rights, as the same sorts of things. In doing so, this utility concept implies that well-being achievements in these distinct areas of human life are the same sort of things and thus interchangeable. As a consequence, utility concepts lead to the conclusion that shortcomings in one area can be compensated by enhancements in other areas. One's overall utility, measured in terms of well-being, could remain the same, or even be enhanced, by offering greater economic freedoms while simultaneously decreasing one's ability to be free from assault. The capabilities informed critique of utilitarian approaches opposes this implication. The second pillar of a capabilities critique of utilitarian approaches suggests that, if and when engaged in aggregation, there is a severe risk of treating some individuals as means to the enrichment of others. Namely, to the extent that utilitarian approaches are in the pursuit of maximisation of aggregated utility, a sacrifice in the well-being of some may be justified if overall utility rises.

The basic, capabilities informed critique of Rawls's theory can also be presented in two claims. The first claim focuses on the central role of the concept of primary goods for questions of justice. Primary goods represent means necessary to pursue individual life plans and conceptions of value, whatever they may be. They are social in nature and include rights, liberties, opportunities, income, wealth, and the social bases of self-respect. A capabilities informed perspective draws attention to the idea that while primary goods encompass a plurality of human goods, the concept cannot take into account the moral significance of the divergence between individuals' ability to convert these social goods into valuable results. That is to say, from a capabilities perspective, Rawls' theory of justice takes insufficient account

see for instance: Crocker, D, 'Functioning and Capability: The Foundations of Sen's and Nussbaum's Development Ethic' (1992) 20 *Political Theory* 584–612; Nussbaum, MC, 'Capabilities as Fundamental Entitlements: Sen and Social Justice' (2003) 9 *Feminist Economics* 33; Sen, A, 'Capabilities, Lists, and Public Reason: Continuing the Conversation' (2004) 10 *Feminist Economics* 77–80; and Alexander, JM, 'Ending the Liberal Hegemony: Republican Freedom and Amartya Sen's Theory of Capabilities (2010) 9 *Contemporary Political Theory* 5–24.

[6] I only provide a brief and simplified outline of what I take to be some of the main and overlapping points of this capabilities critique. There are several other points, including the extent to which utilitarian evaluations of justice exclusively rely on mental states (eg, happiness), that I do not discuss here. For a more comprehensive and elaborate account see: Sen (1999b) (n 2), 58–59 and 72–73; Nussbaum (n 4) 69–81.

of the inequalities between outcomes that individuals will be able to achieve with the means at their disposal. Primary goods are inadequate proxies for what individuals are really able to do and be. Second, a Rawlsian evaluation of justice depends on the identification of the least advantaged position in a society, ie, those who are in social and economic terms considered worst-off.[7] While the concept of primary good encompasses a plurality of human goods, the process of identifying the least advantaged positions relies on measures of income and wealth. In doing so, this part of Rawls' theory (ie, the difference principle) invokes the same capabilities based critique of utility that points to the incommensurability of goods, and the inadequacy of homogeneous measures (often money based measures). Rawls' approach to justice, in its application of the difference principle, fails to adequately recognise that human goods have no common standard of measurement. In short, from a capabilities perspective, both utility based theories and Rawls' theory of justice ultimately allow questions of justice to turn on homogeneous measures that 1) cannot account for the plurality of human goods, and 2) exclude the moral significance of inequalities of individual abilities to convert means into valuable outcomes, ie, individual abilities to do or be things with the resources they have.

B. A Capabilities Based Perspective on Justice and Contract Law

The above description offers two ways to explain why a capabilities approach to minimum justice functions as the basis for the normative framework developed in this book. First, the critiques can be read to offer the basic elements of an argument for the advantages of a capabilities based approach to justice over these dominant, alternative approaches to justice. To the extent that these claims are considered convincing and successful, they provide substantive reasons for the pursuit of a capabilities based normative framework. While I find the critiques compelling, I do not aim to offer an independent argument for the superiority of a capabilities approach to minimum justice over alternative possible choices, as a basis for this book's normative framework. Capabilities theorists and political philosophers are much better positioned to develop the arguments required to defend the various versions, and stages, of capabilities approaches to justice against alternative approaches and there is a rich literature that presents those arguments, as well as the critical responses to them. Moreover, capabilities approaches to justice, including Nussbaum's approach to minimum justice, cannot be sensibly compared to full theories of justice, because 1) they are incomplete, offering elements of a theory of justice, and often 2) their objective and scope are different. Particularly, while theories of justice pursue the outline of the requirements of full justice, Nussbaum's capabilities approach aims to offer the elements of a minimum

[7] See Rawls' second principle of justice, which demands that social and economic equalities are arranged to the benefit of the least advantaged.

justice standard. The choice for a capabilities based approach as the normative framework for minimum contract justice, is substantively propelled by the normative significance of capabilities: it matters for questions of justice, not (only) what resources and means are given to individuals, but what individuals can do and be with those means, ie, what use individuals can make of them in light of their diversity and the diversity of their circumstances. The substantive reasons—advanced and developed in the capabilities literature—for favouring a capabilities based approach are likely compelling to those who are drawn to the normative significance of capabilities to begin with, and less likely to convince others. This book moves forward with the idea that a capabilities approach offers an important illustration of what minimum justice may require of us generally, and of contract law specifically. It does not aim to put that illustration forward as the *only* compelling view, or as a comprehensive proposal that exhausts other requirements of justice. The choice for a capabilities approach to minimum justice is supported by the observation that capabilities approaches constitute an important and influential theoretical paradigm. By articulating minimum contract justice in capabilities terms, this book offers a way for those with an interest in private law theory and contract law specifically, to engage capabilities as they think of contract law's role in a just society more broadly.

A second explanation to pursue a capabilities based normative framework, then, appeals to the fact that the normative significance of capabilities has gained broad appreciation and influence in areas of human development, welfare economics, and political philosopy. The fact that capabilities approaches are widely explored, extended and endorsed, not only lends plausibility (though not necessarily truth) to the normative aspects that capabilities perspectives make visible, but suggests that there is an interesting exploration possible in the extension to contract law. The explanatory, interpretive and normative power of a capabilities perspective for different areas of law has been established, for instance through work that elaborates its close connections to the language of fundamental rights, the legal concept of capacity, and the image of a consumer central in consumer law.[8] But much remains to be examined, in particular as it regards the role of contract law, and private law more broadly, for a society's pursuit and commitment to justice. The elaboration of the connections between capabilities based perspectives on justice and contract law offer a contribution to that broader exploration. The examinations offered in this book can be regarded of interest then, because they can be read to provide further support for capabilities frameworks, or reveal the ways in which this paradigm is inadequate as it regards the implications for contract law. While the book aims to put forth a compelling capabilities

[8] See: Nussbaum, MC, 'The Supreme Court 2006 Term Foreword: Constitutions and Capabilities: "Perception" against Lofty Formalism' (2007) 121 *Harvard Law Review* 4–97; Deakin, S, '"Capacitas": Contract Law and the Institutional Preconditions of a Market Economy' (2006) 2 *European Review of Private Law* 317–41; Benöhr, I, *EU Consumer Law and Human Rights* (Oxford University Press, 2013).

perspective on minimum contract justice, it can also offer an anchor for alternative views of justice to further develop an account of justice implications for contract law. In particular, alternative views may elaborate how a capabilities based standard of minimum contract justice fails in its attempt to capture what we may believe justice entails in our society.

This book's extension of the capabilities paradigm to contract law, offers two contributions: 1) it contributes to an understanding of the scope of capabilities based normative claims of minimum justice, and 2) it offers a novel normative argument within contract theory where capabilities based arguments are largely absent. There are several reasons for the further choice for Nussbaum's capabilities approach. First, this approach is the most advanced, as a theory of justice, albeit a partial account thereof. Second, the approach has close and explicit connections to political and legal insitutions, such that it is possible to articulate its implications for contract law. Specifically, Nussbaum's capabilities approach provides an explicit account of the justificatory basis for the use of state power. While it does not explicitly address the question of contract law's role in a society's pursuit of minimum justice, its implications can be explored as contract law fulfils a central role in determining when state power is available for private pursuits through contract. For contract law then, Nussbaum's version of a capabilities perspective on minimum justice offers the basis for an analysis of the justification of the selective use of state power in recognising, shaping and enforcing contractual relationships between private parties. Third, the partiality of the theory, ie, its focus on minimum justice as opposed to full justice, fits well with the parts of contract law on which this book focuses. Contractual rules on invalidity and immorality set minimum standards for the recognition and enforcement of contractual relations. They offer an account of a society's minimum standards for contractual behaviour and offer a standard for identifying unacceptable consequences of market conduct. Provided that contract law serves a role in a society's pursuit of social justice, the rules that set minimum standards for contractual relations dovetail a minimum account of justice. Thus, this book's account of minimum contract justice, similar to Nussbaum's account of minimum justice, aims to detail only a minimum requirement, and leaves open the extent to, and ways in which other parts of contract law should promote an account of full justice, whatever we believe that account entails.

II. A Capabilities Based Approach to Minimum Justice

The remainder of this section will detail the constitutive elements of a capabilities based approach to minimum justice, developed by Martha Nussbaum.[9]

[9] Martha Nussbaum developed her capabilities approach in the area of political philosophy as a partial theory of justice. See, for a first synthesis of the approach: Nussbaum M, *Women and Human*

This approach expresses the idea that a minimally just society ought to secure certain central capabilities up to a threshold level for all its members, which is compatible with human dignity. There is a central role for the political principles and their supporting (legal) institutions in performing this task. In order to respect the equal dignity of persons, a pluralistic society should commit to political liberalism, endorsing only a political conception of the good life that can be accepted by all who recognise the equal dignity of other human beings. As such, the project of minimum justice builds on the idea that individuals hold the idea of living with others on just and respectful terms, as part of their conceptions of the good. The centrality of justice itself, as part of the good, also includes a notion of global justice. In asking what minimum justice requires of contract law, it is important that living with and towards others on just and respectful terms is a central part of the good. This section discusses the implications of minimum justice for contract law, and for its function in determining what sorts of conduct and relationships are considered permissible, that is to say, what contracts and contract terms can rely on state power for their support and realisation.

A. Central Capabilities

A capabilities approach to minimum justice does not set out principles of justice, which function as a touchstone of how a society should look like if it is to be fully just.[10] Rather, it seeks to put forward a basic benchmark for what a decently just society should secure for all its members as a basic social minimum. The capabilities concept, and an account of the sorts of capabilities that are central to a human life, form the core of a minimum standard of justice. The capabilities concept refers to a space of substantive choice or opportunity to function. As spaces of choice, individuals should remain free regarding the pursuit and achievement of any specific capability.[11] A capabilities approach to questions of justice does not focus on the actual 'functionings' that people have effectuated within the areas

Development: The Capabilities Approach (Cambridge University Press, 2000a); see for an extension of her approach to justice to issues of disability, species and nationality, Nussbaum (n 4); and for the latest, introductory statement of the developments in capability and capabilities discourse: Nussbaum (n 1). Important earlier work illustrates her development of elements of the approach, for example: Nussbaum, MC, 'Nature, Function and Capability' (1988) 1 *Oxford Studies on Ancient Philosophy* 145–84; Nussbaum, MC, 'Human Functioning and Social Justice: In Defence of Aristotelian Essentialism' (1992) 20 *Political Theory* 202–46; and Nussbaum, MC, 'Aristotle on Human Nature and the Foundations of Ethics' in J Altham and R Harrison (eds), *World, Mind, and Ethics* (Cambridge University Press, 1995). However, Nussbaum has made several modifications to her approach, particularly endorsing a political understanding of the capabilities on her list. See: Nussbaum, MC, 'Aristotle, Politics, and Human Capabilities: A Response to Antony, Arneson, Charlesworth, and Mulgan' (2000b) 111 *Ethics* 102–40.

[10] Nussbaum (n 4) 71, 75.

[11] Nussbaum (2000a) (n 9) 86 et seq; Nussbaum (n 4) 79–80; Nussbaum (n 1) 24–25. However, exceptions pertain, see section B below.

articulated as central to human lives, but focuses on the space of substantive freedom, or the ability that people have to choose to function. A capability, ie, an ability to do or be something, consists of the combined existence of 1) internal ability and 2) the external social, material and political preconditions necessary for the effective exercise of this internal ability.[12] An unbridgeable gap may exist between being able to exercise physical control over property and to be able to do so effectively in one's social and political context. For instance, while women are no less internally able than men to control property, they may be socially, politically and legally excluded from the ability to hold property and exercise control over it on an equal basis.[13] Moreover, even when women are able to be property right holders, there may still be social and legal impediments to their ability to exercise them. A salient example is married women's exclusion from legal capacity, which precludes them from independently engaging in contractual relations to exchange their property with others, and consequently hinders their ability to exercise their property rights.[14]

The relevant distinctions that a capabilities perspective makes visible are often illustrated in capabilities literature with introductory examples with the following structure. We imagine two women, living on opposite sides of the globe, neither of them holds property and their lives are characterised by equal levels of functioning and dependence on others around them, who provide for their material needs. Consider the following two descriptions. 1) Dawa renounces all claims to property when she joins an association of faith. She depends on the charity of others to meet her basic needs. If she would choose to do so, Dawa could easily become a holder of property and property rights by altering her relationship with the association of faith: the political principles that shape her society would recognise such rights on an equal basis with others, and there are no social norms in place that obstruct her choice to do so. In her society, Dawa would be able to exercise her property rights by engaging in exchange and contractual relationships with others. 2) Nima is homeless and is not the holder of property and property rights. She is dependent on the members of her community in order to meet her basic needs, and spends most of her days seeking out the charity of passersby. Previously she lived in a small home with her husband, but after his death she was expelled from that home, because the society she lives in does not recognise her politically, socially or legally, as someone who is able to be the holder of a property right.

Although both Dawa and Nima may have equal levels of functioning in relation to their exercise of control over their material environments, their capabilities levels differ vastly due to the external social and political preconditions that shape

[12] For a more elaborate discussion on the distinction between basic capabilities (also: 'rudimentary abilities'), internal capabilities and combined capabilities (also: 'central capabilities') see Nussbaum (2000a) (n 9) 83–86.

[13] On the importance of property rights for self-definition in the context of India, see Nussbaum (2000a) (n 9) 80 and 156.

[14] Hesselink, MW, 'Capacity and Capability in European Contract Law' (2005) *European Review of Private Law* 491–507, 496.

their lives. Dawa has chosen her level of functioning and is able to take leave of the dependence that shapes her current life, whereas Nima lacks this support and the ability to change her dependence. Nima's external conditions have not secured the preconditions necessary for the effective exercise of her internal ability to have control over her material environment. From a capabilities perspective, Nima's situation would be cause for concern in terms of minimum justice, whereas Dawa's situation would not. The example illustrates what minimum justice understood in capabilities terms requires: the social bases for all the central capabilities must be put into place for each individual to be able to function effectively. The focus thus lies in creating and securing an enabling environment for each individual.

There are different accounts of the appropriate selection of capabilities deemed central to a human life.[15] In the context of minimum justice, these accounts point to different areas of life where minimum justice requires a space of substantive freedom. Lists of central capabilities are advanced as tentative proposals, to be worked out for each society. Nussbaum's list of central capabilities represents an account of human entitlements as the evaluative basis of minimum justice claims. Within her approach to minimum justice, all human beings are entitled to a threshold level of these central capabilities.[16] The threshold level of the central capabilities corresponds to what individuals need in a society in order to live a life that is worthy of human dignity.[17] The list contains the following central capabilities:[18]

Life	Being able to live to the end of a human life of normal length; not dying prematurely, or before one's life is so reduced as to be not worth living.
Bodily health	Being able to have good health, including reproductive health; to be adequately nourished; to have adequate shelter.
Bodily integrity	Being able to move freely from place to place; to be secure against violent assault, including sexual assault and domestic violence; having opportunities for sexual satisfaction and for choice in matters of reproduction.
Senses, imagination and thought	Being able to use the senses, to imagine, think and reason—and to do these things in a 'truly human' way, a way informed and cultivated by an adequate education, including, but by no means limited to, literacy and basic mathematical and scientific training. Being able to use imagination and thought in connection with experiencing and producing works and events of one's own choice, religious, literacy, musical. And so forth. Being able to use one's mind in ways protected by guarantees of freedom of expression with respect to both political and artistic speech, and freedom of religious exercise. Being able to have pleasurable experience and to avoid non-beneficial pain.

[15] See for instance Anderson (n 4).

[16] Nussbaum (n 4) 226–227; Nussbaum (n 1) 62.

[17] Nussbaum (n 4) 71; Nussbaum (n 1) 24, 40 et seq.

[18] The list of capabilities is included in full and represents the most recent articulation by Nussbaum (n 1) 33–34, same in Nussbaum (n 4) 76–78

Emotions	Being able to have attachments to things and people outside ourselves; to love those who love and care for us, to grieve at their absence; in general, to love, to grieve, to experience longing, gratitude, and justified anger. Not having one's emotional development blighted by fear and anxiety. (Supporting this capability means supporting forms of human association that can be shown to be crucial in their development.)
Practical reason	Being able to form a conception of the good and to engage in critical reflection about the planning of one's life. (This entails protection for the liberty of conscience and religious observance.)
Affiliation	A. Being able to live with and towards others, to recognise and show concern for other human beings, to engage in various forms of social interaction; to be able to imagine the situation of another. (Protecting this capability means protecting institutions that constitute and nourish such forms of affiliation, and also protecting the freedom of assembly and political speech.) B. Having the social bases of self-respect and non-humiliation; being able to be treated as a dignified being whose worth is equal to that of others. This entails provisions of non-discrimination on the basis of race, sex, sexual orientation, ethnicity, caste, religion, national origin.
Other species	Being able to live with concern for and in relation to animals, plants, and the world of nature.
Play	Being able to laugh, to play, to enjoy recreational activities.
Control over one's environment	A. Political. Being able to participate effectively in political choices that govern one's life; having the right of political participation, protections of free speech and association. B. Material. Being able to hold property (both land and movable goods), and having property rights on an equal basis with others; having the right to seek employment on an equal basis with others; having the freedom from unwarranted search and seizure. In work, being able to work as a human being, exercising practical reason and entering into meaningful relationships of mutual recognition with other workers.

While some capabilities on this list have been subject to criticism, its core represents an overlapping consensus about the sorts of human capabilities that are central to human lives: they appear on other lists of capabilities, as well as in human rights documents. It is compelling that this common core would be included in any list of central capabilities, whatever else a society may endorse on it.

B. Moral Content: Some Freedoms are Bad

The formation of Nussbaum's list of central capabilities is guided by the question of how a life that is worthy of human dignity would look like: which functionings are required to make a life truly human, or, asked differently, which abilities exert a moral claim towards development, because they are evaluated as valuable?[19] The first step in answering this question entails elaborating an account of the activities considered of central importance for the recognition of a human life. At which benchmark do people deny that a human being still exists?[20] The second step aims to raise this benchmark towards a morally rich standard: asking when the engagement in such activities is fully human. A conception of humanity guides the exploration of the second question, which focuses centrally on the value of having control over the shaping of one's own life (rational) and doing so in relation with and to others (social).[21] In this context, two capabilities on the list of central capabilities enjoy a special status: the capability of practical reason and the capability of affiliation. These two capabilities can be described '*architectonic*', as they are the architectural pillars for the entire list: these two capabilities are engaged in all other central capabilities and make any activity become a *human* activity.[22] For instance, the question of whether or not someone is able '*to work as a human being*',[23] asks whether a person is able to work in accordance with their own life plan and conception of the good (practical reason); and whether or not one is able to enter into meaningful relationships of mutual recognition with other workers (affiliation). The list of central capabilities thus has significant substantive moral content, providing a basis for making claims about the circumstances under which human lives are deprived of full human functioning and therefore deprived of human dignity.[24] To recap, the minimum standard of justice focuses on creating, maintaining and protecting an enabling environment in which individuals enjoy substantive freedom to choose the beings and doings that are in accordance with their own life plans and conceptions of the good. The areas of substantive freedom that inform claims of minimum justice are included within an account, eg, a list, of central capabilities.

The beings and doings for which minimum justice requires a social basis are thus qualified. Not all freedoms are protected under the banner of basic justice. While the minimum standard of justice may have nothing to say with regard to many

[19] Nussbaum (n 4) 70. On the methodology behind the articulation of the list see: Katzer, M, 'The Basis of Universal Liberal Principles in Nussbaum's Political Philosophy' (2010) 2 *Public Reason* 60–75.

[20] Nussbaum (2000b) (n 9) 116–124, also Nussbaum (n 4) 71–72.

[21] Nussbaum (2000b) (n 9) 119; Nussbaum (n 4) 71–72.

[22] Nussbaum, MC, 'Women's Bodies: Violence, Security, Capabilities' (2005) 6 *Journal of Human Development and Capabilities* 167–183, 181; Nussbaum (2000a) (n 9) 82.

[23] See: List 'Control over one's environment' under point B.

[24] Nussbaum refers to it as a '*thick vague*' conception of the good. The label is used to contrast with Rawls' primary goods, which he coined a 'thin conception of the good'. See: Nussbaum (1992) (n 9) 214–215.The paper, however, reflects an early articulation of a part of Nussbaum's capabilities approach, which she has later revised and developed towards a *political* conception of the good, a proposed overlapping consensus between otherwise competing conceptions of the good, which serves the political purpose of creating a decently just society.

activities and freedoms,[25] there are also certain freedoms that should be repudiated, and excluded from people's pallets of choice, as a matter of minimum justice.[26] Certain freedoms should be considered as bad on the basis of a list of central capabilities, as they undermine the central capabilities of others. A clear example is men's freedom to have intercourse with their wives, regardless of whether they consent.[27] A slaveholders' freedom to own other human beings would fall within the same category. Indeed, there is broad consensus, not only in denying that people are entitled to such freedoms, but also in deeming such freedoms as bad. Other examples include freedoms that—although not categorically unjust if available in a society—can be used in such a manner that is to be curtailed. An example is the situation in which a person pollutes to the degree that the natural environment of others is destroyed along with the opportunities to provide for their basic needs.

Similarly, the list also provides a basis for making claims about the types of freedoms that should be excluded in light of a person's own basic capabilities. Namely, the approach is not neutral regarding a person's freedom to be excluded from the central abilities to function. In order to be regarded as a human being with dignity, central choices should remain open, even if one would voluntarily agree to be excluded from such freedom.[28] Closing central abilities to function upon one's request, is deeply problematic from a capabilities perspective, as it would require that a society stops treating that person with equal respect. The role of equal respect will be detailed shortly, but let me first detail several possible responses to the approach of minimum justice accounted for so far.

The central capabilities that feature in the approach to minimum justice represent a morally rich content, and define a limited pluralistic account of valuable capabilities. As such, Nussbaum's proposed list has invoked the criticism that it is insufficiently 'objective' (ie, illiberal) and illegitimate with regard to its claim of universal application.[29] This response could affect this book's project of minimum contract justice, in its current form, if the morally rich content of the approach is problematic as a basis for a standard of contract justice in the European context. That is to say, the evaluative standard of minimum justice would be illegitimate if the central capabilities on which it relies are deeply controversial, such that they cannot be understood as representative and compatible with democratic accounts of fundamental human entitlements. In asking questions about the political function of contract law, the question is whether or not the moral content of a capabilities approach is so far from what could be acceptable as a political account of the

[25] Certain freedoms might be subject to demands of full justice, but most are probably not subject to demands of justice at all.

[26] Nussbaum, MC, 'Capabilities as Fundamental Entitlements: Sen and Social Justice' (2003) 9 *Feminist Economics* 33–59, 44–46; also in Nussbaum (n 1) 71–74.

[27] Nussbaum (2003) ibid 45.

[28] See for instance Nussbaum (n 1) 26–27.

[29] See for example Arneson, RJ, 'Perfectionism and Politics' (2000) 111 *Ethics* 37–63 and more recently: Biondi, F, 'Is Martha Nussbaum Really Political Liberal?' (2008) 94 *Archiv für Rechts- und Sozialphilosophie* 311–24 and Katzer (n 19).

good as to render the current proposal irrelevant to the debate. The answer to this question is negative. Any question regarding social justice must provide to some extent an account of the good. The one presented in the current version of the capabilities approach is compelling in part, because, and to the extent to which, it corresponds to internationally articulated accounts. Various capabilities on the list represent areas of freedom and ability widely regarded as central to human lives. For instance, these central capabilities are articulated as human rights and fundamental entitlements in internationally endorsed documents, and feature as central categories for measurements regarding well-being, development and opulence.[30] This reflection can also offer the beginning of a response to another line of criticism, namely that the (academic) articulation of a list of central capabilities fail to meet requirements of procedural justice. In this view, the central capabilities are not (only) controversial in moral content, but instead, fail to meet justice requirements for the process of the formation of a list. However, if a list is interpreted as a proposal, illustrative of how minimum justice requirements function, capabilities identified through an appropriate procedure (to be defined by full justice) can be substituted for the central capabilities currently listed. The anchoring idea of the capabilities approach to minimum justice is that members of the human species are entitled to certain central capabilities, whereas the articulation of their specific content is tentative and proposed as a starting point for further political debate. For this book's project, this means that we can look at European constitutional values and fundamental rights documents, in order to see which central capabilities are currently considered objects of broad consensus and endorsement.[31] In this context, the book's project relies on central capabilities that are objects of both European, and international consensus, such that it can respond to potential controversy regarding their moral content and criticism regarding their procedural identification. As such, these central capabilities are compelling elements of a political conception of the good: ie, a conception that has the function to ensure minimum justice in a society characterised by circumstances of plurality.

C. Equal Respect in a Pluralistic Society

The project of minimum contract justice advances from a capabilities account that articulates a minimum standard of justice for a society that shows equal respect to individuals who hold different values, and who are characterised (internally and through their external circumstances) by individual differences.[32] Its moral

[30] The capabilities approach in this form is understood as a species of a human rights approach. See: Nussbaum (n 4) 78 and 284 et seq.; also Nussbaum, MC, 'Capabilities and Human Rights' (1997) 66 *Fordham Law Review* 273–300.

[31] The legally binding status of the Charter of Fundamental Rights of the European Union is equal to that of the founding treaties.

[32] Nussbaum (2000a) (n 9) 31–32.

content must be understood in this context, ie, serving the political purpose of creating a decently just society.[33] By putting forth the moral content of a capabilities approach, as a political conception of the good, the account represents a politically liberal project.[34] Political liberalism refers to the idea that in a pluralistic society (ie, a society in which individuals hold conflicting and competing comprehensive conceptions of the good), the state is to show equal respect to all its members by refraining from the endorsement of a particular comprehensive conception.[35] Instead, the state is to adhere to a set of political principles that serve basic justice.

From a capabilities perspective, a society ought to show equal respect to all its members by ensuring that each individual has the ability to formulate, hold and pursue *reasonable* conceptions of the good on equal grounds with others. Respect can be described as

> (…) a way of regarding and treating persons, closely related to the Kantian idea of treating humanity as an end and never as a mere means. Respect is thus closely linked to the idea of dignity, to the idea that humanity has worth and not merely a price. Equal respect would then be respect that appropriately acknowledges the equal dignity and worth that persons have as ends.[36]

From this account follows the idea that the political institutions, which bind those whom they govern, are not to grant privileges to some over others by adhering to a particular comprehensive conception of the good, as it may support the life plans of some individuals, while barring those of others. The result of such a structure would be one in which some individuals would be denigrated continuously:

> When the institutions that pervasively govern your life are built on a view that in all conscience you cannot endorse, that means that you are, in effect, in a position of second-class citizenship. Even if you are tolerated (…), government will state, every day, that a different view, incompatible with yours, is the correct view, and that yours is wrong.[37]

In this conception of political liberalism, the qualification of equal respect to individuals who hold *reasonable* conceptions of the good is informed by the idea of equal respect itself.[38] A reasonable individual is one who accepts equal respect as a political value, and who holds a conception of the good that is compatible with equal respect in the political realm.[39] Conversely, unreasonable individuals are those who hold unreasonable conceptions of the good, ie, conceptions that are incompatible with respecting others as equals for political purposes. An example

[33] Nussbaum, MC, 'The Good as Discipline, the Good as Freedom' in DA Crocker and T Linden (eds), *Ethics of Consumption* (Rowman & Littlefield Publishers, 1998) 318; Nussbaum (2000a) (n 9) 76; Nussbaum (n 4) 79; Nussbaum (n 1) 89.

[34] For critical views on Nussbaum's liberalism, see references in n 29 in this chapter.

[35] For instance, Nussbaum (n 4) 70. Elaborately discussed in Nussbaum, MC, 'Perfectionist Liberalism and Political Liberalism' (2011) 39 *Philosophy and Public Affairs* 3–45.

[36] Nussbaum (2011) ibid 18.

[37] Ibid 35.

[38] Ibid 20.

[39] Ibid 33.

of an unreasonable conception of the good is, for example, one which considers unproblematic the use of individuals of a darker skin colour as a means for the ends of people with lighter skin colour; the use of women as a means for the ends of men; or the use of individuals of certain nationalities as a means for the ends of individuals with other nationalities. Reasonable conceptions of the good thus share an overlap ('overlapping consensus') defined as the idea of equal respect as a political value. Minimum contract justice seeks to advance on the basis of a capabilities approach that expresses such overlap, ie, a substantive account of an overlapping consensus that can be acceptable to reasonable citizens for the political purpose of creating a minimally just society. An important part of that account involves the idea that the significance of central capabilities extends beyond national borders.

D. A Capabilities Approach to Justice Beyond Borders

A core feature of the capabilities approach to minimum justice is the idea that certain basic capabilities represent fundamental entitlements of each human being. Their normative significance is independent of institutional recognition and extends beyond the political structures that could secure them coercively. On a moral basis then, everyone has moral duties to secure these capabilities.[40] In order to protect individual lives from this overwhelming and capabilities undermining task, these duties are derivatively assigned to institutional structures.[41] One way of understanding and identifying the institutional structure responsible for securing basic capabilities is through Rawls' concept of the basic structure. Nussbaum locates, for instance, the responsibility for securing basic capabilities in the basic structure of society, ie, 'that set of institutions that determines people's life chances pervasively and from the start of a human life.'[42] One way of interpreting the responsibility for minimum justice is to understand the basic structure of a society as coinciding with the state. In this context, the central capabilities are, in the first place, fundamental entitlements that citizens have towards their own states, ie, the basic structures of their societies.[43] An important reason for considering central capabilities, and minimum justice, as a primary task of the basic structures of the society in which individuals live, refers to the process of formation of the list (discussed above). In short, it emphasises the moral importance of a democratic connection between the basic structure of the state and the fundamental political entitlements of its members. At its core is the idea that central

[40] Nussbaum (n 4) 307 also Nussbaum, MC, 'Reply: In Defence of Global Political Liberalism' (2006) 37 *Development and Change* 1313–28, 1317.

[41] Nussbaum (n 4) 307–10.

[42] Nussbaum (n 4) 311. See Rawls, J, *A Theory of Justice* (Harvard University Press, 1971) Chapter 1, section 2.

[43] Nussbaum (n 4) 255 et seq; Nussbaum (n 1) 166 et seq.

capabilities should not be imposed on others; rather, individuals should have control over their articulations and specification in the societies in which they live.[44] Another interpretation, understands the connection between the responsibility for minimum justice and the basic structure as one that relies on influence and implementation. The basic structure of society consists of those institutions that are influential for the central capabilities of individuals. The reason to highlight the connection between the state, coinciding with the basic structure of society, and state membership is because of its influence for the lives that individuals are able to live.

The primacy of human central capabilities is reflected in efforts to extend the capabilities approach to global justice. The capabilities approach to global justice seeks to address the disproportionate distribution of advantage and disadvantage from global cooperation that shapes the lives of individuals in different nations in the world. In this context, the power of more prosperous states works in their favour, creating unfair conditions of global competition, thereby contributing to the (continued) existence of global inequality in the capabilities of individuals and persistent capabilities deprivation in less advantaged nations.[45] Although there is no global structure that is politically coercive within the global context, similar to basic structures within states, there are important institutions and structures that create and sustain global inequality. On a global level, these institutions and structures guide the allocation of the responsibility for global justice.[46] The allocation on a global level corresponds structurally to the state and its institutional structure. In the absence of a political coercive global structure, the concept of the basic structure has a non-political, ethical counterpart. Namely, the responsibility to address global injustice is placed within the structure that influences, globally, the life chances that people have. One may think, for example, of international institutions, such as the World Bank and the International Monetary Fund, or of the responsibility to work towards just global trade agreements. But private actors may also have the responsibility to secure basic capabilities; for instance, multinational corporations may have the responsibility to enhance the capabilities of those who are located in the areas of their operations.[47] In this context, Nussbaum also references the responsibility of consumers to 'bring pressure to bear on a corporation to perform better than it has been performing'.[48] The latter reflects the recognition that individual positions of advantage and disadvantage are causally connected. A denial of that connection '(…) cannot possibly be made about distant people in today's world. Even were the global economy not unfair to poorer nations, it engages us with them and gives us reason to think responsibly about how those engagements should continue'.[49]

[44] Nussbaum (n 4) 257.
[45] Nussbaum (n 1) 175.
[46] Nussbaum (n 4) 306–24.
[47] Nussbaum (n 1) 315–23.
[48] Nussbaum (n 1) 318.
[49] Nussbaum (n 1) 116.

The responsibility for advancing and supporting capabilities globally, and its connection to institutions that are part of domestic basic structures, such as contract law, can be interpreted in different ways. First, the responsibility for supporting and enhancing central capabilities on a global level lies with institutions and institutional structures that influence the central capabilities of individuals, regardless of their state membership. In asking what people across the world are able to be and do (ie, which capabilities they have) and which preconditions for capabilities are lacking in their worlds, attention goes to the basic structures that underlie cooperation extending across national borders. In this view, there is no principled reason why domestic basic structures are exempt from scrutiny in this context if they shape or maintain the cooperative structures with others elsewhere, in ways that are detrimental to their abilities to live decent lives. Thus, although it cannot be politically coerced, moral responsibility exists for the enhancement of the capabilities of those across borders. State membership (ie, nationality) is *morally irrelevant* to the question of whether or not an individual has a fundamental entitlement grounded in justice, and, for the question of whether or not others have a moral duty to support and protect them.[50] Second, the responsibility for supporting and enhancing central capabilities on a global level is not just part of a global justice approach, but also reflects part of a conception of minimum justice in which the normative significance of central capabilities extends beyond national borders. This expresses the idea that minimum justice is incompatible with the use of individuals of certain nationalities as a means for the ends of individuals with other nationalities. The constitutive elements of the capabilities approach to minimum justice, and notably the basic claim that reasonable conceptions of the good embrace the idea that justice itself, presuppose that individuals can accept that each human being (and not just each member of one's society) has basic entitlements founded on justice. The underlying purpose of cooperating and living with and towards others is found, not exclusively in mutual advantage, but in the creation of a decently just world in which each person enjoys the central capabilities.[51] The approach to minimum justice and its demands on the basic structure thus ensconces deeply this conception of the good.[52] The latter carries moral judgements beyond national borders and a critical reflection on the way in which domestic engagements sustain or contribute to global injustice. The global interconnectedness and interdependence that is characteristic of today's world brings forward claims founded on justice, highlighted in a context of global inequality. These claims also resonate when we consider the ways in which the domestic basic structures of prosperous societies contribute to shaping cooperative structures that extend national borders. These two lines of thought provide different interpretations of how the universal significance of basic capabilities relates to contract law,

[50] Nussbaum (n 4) 279–80 and Nussbaum (n 1) 114–15.
[51] Nussbaum (n 4) 273–275.
[52] Nussbaum (n 4) 158.

if at all. The first view, connects claims of global justice to a global institutional structure, in which contract law may play a role, while the second points to the way that a notion of global justice is ensconced in the minimum standard of justice itself, for which a society's basic structure is responsible. In the latter view, the normative significance of central capabilities across national borders is pertinent to contract law, if the latter is part of the responsibility bearing structure for minimum justice. This book will proceed with the latter line of thought, as its central project is to detail the implications of minimum justice for contract law, that is to say, the question whether a society can claim to be minimally just if it supports contractual relations (of its own members) that are detrimental for others elsewhere. The question addressed in the remainder of this chapter is therefore whether or not contract law is, or parts of it are, subject to the demands of minimum standards of justice.

III. Contract Law and the Responsibility Bearing Structure of Society

The second part of this chapter examines the question whether or not contract law, and specifically the rules concerning contractual immorality and invalidity, should be understood as subject to the demands of minimum justice. This section will focus in particular on the concept of the basic structure of society, or society's responsibility bearing structure, which functions as an influential concept for the sphere of application for the requirements of minimum justice. Whether or not contract law has a role in serving, enhancing and securing minimum justice, depends on whether we should understand the responsibility bearing structure of society to include contract law, or parts of it. How can we identify 'responsibility bearing' (basic) structure from institutions that are 'non-responsibility bearing'? In order to consider contract law in light of minimum justice, we must reflect on its political function, and examine the role that it plays in human lives. Can a capabilities approach to minimum justice be neutral towards contract law? If the rules that define the structure of contractual relations, eg, rules on contractual immorality, are basic structure, as is argued here, this entails that they must be constructed, in conjunction with the entire basic structure, in ways that are compatible with minimum justice. What are the implications of minimum justice for the defining structure of contractual relations?

An influential concept for the selective application of principles of justice is Rawls' basic structure of society. On the first pages of *A Theory of Justice*, Rawls describes it as 'the way in which the major social institutions distribute fundamental rights and duties and determine the division of advantages from social cooperation'.[53] Those institutions that establish and determine the social processes that

[53] Rawls (n 42) 6.

produce distributions of advantage and disadvantage in a society, the institutions that determine life chances from the start, are the 'primary subject of justice'.[54] Rawls' concept of the basic structure has been subject to diverging interpretations and consequent discussion concerning the question of whether or not (parts of) contract law should be understood as included in it.[55] Notably, Rawls writes that the principles of justice 'may be irrelevant for' (...) 'the fairness of voluntary cooperative arrangements or procedures for making contractual agreements'.[56] However, the discussion on Rawls' conception of the basic structure, and the ambiguity associated with its relation to contract law arise from other entries in his writings, which include somewhat different formulations of the concept and its distinctive features. The slightly different descriptions appear in passages where Rawls refers to: 1) the distinction between 'the basic structure and the rules applying directly to individuals and associations and to be followed by them in particular transactions';[57] 2) both coercive and non-coercive institutions;[58] and 3) the inclusive idea that basic structure institutions are identified by their pervasive influence on life chances.[59] These allegedly diverging conceptions of the basic structure have been subject to debate concerning similarly diverging implications for the question of whether or not contract law should be properly understood as being subject to Rawlsian political philosophy.

There are at least three versions of the interpretation of the relationship between Rawls' basic structure and contract law.[60] A narrow conception of the basic structure excludes contract law as a whole, and limits the understanding of the basic structure to constitutional liberties and the system of tax and transfer. On the other side of the spectrum we find the broadest interpretation, which includes contract law and any aspect of social life that affects an individual's life chances pervasively and from the start. Between these understandings of the basic structure, there are selective interpretations which include, for instance, only parts of contract law that have distributive effects, or only parts, which are legally coercive. The first, narrow, conception considers Rawls' theory of justice to be neutral towards the way in which contract law is constructed, ie, contract law and the range of alternative outcomes that it can produce, are irrelevant for questions of a socially just distribution. More inclusive conceptions hold that contract law, or

[54] Rawls (n 42) 6–7.

[55] The question is answered in the affirmative by Kronman, AT, 'Contract Law and Distributive Justice' (1980) 89 *The Yale Law Journal*; Murphy, L, 'Institutions and the Demands of Justice' (1999) 27 *Philosophy & Public Affairs* 251–291; Kordana, KA and DH Tabachnick, 'Rawls and Contract Law' (2005) 73 *The George Washington Law Review* 598–632; different by Ripstein, A, 'Private Order and Public Justice: Kant and Rawls' (2006) 92 *Virginia Law Review* 1391–1438.

[56] Rawls (n 42) 7.

[57] Rawls, J, *Political Liberalism* (Columbia University Press, 1993) 268–69.

[58] Notably, his inclusion of the family in the basic structure, see discussion in Nussbaum (2000a) (n 9) Chapter 4.

[59] Rawls (n 42) 7.

[60] See Kordana and Tabachnik (n 55).

at least some relevant parts of it, should be constructed in conjunction with the basic structure as a whole, in a way that aims to satisfy the principles of justice. In a Rawlsian understanding, this could mean that (the relevant parts of) contract law should serve to maximise the position of the least well-off.[61] It remains subject to debate what the best or most persuasive Rawlsian interpretation is of the concept of the basic structure, and consequently how we can best understand its relationship to contract law.[62] However, if we examine the function of the concept of the basic structure through its normative significance for individual capabilities, the relationship between demands of justice and contract law is less ambiguous. While one can maintain, from a Rawlsian perspective, that contract law is to be excluded entirely from the basic structure, a similar argument is difficult to produce in the context of this book's capabilities perspective to minimum justice.

A capabilities based pursuit of minimum justice is oriented towards the creation of a right outcome, ie, securing the central capabilities up to the threshold level to all individuals.[63] The basic structure, or the responsibility bearing structure, should work towards a minimally just society. The central capabilities function as independent criteria for evaluating the procedure and social processes that produce the outcome.[64] A society can only be evaluated as minimally just, if, and only if, the central capabilities are secured up to an appropriate threshold level. This orientation towards a just substantive outcome guides the type of argument that needs to be made in order to identify the social processes and institutions that are 'responsibility bearing' (basic) structure. It also informs the role and underlying reason for focusing on an institutional responsibility bearing structure to begin with, as it safeguards individual freedoms and the lives people are able to live. The importance of capabilities informs the normative significance of the responsibility bearing structure from the start.[65]

Similarly, the capabilities that are central for evaluations of justice provide guidance for thinking about what is and is not part of the responsibility bearing structure and, for the allocation of responsibility to particular institutions. The identification of the responsible institutions for securing and enhancing individual capabilities is not removed from the orientation towards human lives: what matters is the role an institution or social process plays in relation to the central capabilities of individuals. What role does an institution play for the lives that people are able to live? Would alternative constructions be able to make significant

[61] Kordana and Tabachnik (n 55) 621–22.

[62] See for an important recent contribution: Scheffler, S, 'Distributive Justice, the Basic Structure and the Place of Private Law' (2015) *Oxford Journal of Legal Studies* 1–23.

[63] Nussbaum identifies this as the 'deepest difference' between her partial theory of justice and Rawls' theory of justice. Nussbaum (n 4) 81 et seq.

[64] Rawls' theory of justice contrasts with capabilities oriented pursuits of justice in this sense. See Nussbaum (n 4) 82–83 and Rawls (n 42) 74–75.

[65] Although people may be responsible for securing the central capabilities to all, the burden of the pursuit of minimum justice is not to fall on individuals, as this would undermine individual capabilities and would therefore be counterproductive. See Nussbaum (n 4) 306 et seq.

contributions in creating or securing central capabilities, ie, in a society's pursuit towards minimum justice? It is these sorts of questions that help guide the question whether contract law should be considered as a responsibility bearing, basic structure. That is to say, whether contract law, or parts of it, is subject to the requirements of minimum justice depends on the role it plays in the central capabilities that are important for individuals. Thus, we must first ask what role contract law, and in particular rules of contractual immorality, play in society and how they influence individual lives as they interact with one another.[66]

A. The Significance of Contractual Relations for Human Capabilities

To be able to say something about the role of contract law in society and individual lives, I will discuss contract law as the law governing economic transactions and market exchanges in particular. So let me first elaborate on the relationship between market exchanges and capabilities.

In modern societies, the ability to engage in exchange, to participate in the market, is not akin to participating in a game one happens to enjoy and is able to afford. Rather, the ability to engage in market exchanges is important for the pursuit of one's life plan, whatever it may be. The market plays a prominent role in people's lives, which is most evident when we directly ask how people function in the areas of the central capabilities, ie, abilities to achieve valuable functionings. For instance, how do people obtain adequate nourishment or adequate shelter, how do people obtain a decent education and execute control over their material environment?[67] The answers to these questions have in common that people participate in market exchanges, primarily, to achieve valuable functionings.

One way to understand the importance of the ability to participate in the market is by articulating it as a capability, that is to say, as 'the substantive freedom to realize, through participation in the market, a range of desired end-states and activities'.[68] This conceptualisation of market exchange does not straightforwardly show its relationship to minimum justice, unless a close connection can be made between the ability to engage in market exchange and the central capabilities that should function as benchmarks for normative evaluations of justice.[69] If we take Nussbaum's capabilities list as a guideline, we see that it does not articulate the

[66] The question of whether or not contract law is drawn into the basic structure as a whole, or if only some parts are to be considered basic structure, need not be answered conclusively here, good arguments for the former position are made by Kordana and Tabachnick(n 55) 598–632, 617–19.

[67] See also: Study Group on Social Justice in European Private Law, 'Social Justice in European Contract Law: A Manifesto' (2004) 10 *European Law Journal* 655.

[68] Deakin (n 8) 340. See also Deakin, S and A Supiot (eds), *Capacitas: Contract Law and the Institutional Preconditions of a Market Economy* (Hart Publishing, 2009).

[69] Compare: Sen (1999b) (n 2) 25–26 and Nussbaum (2003) (n 26) 44–46; Nussbaum (n 1) 71. By contrast, Sen seems to adhere to the idea that the ability to transact with others is a valuable activity per se, in the same way that having conversations is valuable, ie, as a mode of social interaction. It seems

ability to participate in market exchange as a central human capability. In this context, the ability to participate in the market would not directly and independently influence our evaluation of minimum justice. We can imagine a human society in which the absence of the ability to engage in market exchange is not problematic for human dignity, like the absence of the ability to be adequately nourished would be. In other words, a person's inability to participate in market exchange is not reflective of a lack of human dignity *per se*. However, for modern societies, we can think of the ways in which the ability to engage in market exchange is of crucial importance to human lives, that is, important for the central capabilities that may figure on a list such as the one articulated by Nussbaum.

What sorts of desired end-states and activities may be entailed in the substantive freedom of individuals to engage in market exchange? Only insofar as market exchange is entailed in desired end-states and activities that are pertinent to central capabilities, would they be salient for minimum justice. There are at least two ways in which these relationships can be construed. First, market exchange is the primary mechanism through which individuals fulfil some of their basic needs, such as obtaining food, income, and shelter. If individuals are unable to, or excluded from, obtaining these goods through market exchange it would seriously impact on their abilities to function in valuable ways and in areas that are directly relevant for evaluations of justice. Second, the ability to engage in exchange is also relevant for the control over one's material environment. The latter not only entails the ability to hold property and have property rights on an equal basis with others, but also the freedoms that individuals have to exercise those rights. The ability to hold property and property rights seems devoid of real meaning, if these do not include, centrally, the possibility to exchange.[70] In particular, if holding property rights on an equal basis with others is an important benchmark for minimum justice, this would simply exclude a structure in which the ability to exercise those rights would be constructed unequally. In other words, if the capability to exercise control over one's material environment is central to justice, and it is to be constructed on an equal basis for each individual, then the ability to engage with others in economic exchanges should be constructed with a similar concern for equality.

Both connections suggest that the ability to engage in market exchange is not valuable per se, but only insofar as it is entailed in other valuable pursuits. In this context, the interdependence between central capabilities is of special significance.[71] Deprivation in one area can undermine valuable functioning in other

that any restriction on contractual freedom, ie, the ability to transact, would entail a loss of something valuable from that perspective. See: Sen (1999b) (n 2) 6–7.

[70] Nussbaum does not discuss contract law, or the importance of freedom of contract explicitly, but the latter must be entailed in her discussion about property rights, since the effective exercise of property rights necessarily includes the/some ability to engage in transactions. See, in Nussbaum (2000a) (n 9), eg, 156 and further Chapter 4, 282.

[71] See for instance Nussbaum (n 4) 289–90 on the relationship between economic and social entitlements and political liberties.

areas. For instance, the inability to be adequately nourished quickly erodes not only the ability to live a life of normal length, but also the architectonic capabilities of practical reason and affiliation. Pervasive need can push people into activities—including exchanges with others—that have detrimental effects on their abilities to function in valuable ways. Market exchanges can be sources or facilitating factors of capability deprivations and therefore infringements of fundamental entitlements.[72] Moreover, in a similar sense, market exchanges and the structure of the market overall can have adverse effects on the capabilities of others. For questions of minimum justice, market exchanges can be potential sources of capability deprivation and it is an area of human interaction where questions of justice pertain. To recap, these market exchanges can be considered to be of significance for central capabilities in at least three ways. First, market exchanges are the mechanisms through which individuals fulfil a set of basic needs in terms of consumption goods such as food and clothes. Second, the ability to engage in market exchange is implied within a meaningful understanding of the ability to have control over one's material environment and stands in an interdependent relationship with other central capabilities. Third, the market and market exchanges can be properly understood as potential sources or facilitating factors of capability deprivation.

The significance of contractual relations and contract law for human capabilities can be elaborated through this discussion of economic transaction and market exchanges. Namely, contract law can be described, in a broad sense, as the law that governs economic transactions. In particular, contract law is the institution that specifies the conditions under which economic transactions become *contracts*, ie, transactions that are legally enforceable. People can, in principle, engage in transactions and exchange with others on the basis of the conditions and terms they wish, and markets form wherever supply and demand meet. However, in the context of the questions of minimum justice at issue, the transactions that I refer to here are market exchanges that are supported by state power.[73] 'The market' is governed by legal structures, notably by contract law, which makes available the legal enforcement of transactions for exchange, and determines the rights and obligations between transacting parties, and the consequences of breach. In other words, contract law determines which transactions the state would be willing to enforce and how. Contract law is the institution that transforms a limited and favoured set of transactions between individuals into *contracts* between private parties. The transformation is limited as contract law's conditions are selective, excluding from the contractual recognition a range of transactions that private

[72] From a capabilities viewpoint on minimum justice, the central capabilities should be effectively achievable in a decently just society, it follows that the state has reasons, based on justice, to intervene where the market or private parties represent an impediment to individuals' real abilities to function in valuable ways. Nussbaum (n 4) 286–87.

[73] 'The market' refers to the manner of exchange that is legally recognised and has a formal and official character, as opposed to 'black' markets, which function underground or outside of the structures established as legitimate.

actors pursue. In addition, the transformation of a transaction into a contract is favourable, because the power of the state becomes available to coerce people into behaving in accordance with what they have agreed upon with others. Public support is not equally available for transactions that lack contractual status. Moreover, contract law's rules reflect the norms about how people are to behave towards each other, and others more broadly, when engaging in market transactions. Thus, the selective enforcement of transactions as contracts also expresses state approval, and provides recognition to those activities and pursuits that comply with the (minimum) standards articulated in the rules of contract law. There are thus great advantages attached to the recognition of a transaction as a contract.

Market exchanges are important for the lives that individuals are able to live and contract law, as the institution that governs economic transactions broadly, organises the advantages and disadvantages that are attached to particular market pursuits. In fulfilling this role, alternative constructions of contract law can do better or worse for people and the lives they are able to live. Contract law determines if and under which conditions the state will support market exchanges, and determines which sorts of transactional outcomes and implications are acceptable. It thus also determines to what extent, if at all, capability deprivations are salient for the availability of public enforcement mechanisms. Because contract law is an institution that is pertinent for individual capabilities, it must be considered part of the responsibility bearing structure of a society that strives for minimum justice. The following section will assess what this responsibility entails for contract law, in particular for those rules concerning contractual immorality and invalidity.

B. The Defining Structure of Contractual Relations

In descriptions of contract law, the binding nature of contract and freedom of contract are often referred to in the same sentence, as expressions of party autonomy.[74] The principle of freedom of contract, considered as a fundamental principle of contract law, reflects the idea that private parties are free to choose whether or not to enter into a contract, with whom and on which terms. Freedom of contract is described both in negative terms, as freedom from state control or intervention, and in positive terms, as the ability to engage in contractual relationships as a form of individual self-realisation.[75] Yet, party autonomy and the principles of freedom of contract do not govern the defining structure of contract itself.

[74] See for instance: Köhler, H, *BGB Allgemeiner Teil* (33 Auflage edn Verlag CH Beck, 2009) 32; Asser/Hartkamp & Sieburgh 6-III (ed), *Mr Asser's Handleiding tot beoefening van het Nederlandse recht. 6. Algemeen overeenkomstenrecht* (Kluwer, 2010) nr 41; Whittaker, S, 'Introductory' in H Beale and AS Burrows (eds), *Chitty on Contracts Volume 1 General Principles* (Sweet & Maxwell, 2008) nr 1-010.

[75] For instance: Loth, MA, *Dwingend en aanvullend recht* (Monografieën Nieuw BW A-19, Kluwer, 2009) nr 14 and for an in-depth historical analysis of the principle see: Atiyah, PS, *The Rise and Fall of Freedom of Contract* (Clarendon, 1979).

A primary function of contract law is to determine which agreements between private parties will be legally recognised and may be enforced by means of state power. Rules on contractual immorality are part of the broader set of contract law rules that serve this function. The latter, broader set of rules lays out the requirements on contractual validity. This set includes rules that pertain to the qualities of the contracting parties, for example rules that determine legal capacity and use age as a proxy for the ability to make independent judgements. Other rules pertain to the circumstances surrounding the formation of parties' consent and intention, such as rules on defects of consent. Within this broader set of rules on contractual validity, rules on contractual immorality represent the substantive standards of morality with which agreements, if they are to be recognised as *contracts*, must comply. They function as a minimum standard for the content and implications of contracts, ie, rules on contractual immorality establish substantive benchmarks for the scope of contracts. These substantive standards identify not only those arrangements that are strictly regarded and labelled 'immoral', but also those that are illegal or otherwise contrary to public policy or *ordre public*.[76]

Jointly, rules on contractual validity define what qualifies as a contract, ie, an agreement that is legally binding between private parties and recognised as such by society as a whole. They provide insight into how the legal system recognises contracts among a variety of agreements that private parties may engage in. They provide the criteria that distinguish contracts from other sorts of relations that may appear to be very similar to contractual relations, but lack the legal significance and status of contracts. Although people may wish to refer to all types of agreements as 'contracts', what is legally recognised in a society, and supported *as a contract*, depends on the legal standards set out by rules of contractual validity. In other words, rules of contractual morality are part of the set of rules that outline the basic or *defining structure of contract*. Parties cannot deviate from these standards.[77] They do not have the freedom to decide between themselves what they consider to be immoral as contractual behaviour; the legal standards are determined exogenously to private parties' conceptions of the good. When it comes to contractual immorality, agents of the state determine *that* contracts can be immoral and invalid (eg, the legislator through a civil code) and determine *which* contracts are immoral and invalid (eg, the courts). The question of whether or not an agreement is legally binding—whether or not it is a contract—is thus dependent on normative standards exogenous to standards that the parties may hold and share between them.

[76] Taken as a whole, the category of substantive standards on contractual behaviour is commonly dealt with under headings of immorality or illegality in comparative legal studies and treated in national legal systems under various headings, including those of good morals and public policy. See for instance: Basedow, J et al (eds), *The Max Planck Encyclopedia of European Private Law Volume I* (Oxford University Press, 2012).

[77] They are mandatory rules of law. See: Loth (n 75).

At this point, it is important to highlight one purpose of contractual immorality, which is to avert the negative externalities that private agreements may have on third parties or society as a whole. All agreements have external effects simply because they exclude others from engaging in the relationship which parties seek to form. On the basis of contractual immorality, a distinction is made between those effects that are considered acceptable, and those that are not. As a whole contract law conveys to those who are governed by it, how they are to behave towards each other, and towards others, when engaging in contractual relations. Contractual immorality reveals when self-interested pursuits are devoid of recognition and support, due to unacceptable effects on others. Contractual immorality sets a minimum standard for contractual conduct in a society, ie, for economic and social cooperative structures between private persons. The rules on contractual immorality are part of the defining structure of contractual relations and they reveal when self-interested pursuits are devoid of recognition and support, due to unacceptable effects on others.

Depending on one's conception of contract law, one may think of the relation between the involvement of the state in determining the defining structure of contracts and the freedom of private parties to shape their own contractual relationships, to be one of tension as it relates to substantive standards. How should a society that strives for minimum justice understand this relationship? Can a society that strives towards minimum justice be neutral towards the way in which contractual immorality is constructed given: 1) the fact that contractual immorality imposes on market-based exchanges substantive moral requirements; and 2) the importance of markets and market-based exchanges in people's lives? It should be emphasised that the question is not whether or not a minimum capabilities based standard of justice requires the existence of rules pertaining to contractual immorality, or even rules of contract law altogether in an abstract sense, ie, for every imaginable type of human society. Rather, the question is raised in a contextual setting, and asks whether or not a society that strives for minimum justice can be indifferent to diverging conceptions of contract law in modern societies, given the fact that 'contract law' exists. Thus, the question takes for granted the availability of state power for the enforcement of contracts between persons as an established institution.

C. Diverging Conceptions of Contract Law

Various conceptions of contract law diverge significantly in their understanding of the appropriate relation between this area of law and the involvement of the state. These diverging conceptions correspond to different normative ideas about how contract law should be constructed, specifically, in relation to aims of social justice. The main differences come to the fore, particularly, in the debate about the distinction between private and public law. This debate does not concern the positive distinction between private law, as governing the (horizontal) relations between private persons, and public law, as governing the (vertical) relation between the state (acting as a state) and its citizens. Rather, the debate concerns a distinction in a more ideological sense, regarding the underlying ideas and assumptions about the principal differences between private and public law.[78] This debate has gained renewed impetus particularly in the course of the development of new transnational European instruments of contract law.

On the one hand, contract law is understood as an area of law that is autonomous and independent from public or political goals and aims.[79] Contract law's rules are to be understood in terms of expressions of contracting parties' will, as if they were their own legislators through contract. In a classic view that renders contract law principally distinct from public law, private law is said to deal with the restoration, or correction, of a wrong that has occurred between interacting parties.[80] The underlying structure of contract law aims to achieve corrective justice between contracting parties. In a normative sense, this area of law should be free from political considerations because they would interfere with the autonomy of persons. Contract law is to remain politically neutral, in order to assure that individuals are able to express their autonomous choices without being burdened by public goals. According to this view, contract law is distinctly *not* to be concerned with social (distributive) justice.[81] In fact, contract law should not be concerned with any goals that are external to this area of law at all. Contract serves its own—internally coherent—goals that are distinct from public goals such as efficiency or social justice. It is an area of law that is independent and intelligible in its own terms, that is to say, contract law has an intrinsic beauty that would be blemished by external (public) goals. In other words, contract justice is separate, as a matter of principle, from the requirements of social justice. In this classic conception of contract law, substantive standards that would serve the pursuit of minimum justice cannot be identified as anything other than an *infringement* of party autonomy, ie, freedom of contract.

The ideological distinction between private and public law that is maintained in a classic view of contract law has been deconstructed by legal realism, in particular, by critical legal studies.[82] The basic viewpoint follows the logic that every legal rule is in essence a form of state regulation. Contract law cannot be considered

[78] This debate corresponds to the debate about corrective and social justice in private law. See for example: Gordley, J, *Foundations of Private Law* (Oxford University Press, 2007) Chapter 1; Weinrib, EJ, *The Idea of Private Law* (Harvard University Press, 1995) Chapter 1; Smith, SA, *Contract Theory* (Oxford University Press, 2004) Chapter 2.

[79] See notably the conception of private law as argued by Weinrib (n 77) and Weinrib, EJ, *Corrective Justice* (Oxford University Press, 2012).

[80] Weinrib (n 78) Chapter 3.

[81] Weinrib (n 78) 61–63.

[82] Kennedy, D, 'Form and Substance in Private Law Adjudication' (1976) 89 *Harvard Law Review* 1685–1778; Kennedy, D, 'The Political Stakes in "Merely Technical" Issues of Contract Law' (2002) 10 *European Review of Private Law* 7–28; Schwartz, LB, 'With Gun and Camera through Darkest CLS-Land' (1984) 36 *Stanford Law Review* 413–64; Horwitz, MJ, 'The History of the Public Private Distinction' (1982) 130 *University of Pennsylvania Law Review* 1423–28.

as anything other than an allocated form of public state power. Namely, the state determines the boundaries of the realm of life that is governed by its rules, enacts the rules as law, and exercises state power in the enforcement of contractual rights and obligations. This view emphasises that the state shapes social life through contract law and does so, in accordance with normative ideas about how this should be structured.[83] According to this conception, labelling contract law as 'private law' indicates that it governs the relations between private persons (in the positive sense). It does not connote that it can, is or should be divorced from public or political considerations. In the absence of a principled distinction between private and public law, it is not illegitimate for the state to pursue social justice aims through contract law. In other words, contract justice cannot be separated from social justice on principle. As such, the contractual immorality and invalidity of mutually beneficial contracts are not necessarily explained in terms of *infringements* of party autonomy, ie, freedom of contract. Indeed, the contractual immorality and invalidity of mutually beneficial contracts may be justified directly by a notion of contract justice that reflects a notion of social justice.

The denial of a principled distinction between private and public law, has led towards the claim that social justice is not only legitimately pursued through contract law, but that, as a matter of fact, contract law necessarily reflects an idea of social justice adhered to by the state.[84] This point is made in reference to contract law's role in regulating market transactions. If the market is the primary mechanism through which wealth and power is allocated in modern societies and contract law regulates market relations, then contract law decides the relevant sources of power, and importantly the relevant sources of weakness, which determine market outcomes.[85] As such, a predictable pattern of advantage and disadvantage in an important social area of life is endorsed and shaped through contract law. In other words, by enacting a particular set of rules through contract law, a state establishes a particular market order, which is attached to a predictable pattern of advantage and disadvantage, ie, a predictable distributive outcome.[86] Thus, according to this view, a notion of contract justice necessarily reflects a notion of social justice.

Both views regarding the distinction between private and public law, and consequently, the nature of contract law in relation to social justice, find articulation in current contract law theories. The classic view is hard pressed to explain the existence of modern rules of contract law, which are purposely used to achieve or prevent substantive outcomes that correspond to public aims.[87] Mandatory rules of

[83] Singer, JW, 'Things that We Would Like to Take for Granted: Minimum Standards for the Legal Framework of a Free and Democratic Society' (2008) 2 *Harvard Law & Policy Review* 141–42.

[84] Collins, H, *The Law of Contract*, 4th edn (Cambridge University Press, 2003) Chapter 1; Study Group on Social Justice in European Private Law (n 67).

[85] Kronman (n 55) 496; Collins, ibid 13.

[86] Collins, ibid 12–13. Also: Singer (n 83) 141–142.

[87] For instance, as they correspond to notions of social justice, but also to efficiency in terms of enhanced market functioning.

contract law, which, for instance, aim to protect consumers, are the leading examples in this context. Conceptions of contract law that deny a principled distinction between private and public law altogether, are challenged to capture the distinctive features of contract law and its distinct internal normativity. A capabilities based understanding of minimum justice can, however, not be neutral towards these various conceptions of contract law, especially towards the way in which contractual immorality is constructed.

D. A Capabilities Based Understanding of Minimum Contract Justice and Immorality

If the market and market relations are important to the central capabilities of persons, a capabilities standard of minimum justice cannot be neutral in relation to the way in which freedom of contract is constructed. Indeed, market exchanges form important means through which to pursue valuable ends, but they can also undermine the central capabilities, both of contracting parties and of others. A capabilities based standard of minimum justice of course says nothing directly about such exchanges, or their terms, considered individually. The requirements of minimum justice apply to the structure as a whole, not to individual or specific transactions on the market. However, as stated previously, the construction of freedom of contract reflects a defining structure for market exchanges in general. That is to say, it reveals the types of market relations considered acceptable in a society, ie, those recognised as contracts and enforceable by means of state power.

Contractual immorality functions as the basis for determining the selective availability of state power for the enforcement of agreements between persons. For instance, norms of good morals construct certain contracting options and outcomes as closed. Contract law could be alternatively constructed if selective enforcement on the basis of substantive standards would be excluded from its rules. In this case, state power for the enforcement of mutually beneficial agreements would be available independently of the substantive content or outcomes of agreements for the parties. Such a construction would not necessarily be problematic under the classic view of contract law. Namely, provided that an agreement is mutually beneficial, party autonomy deserves respect regardless of what persons may define as beneficial for themselves. Imposing on their choice an assessment that is based on normative standards exogenous to what they have agreed to in the absence of defects of consent represents an infringement of their autonomy.[88] To exclude contracting options from the availability of state enforcement is only justified on the basis of a denial that an agreement is mutually beneficial (ie, without defects of consent) according to this view. In order to justify that mutually beneficial contract options are excluded from recognition and enforcement,

[88] See Kordana and Tabachnick (n 55) 599; 626–29.

something external to party autonomy must be considered of overriding importance. In other words, the justification must be found external to contract law, ie, the state must find a justification for imposing external constraints on contractual relations. In refusing to recognise and enforce a mutually beneficial agreement, the state must say: even though your freedom to contract is valuable by its very nature, something other of value has priority over its exercise in this particular case. Or in other words, the state must say that it will impede on one's party autonomy in light of a normative standard that takes priority.

However, in the context of a capabilities based approach, there is no reason to maintain that substantive norms must be understood as external constraints on contractual behaviour, nor that freedom of contract must be recognised as a valuable freedom per se. Instead, freedom of contract and contractual relations must be read in a different light. Namely, what is recognised *as* a contractual relation is in a direct sense constructed by the state, ie, the rules of contract law. Indeed, although people may wish to refer to all types of agreements as contracts between themselves, what is recognised in a society as truly *being a contract* depends on the question whether or not it complies with the substantive standards set by the state. In other words, there is nothing external about the substantive norms that shape freedom of contract. That is to say, they do not impose constraints on existing contractual relations (as if they were phenomena of nature), but they construct what contractual relations really are in a defining way. This line of reasoning is analogous to a capabilities based approach to the relation between the family and the state. For instance, in this context Nussbaum states:

> For there is really no entity, 'the family', into which the state either does or does not intervene. People associate in many different ways, live together, love each other, have children. Which of these will be given the name 'family' is a legal and political matter, never one to be decided simply by the parties themselves.[89]

Similarly, the institution of contract is from the outset established as a legal and political matter by the rules that outline its defining features. There are other sorts of agreements that private parties engage in and pursue, but not all of them will be recognised by the term contract. Although both the family and contracts may invoke the idea that they are somehow 'private' and should be separate or free from state intervention, this should not obscure the importance of their underlying political legal structure for questions of justice. If contract law is responsible for constructing, in conjunction with other institutions, the defining structure of contractual relations (state supported exchange between market actors), it must do so in a way that is compatible with the requirements of minimum justice. The ways in which requirements of minimum justice bear on contract law inform a standard of minimum contract justice, and the subject of minimum contract justice is the defining structure of contractual relations, which includes rules on contractual immorality. From a capabilities perspective we can say that minimum contract

[89] Nussbaum (n 2000a) (n 9) 262.

justice requires that freedom of contract is constructed as to create an enabling environment in which persons have the ability to pursue *valuable* functionings through market exchange on an equal basis with others. In this view, the state only impedes one's freedom of contract, if it fails to secure the ability for persons to engage in valuable functionings through contractual relations.[90] This is an important qualification that reflects the moral content informed by basic capabilities. This political conception of the good, as ensconced in the capabilities approach to minimum justice, also provides a basis for identifying contracting options that should not be constructed as open, because they are incompatible with the standard of minimum justice to which a society adheres. By excluding those contracting options from the support of state power for recognition as legitimate market transactions, society safeguards itself from involvement in activities that are not only not considered valuable, but which may be considered patently bad.[91] Rules on contractual immorality then function as a way to protect individuals' basic abilities to engage in valuable functionings, and shield from contractual recognition, for instance, exploitative endeavours that impair individual basic capabilities. As such, a capabilities perspective provides a basis for a standard of minimum contract justice. Namely, the recognition and enforcement of agreements is to be compatible with the requirements of minimum justice as it applies to the basic structure as a whole. A capabilities approach to minimum contract justice identifies those agreements that are incompatible with securing and protecting basic capabilities, ie, those agreements that should not be recognised as contracts.

There are several theoretical approaches to contract law that seem favourable to this understanding of minimum contract justice. For instance, Shiffrin offers support for the idea that a society's commitments to justice could produce reasons to refuse the recognition and enforcement of certain agreements. She states that a society may have 'self-regarding reasons' to refuse support to private pursuits 'on grounds that it would implicate her and use her energies in a way she disapproves of'.[92] This position relies on the idea that political and public values identify and distinguish unworthy pursuits (eg, exploitative or unfair arrangements) from those that deserve contractual enforcement and support. Shiffrin's theoretical approach does not detail the content of the political and public

[90] As a minimum standard of justice, there are many activities on which Nussbaum's capabilities approach is neutral. That is not to say that those activities would not be relevant to justice in a fuller sense, ie, a complete theory of justice may demand more than securing a threshold level of capabilities. However, such demands are outside the scope of discussion for the purpose of this book.

[91] A similar justification is provided by Shiffrin, SV, 'Paternalism, Unconscionability, and Accomodation' (2000) 29 *Philosophy and Public Affairs* 205–50 in relation to the unconscionability doctrine where she states: 'But Self-Regarding Refusal is propelled by C's self-regarding reasons, namely her refusal to lend herself to an unfair or exploitative project on grounds that it would implicate her and use her energies in a way she disapproves of. By analogy, it seems then that a state's refusal to enforce an unconscionable contract could reflect an unwillingness to lend its support and its force to assist an exploitative contract because it is an unworthy endeavor to support' (at 227–28).

[92] Shiffrin (n 91) 205–50, 227–28.

values that offer 'self-regarding refusal' grounds.[93] But to the extent that a society were to endorse a capabilities standard of minimum justice, this framework could inform reasons for self-regarding refusal, such that in principle, Shiffrin's account appears favourable, or at least compatible, with the contract law implications that follow from this books' capabilities based interpretation of minimum contract justice.

Another contract theory that seems favourable, is the contract theory advanced by Dagan. In Dagan's theory of contract law, contract serves the Razian ideal of 'autonomy as self-authorship'. A society that aims to be just, pursues an ideal of human flourishing, in which legal institutions, such as contract law, enhance and empower individuals to be the authors of their own lives. This contract theory envisages a pluralist contract law that embraces various contract institutions 'insofar as they have the potential to add valuable options of human flourishing that significantly broaden people's choices'.[94] Dagan comes to an interpretation of contract law's selective support for private arrangements that is distinctly capabilities friendly. Namely, in his qualification of Raz's idea that contract law is primarily supportive of, and thus follows, existing moral and social practices, Dagan emphasises contract law's enabling function to make valuable choices.[95] If contract law's role is to enhance individuals' abilities to pursue their life plans through valuable arrangements with others, this interpretation comes very close to the capabilities based interpretation presented in this book.[96] Namely in this theory, contract law's selective support (ie, enforcement) is based on the idea of human flourishing itself: contract law's goal is to enhance human flourishing and gives preference to agreements that contribute to this goal. Arrangements that are contrary to the ideal of human flourishing in terms of autonomy as self-authorship, need not be embraced within contract law's framework, ie, those arrangements need not be recognised as contract institutions. In this view, when contract law refuses contractual recognition to certain arrangements, ie, those incompatible with the overall goal of human flourishing, it need not invoke moral conceptions external to contract theory, but can rely on the internal function of contract law itself.

[93] At the core of Shiffrin's theory of contract is the idea of a 'flourishing political society' in which contract law enables and supports the conduct of morally decent persons. In this account, moral decency entails the recognition of the moral importance to keep one's promise and to be faithful to one's commitment; it does not directly address the question of the moral decency of a commitment's content or implications.

[94] Dagan, H, 'Autonomy, Pluralism and Contract Law Theory' (2013) 76 *Law and Contemporary Problems* 19–38, 33.

[95] See also: Dagan, H, 'The Utopian Promise of Contract Law' (2016 Forthcoming) *University of Toronto Law Journal*.

[96] The approaches diverge as Dagan's theory of contract represents a perfectionist liberal ideal, whereas a capabilities based approach to minimum contract justice represents a politically liberal alternative. See on this distinction: Nussbaum (2011) (n 35) 3–45.

An economic theory of contract law could also be favourable to this book's conclusions. Economic analyses of contract law assume that contract law should promote economic efficiency, and contract law rules are evaluated on the basis of their ability to facilitate and encourage economic efficient outcomes. In economic theory, externalities refer to a wide range of effects of transactions on third parties, ie, parties not directly involved in the transaction. Harmful or negative externalities cause efficiency problems through market failures, because transactions fail to reflect true costs, as costs are partly externalised onto others. Negative externalities translate into welfare losses, because third parties and society as a whole bear costs that accompany transactions between private parties. From an economic perspective, then, there is a justification, namely inefficiency, for denying contractual recognition and support to arrangements between private parties that externalise costs onto others. Economic contract theory would support contract law rules that exclude agreements that impose negative externalities on others from contractual recognition, but may still diverge from this book's capabilities based interpretation of minimum contract justice as to which capabilities impairing contractual implications would count as negative externalities (see Chapter 3, section III, B).

3

Sweatshops and Consumer Contracts

Many people share the idea that sweatshops are characterised by deplorable production conditions; that these conditions are morally objectionable; and that certain market conduct is causally linked to the continued existence of sweatshops. These ideas are explored in this chapter. What do people mean when they use the term 'sweatshop'? What are the most common arguments that address the moral status of sweatshops? And how is consumer conduct linked to sweatshop conditions? This chapter turns to the role of sweatshop good-consumption and provides the background for a test case on sweatshops developed in the subsequent chapters. This case examines and tests the hypothesis that a consumer contract is invalid for immorality, if parties exchange money for clothes that are made under sweatshop conditions.

The first part of this chapter is dedicated to describing the most common sweatshop features as they are referred to in studies on sweatshops in the garment industry. There is no univocal, strict definition of the term that is widely shared between those who study sweatshops. Yet, all studies depict and scrutinise a similar set of common practices and conditions. The first part of the chapter aims to detail these common conditions, and taken together, capture the descriptive core of sweatshops, without providing a strict definition. The second part of this chapter details the context in which sweatshops exist, and have persisted over time. Sweatshops are particularly endemic in the garment industry, and structural features of its global supply chains can be identified as contributing and causal factors. This part also describes the market dynamics that link demand conditions and supply factors within the garment industry to sweatshop conditions, specifically for those segments that engage in fast fashion strategies. This description shows how the demand side of the market, namely consumer conduct, contributes to sweatshop conditions. It enables the identification of particular terms in consumer contracts that have problematic implications for the lives that others are able to live. Specifically, this part aims to show that consumer transactions are directly linked to the supply factors that incentivise conditions that form the descriptive core of sweatshops.

The chapter proceeds with an overview of the main arguments brought to the fore in the debate on the objectionable status of sweatshops. This section does not take on grand questions of moral theory (what, if anything, is wrong with sweatshops?), or even aim to detail a comprehensive overview of all questions and arguments raised by those who do turn to these questions. Instead, by offering a brief insight into the dominant arguments that defend the morally objectionable or morally legitimate status of sweatshops, this section aims to show that, and how, sweatshops raise moral concerns. The final section illustrates a capabilities perspective on the example of sweatshops as externalities of market transactions and illustrates why sweatshops evoke questions of contractual immorality and invalidity. In the context of the book, sweatshops serve as an example of production conditions that are scrutinised and identified as (morally) objectionable, and which are generally referred to as deplorable. For the purpose of the book's normative argument, it is important to show that these conditions are problematic from a capabilities perspective: sweatshop conditions impair important basic individual capabilities. Within the context of this book, sweatshops serve as an illustrative example for the capabilities based argument. This chapter is devoted to establishing the plausibility that there are consumer transactions made on Europe's internal market that impair the basic capabilities of others elsewhere. It argues that the morally objectionable status of sweatshops taints consumer transactions for sweatshop goods, not only because of epistemic dimensions that link sweatshop conditions to the consumption of sweatshop goods, but because the former represent a necessary implication of the latter. The argument speaks of the way in which consumer conduct and consumer contract terms for sweatshop goods are directly linked to sweatshop conditions. As the previous chapter shows, the capabilities based framework dovetails with other normative perspectives on this matter. We may also be able to identify a broader set of production conditions as deplorable, morally objectionable, and incompatible with this book's normative, capabilities perspective. Thus, while this book focuses on establishing the arguments around the issue of sweatshops, the hypothesis that consumer contracts are invalid for immorality may be extended to other cases, and could be supported by capabilities based arguments, alongside those that develop from other normative perspectives.

I. Sweatshops

This section provides a descriptive overview and background on the defining features of sweatshops, as they are detailed in studies on sweatshop conditions in the garment industry. These sweatshop features overlap with those described in mainstream media sources, where they figure as one of many examples of supply conditions that are subject to (moral) criticism. The types of harm that are allegedly caused throughout the supply chains of popular goods are numerous, ranging from human rights violations and animal cruelty, to environmental damage. A well-known example of the latter, highlighted in media reports, concerns Shell's involvement in gas flaring activity in the Niger Delta, which has caused environmental damage over a time span of more than 50 years.[1] Gas flaring is notorious for its contribution to greenhouse gases and severe health problems for local residents. Oil spills have caused water contamination, the loss of fisheries, plants and vegetation, which in turn has led to economic deprivation for Nigerian farmers who have lost their source of income.[2] Another much-publicised example concerns industrialised agriculture, which has been critiqued for its low levels of animal welfare. The industry is castigated for using methods of animal production that cut costs at the expense of animal and human welfare, causing threats to public health and the environment.[3] And, in the area of human rights violations, chocolate manufacturers are blamed for creating conditions in which cacao-farmers resort to child slavery by bargaining for increasingly lower prices.[4] All these examples illustrate a spectrum of criticism in the public sphere relating to a variety of production conditions in which our goods are made. Consumers subsequently buy these goods and contract law governs these transactions.

The case of sweatshops in the supply chains of popular consumer goods can be counted amongst the examples that invoke moral scrutiny. In mainstream media reports, the term is used in relation to the example with which this book began: a corporation was discredited for outsourcing the production of popular consumer goods to a supplier abroad with allegedly unsafe and low standard working conditions. The corporation confirmed the claims made in the media reports, referring to the use of n-hexane, the occurrence of suicides and involuntary labour, unsafe working conditions, falsification of wage statements and bribery in the supply chain.[5] These production conditions correspond to the way in which sweatshops are described in other contexts, particularly as they occur in supply chains of the garment industry. The garment industry has been the object of elaborate studies, which unanimously assert that sweatshops are endemic and structural features of

[1] Associated Press, 'Nigerian Farmers Sue Shell in Dutch Court' www.theguardian.com/world/2012/oct/11/nigerian-farmers-sue-shell-dutch, accessed 10 September 2015.

[2] Together with several Nigerian farmers, Friends of the Earth Netherlands (a non-governmental organisation (NGO)) started judicial proceedings against Shell Nigeria and Royal Dutch Shell for compensation for damages. Recently, the Rechtbank Den Haag held Shell Nigeria liable for the damages of one Nigerian farmer, because under Nigerian law they breached a duty of care to prevent his damages. See: Rechtbank's-Gravenhage, 30 January 2013, LJN BY9854.

[3] For instance: 'Hoogleraren: Maak Einde aan Intensieve Veehouderij' *Het NRC Handelsblad, Online Edition*, accessed 15 September 2015.

[4] In the Netherlands, a Dutch consumer, four alleged former child slaves from Burkina Faso, and 2136 other 'worried consumers' demanded prosecution by the Dutch state of the aforementioned consumer for buying chocolate made with cacao picked by child slaves ('Opzetheling' referring to the handling of unlawfully obtained goods under Art 416 Dutch Criminal Code). See: Chocolate slavery: Gerechtshof Amsterdam, 5 April 2007, LJN BA2373.

[5] Apple Supplier Responsibility 2011 Progress Report. Available at: http://images.apple.com/supplier-responsibility/pdf/Apple_SR_2011_Progress_Report.pdf; also in Apple Supplier Responsibility 2012 Progress Report. Available at: http://images.apple.com/supplier-responsibility/pdf/Apple_SR_2012_Progress_Report.pdf. The reports respond to violations of their code of conduct, including issues such as excessive working hours, unpaid overtime and involuntary labour.

its global supply chains.[6] In this book, the case of sweatshops is singled out as a basis for a case study, to be the focus of questions of contractual immorality in the subsequent chapters.

The word *sweatshop* has been primarily associated with dispersed workspaces located in the homes of agents who obtained work orders from manufacturers, for which they employed workers whom they compensated poorly with low pay.[7] However, over the course of the twentieth century, the term transposed into the context of fully-fledged factories, denoting primarily low standard working conditions in the manufacturing stage of globalised supply chains. Although there is no univocal agreement on the exact definition of a sweatshop, studies into sweatshops nevertheless reveal a descriptive core that includes features concerning wage, working hours, health and safety standards, elements of force and coercion, and degrading practices.[8]

From the outset of its usage, the term denotes a very low wage received by workers, indicated by various benchmarks.[9] Some refer to the structural violation of minimum wage legislation, if in place and applicable. However, the applicability of such legislation can be displaced for the sake of trade, as is the case in Exporting Processing Zones.[10] As a standard, minimum wage legislation is also said to disguise the deprivation characteristic of workers' lives. The claim is that even in cases where workers receive the minimum wage, they remain in poverty and are unable to fulfil the basic needs of their family members.[11] Others therefore refer to 'living

[6] See: Klein, N, *No Logo* (Macmillan, 2003); Ross, RJS, *Slaves to Fashion* (University of Michigan Press, 2004)13. Bonacich, E and RP Appelbaum, *Behind the Label: Inequality in the Los Angeles Apparel Industry* (University of California Press, 2000) show that sweatshops have also been located in affluent countries, where vulnerable groups (eg, illegal immigrants) make up the majority of the workforce 169–75.

[7] See Ross ibid, 13–19, for a discussion on the historical development of the term sweatshop.

[8] For an elaborate description of these practices see: Varley, P et al, *The Sweatshop Quandary: Corporate Responsibility on the Global Frontier* (Investor Responsibility Research Center, 1998) Chapter 4, 59–80; Ross (n 6) 19–24; Bonacich and Appelbaum (n 6) 175–95.

See various definitions of the term 'sweatshop' in: Bonacich and Appelbaum (n 6), who refer to the structural violation of legal standards, including the failure to pay a living wage that enables a family to support itself at a 'socially defined, decent standard of living', 3–4; Arnold, DG and LP Hartman, 'Worker Rights and Low Wage Industrialization: How to Avoid Sweatshops' (2006) 28 Human Rights Quarterly 676–700 who refer to sweatshops as 'any workplace in which workers are typically subject to two or more of the following conditions: income for a 48 hour workweek less than the overall poverty rate for that country; systematic forced overtime; systematic health and safety risks due to negligence or the willful disregard of employee welfare; coercion; systematic deception that places workers at risk; and underpayment of earnings'; Zwolinski, M, 'Structural Exploitation' (2012) 29 Social Philosophy and Policy 154–179 who points to the fact that the definition of sweatshops centrally takes on a pejorative meaning. The term sweatshop refers to 'a place of employment in which worker compensation or safety is compromised, child labor is employed, and/or local labor regulations are routinely disregarded in a way that is prima facie morally objectionable' (p 11).

[9] Ross (n 6) 16–18.

[10] EPZs are described as industrial enclaves where manufacturing for export occurs under regulatory regimes that offer businesses economic advantages, see for instance Varley et al (n 8) 21; Rosen, EI, *Making Sweatshops: The Globalization of the U.S. Apparel Industry* (University of California, 2002) 25–26.

[11] Ross (n 6) 27; Varley et al (n 8) 61; Bonacich and Appelbaum (n 6) 181–82.

wages' as a benchmark for identifying low wage levels in sweatshops.[12] The notion of a 'living wage' refers to the ability of a family to support itself at a decent standard of living, defined in terms of the fulfilment of basic needs, such as food, shelter and basic health care. Along with low wages, sweatshops are also described in references to practices that lead to discrepancies in formal statements of wage and actual income. These practices include firing and re-hiring, which allows employers to pay a 'training-wage' during extended probation time that is below the minimum wage.[13] Moreover, fraudulent records may show that workers receive the minimum wage, but actual paid wages may fall far below the stated wage and far below the applicable legal benchmarks, if in place and applicable. The discrepancies between formal wage statements and actual income have various causes. Wage statements (if they exist to begin with) may not show the actual amount of hours that workers have put in.[14] Moreover, while (unexpected) overtime is a systemic feature of sweatshop work, it often remains uncompensated. Additionally, wages are reported to be deduced on the basis of mistakes, refusals to work overtime, failures to reach daily quotas, and for taking breaks for lunch, bathroom visits and talking during work. Other practices that contribute to discrepancies include the deduction of excessive amounts for workers' transportation, housing and food that is provided by employers. Those who work in sweatshops are often confined to designated living spaces close to the factories and are required to buy supplies from shops owned by their employer. Rent and available goods are often priced excessively high, contributing to the inability of many workers to support their family members elsewhere or to save money to support their departure from sweatshop labour.

Another feature of sweatshop labour is the excessively long working days and workweeks. Workweeks of 60–80 hours are commonly described, as well as frequent (and often uncompensated) overtime.[15] Overtime is purportedly imposed on workers either through physically enclosing them in buildings or by means of threats.[16] Common examples include the threat to be fired or to lose earned wages through penalties for non-compliance with supervisors' orders. Next to low wages and long working days, sweatshops are also described to operate under unhealthy and unsafe working conditions, such as overcrowding, lack of ventilation, unsafe equipment and materials, unsanitary toilets, and lack of clean water. These conditions lead to ailments such as asthma, bronchitis and tuberculosis.[17] Moreover, the lives of workers are endangered by the practice of locking workers in factory

[12] Bonacich and Appelbaum (n 6) 3–4.
[13] Varley et al (n 8) 62–63.
[14] Varley et al (n 8) 63.
[15] Varley et al (n 8) 64.
[16] Arnold, DG and NE Bowie, 'Sweatshops and Respect for Persons' (2003) 13 *Business Ethics Quarterly* 229; Varley et al (n 8) 72.
[17] Arnold and Bowie, ibid, 66–68.

buildings—closing doors and windows from the outside, which leads to a high number of deaths in the event of a fire or a collapse.[18]

Other sweatshop features that studies consistently make mention of are degrading and abusive practices including mental and physical abuse by superiors.[19] A large portion of people who work in sweatshops in the garment industry are women, who are vulnerable to specific forms of abuse. There are reported cases of verbal and physical abuse, which include documented cases of rape and beatings.[20] Moreover, sweatshop regimes are generally described by practices that reveal a high level of control over basic human freedoms. Notably, sweatshop regimes are characterised by severe restrictions on workers' freedoms to interact socially with others during their work, receiving fines for talking. They are restricted from eating and from making use of basic sanitary facilities during work hours.[21] In reported cases, restrictions to leave the workplace in order to receive medical care have resulted in health hazards, miscarriages and death.[22] Lastly, reports make mention of the suppression of worker unions by supply chain actors.[23] Such suppressive actions include: firing, blacklisting, the bribing and threatening of organisers and participants of union initiatives.[24]

Taken together, these features—inadequate wages, long working days, health and safety hazards, elements of force and coercion, and degrading practices—form a descriptive core of the term sweatshop. These features exist and persist in the context of the garment industry where several characteristics contribute to the market dynamics that directly link consumer-transaction terms to these sweatshop conditions. Especially in those segments of the industry that are engaged in fast fashion strategies, demand conditions drive the sorts of supply factors that require sweatshop conditions in global supply chains.

II. Context: Sweatshops in the Garment Industry

A. Outsourcing

The production of clothing has moved (with the production of many other goods) to developing countries during the last three decades of the twentieth

[18] A much referred to example is the New York Triangle Shirtwaist Factory fire in 1911, where 141 workers died. Armbruster-Sandoval, R, *Globalization and Cross-border Labor Solidarity in the Americas: The Anti-Sweatshop Movement and the Struggle for Social Justice* (Routledge, 2005) 2. There are contemporary equivalents, see in 2012: 'Dhaka Bangladesh Clothes Factory Fire Kills more than 100' www.bbc.com/news/world-asia-20482273, accessed 10 September 2015 and in 2010: 'Bangladesh Clothes Workers Die in Factory Fire' www.bbc.com/news/world-south-asia-11991807, accessed 15 September 2015.

[19] Varley et al (n 8) 6869.

[20] Bonacich and Appelbaum (n 6) 189.

[21] Ross (n 6) 23; Bonacich and Appelbaum (n 6) 191–92.

[22] For an overview of cases see: Arnold and Bowie (n 16) 221–42, 227–31; Varley et al (n 8) 66.

[23] Bonacich and Appelbaum (n 6) 123.

[24] Varley et al (n 8)78–80; Bonacich and Appelbaum (n 6) 123.

century. This move is part of the broader development of globalisation in which the competitiveness of corporations depends to a large degree on their ability to take advantage of the opportunities made available by the increasing scope of business environments.[25] Corporations have used internationalisation strategies to achieve or maintain competitiveness and are able to capitalise on the supply of factor conditions (ie, land, labour and capital) abroad.[26] Previously, many manufacturers therefore moved their own facilities for production abroad, but internationalisation is more often observed in the cross-border extension of supply chains through the outsourcing of production. Outsourcing is a specific strategy in which corporations subcontract activities to other business entities in order to increase competitive advantage.[27] For most garment corporations, production is outsourced completely to other entities.[28] In turn, these entities can also engage in outsourcing activities, such that actual production activities are distributed among a high number of factory facilities. This strategy provides many benefits for corporations such as increases in capacity, flexibility, specialisation and cost reduction.[29] Corporations give orders for their goods to contractors and agents in the supply chain, who serve as middlemen between the retail and production level. These practices increase the distance between the beginning and end of the supply chain, as well as the number of players with which the corporation is directly or indirectly engaged. This strategy allows corporations to become more flexible in their ability to have orders fulfilled and meet the demands of the market. This flexibility is important for corporations in the garment industry given the nature of the demand and competition within the industry. Especially for corporations who rely on fast fashion strategies, it is pivotal that supply factors can respond quickly, and at low cost, to unpredictable, consumer trends (see section C below). By outsourcing production processes, corporations eliminate the need to make investments, and long-term commitments to any one supplier or location.[30] Subcontracting to various suppliers provides corporations with the freedom to move quickly towards the best available competitors. The purchasing processes in place are set up in support of this freedom. For example, some large retailers make use of fully electronic auction processes for their orders.[31] In such a system, contractors are placed in direct competition with each other. Suppliers are assessed in the first place on their costs, but also on their ability to offer short lead-times (ie, time from the beginning to the completion of the production process) and flexible means of production. The ability to fulfil an order quickly and to limit the time from the moment that demand emerges to the in-store availability of products is pivotal for supplier success. Where demand is subject to quick shifts, retailers seek to supply products to the market as soon as possible to capture and profit from

[25] Armbruster-Sandoval (n 18) 8.
[26] Rugman, AM, *International Business*, 3rd edn (Prentice Hall, 2003) 17.
[27] Ibid 276.
[28] Varley et al (n 8) 84–85; Bonacich and Appelbaum (n 6) 136.
[29] Varley et al (n 8) 85; Arnold and Bowie (n 16) 225–26.
[30] Bonacich and Appelbaum (n 6) 136.
[31] Hearson, M, *Cashing In* (Clean Clothes Campaign, 2009) 47.

such trends. Consumer demand for products that follow fashion trends requires supply factors that can deliver low cost products, developed in short cycles, in a high variety of styles. Due to quick shifts in demand, supply factors must be able to deliver short lead-times, and frequently fulfil orders for a low number of pieces of the same style, colour and sort. Contractors thus seek to improve on features in their production process that advance low cost, flexibility and short lead-time; these are features that contribute to a supply chain that is responsive to consumer fashion trends. Studies on sweatshops point to the incentives created within such systems towards sweatshop conditions in the garment industry.

Outsourcing production to low cost production locations is an advantageous strategy in the labour-intensive garment industries, as globalisation offers the opportunity to make use of low cost labour sources in other countries.[32] Economic studies have revealed diverging correlations between the globalisation of production and the wage levels and working conditions at production level.[33] On the one hand, globalised production is said to create employment options with higher wage levels than would otherwise be available, while, on the other hand, other researchers point to adverse effects on working conditions due to unequal bargaining power.[34]

B. Bargaining Power

Studies on sweatshops point to systemic features in the garment industry that place retailers in powerful bargaining positions in supply chains.[35] At the beginning of the supply chain, clothes are manufactured in factories owned by contractors and sub-contractors who employ garment workers. The barriers to enter the market at this level are relatively low (ie, low start-up costs) and the number of players is high, which leads to a high level of competition.[36] At the end of the supply chain, the number of players involved is relatively low. The barriers to enter the market at the retail level are high, making control and power concentrated to the extent that a small number of retailers control a big market share. Furthermore, the high level of concentration is also the result of the consolidation of retailers, and so-called manufacturers.[37] Manufacturers are not involved in the actual production of clothes, but in activities of design and branding.[38] Consolidation occurs on

[32] Rugman (n 26) 279; Varley et al (n 8) 61.

[33] Powell, B, 'In Reply to Sweatshop Sophistries' (2006) 28 *Human Rights Quarterly* 1031–42, for a different view, see: Miller, J, 'Why Economists Are Wrong About Sweatshops and the Antisweatshop Movement' (2003) 46 *Challenge* 93–122.

[34] See references in n 33.

[35] Armbruster-Sandoval (n 18) 5–7.

[36] Bonacich and Appelbaum (n 6) 8–9; Armbruster-Sandoval (n 18) 5–8.

[37] Bonacich and Appelbaum (n 6) 13–15, 89–96.

[38] Klein (n 6): 'What was changing was the idea of what (…) was being sold. The old paradigm had it that all marketing was selling a product. In the new model, however, the product always takes a back seat to the real product, the brand, and the selling of the brand acquired an extra component that can only be described as spiritual' (p 21). '(…) Brand X is not a product but a way of life, an attitude, a set of values, a look, an idea' (p 23).

the one hand, where retailers take on the activities of designing and branding the clothes they sell, and on the other hand, where corporations originally engaged solely in the design and branding of clothes move into retail, in effect merging the two levels in the supply chain to one.[39] A high concentration at the end of the supply chain gives corporations at this level increased bargaining power. A relatively low number of retailers and manufacturers place their orders for the production of clothes with a high number of contractors around the globe who compete on their ability to produce at low cost. The bargaining power at the end of the supply chain reportedly results in practices that adversely affect the working conditions at the beginning of the supply chain, and contribute to the overall context in which sweatshops continue to exist. In particular, the bargaining power of retail and manufacturing corporations results in the practice of top-down price dictation.[40] Price dictation refers to the ability of powerful corporations to set the price levels for the orders they need fulfilled, and the inability of competing contractors to negotiate prices that cover certain cost levels of production. The result is described in terms of a race to the bottom, or downward squeeze of all determinants of production costs such as wages, health and safety standards and overall working conditions.[41] To the extent that competing contractors are unable to negotiate minimum price levels, the downward squeeze can result in sweatshop conditions. This is particularly so in cases where production facilities have been tailored to process orders for particular retailers and manufacturers, such that facility adjustments are costly. In such cases, accepting orders for prices that do not cover costs is described as a preferred alternative over leaving facilities unproductive.[42] Powerful bargaining positions at the retail level of the supply chain can thus be considered to be among the features that make up a context that contributes to the (continued) existence of sweatshop conditions.

C. Fashionability and Flexibility

In part, the need for corporations to develop and make use of flexible means of production in the garment industry is driven forward by consumer demand, especially in those segments that pursue fast fashion strategies.[43] Generally, the demand for clothing is subject to seasonal fluctuation, and is highly unpredictable. Yet, the success of retailers and manufacturers who rely on fast fashion strategies

[39] Armbruster-Sandoval (n 18) 7; another reason for the increased concentration of power is due to mergers and acquisitions at the retail level during the 1980s and 1990s. Bonacich and Appelbaum (n 6) 80–86.

[40] Ross (n 6) 129–30 and 145; Armbruster-Sandoval (n 18) 7; Bonacich and Appelbaum (n 6) 89–96.

[41] Armbruster-Sandoval (n 18) 8–9; Appelbaum, RP et al, 'The End of Apparel Quotas: A Faster Race to the Bottom?', p 2 http://escholarship.org/uc/item/40f8w19g, accessed 10 September 2015.

[42] Varley et al (n 8) 21, 94–95.

[43] Varley et al (n 8) 85.

depends decisively on their ability to meet almost immediately the rapidly shifting demands of their customers. Namely, fast fashion evolves around the ability of retailers to make fashionable products available at a low cost to consumers who wish to buy and wear clothes when they are trendy, and only for the duration of the trend. When a new trend is set, a retailer should be able to supply new products immediately at a price level that is affordable for consumers who routinely replenish their wardrobes. It requires that retailers are able to tap into current trends and anticipate potential upcoming developments. Such retailers cannot simply develop and design collections on seasonal cycles, but must be engaged in trend spotting by keeping a close connection to fashion bloggers, trend setters, and the resulting consumer demand. The supply factors that are important to such retailers must be capable of responding to unpredictable, fast-shifting consumer demand, and be able to cater to it as soon as it appears. As such, the market dynamics in the garment industry reveal direct links between consumer-transactions and sweatshop conditions. The sort of consumer demand that fast fashion retailers fulfil is unpredictable and requires the ability of retailers to offer almost immediate supply at low costs, as demand appears. The supply factors that are pivotal to that ability require high flexibility and short lead-times at low production costs. Studies point to the fact that these dynamics incentivise sweatshop conditions in the garment industry, as these conditions serve low cost production and subject workers to practices that serve short lead-times and the flexible fulfilment of orders.

III. The Debate on the Moral Status of Sweatshops

After having described the descriptive core of sweatshops, and detailing some of the important features of the garment industry that contribute to the context in which sweatshops (continue to) exist, the chapter now turns to an overview of the main arguments brought to the fore in the debate on the question: what, if anything, is wrong with sweatshops? The debate concerning the moral status of sweatshops addresses various dimensions concerning sweatshops, including the roles and the moral duties of specific actors, such as corporations (and groups within corporations, eg shareholder, management) and consumers. These discussions have generated different arguments, predominantly focused on the evaluation of divergent proposals and their potential to improve or worsen sweatshop conditions, notably voluntary codes of conduct and legal regulatory measures.[44] The purpose of this section is not to bring to the fore a comprehensive overview of all questions and arguments raised, or to take on grand questions of moral theories and their application to sweatshops. Instead, a general overview of the dominant arguments used to substantiate either the moral legitimacy or the

[44] See for example, Powell, B, and Zwolinski, M, 'The Ethical and Economic Case Against Sweatshop Labor: A Critical Assessment' (2012) 107 *Journal of Business Ethics* 449–72, 457 et seq.

moral objectionability of sweatshops, aims to show why sweatshops raise moral concern.[45] As such, the overview functions to illustrate why this book proceeds with a sweatshop test case to evoke questions of contractual immorality and invalidity.

A. The 'It's a Choice' Argument

The most active and forceful contribution in defence of sweatshops comes in the form of the mainstream libertarian position on sweatshops.[46] Arguments of this sort are primarily articulated with regard to conditions of low wage and long working hours, rather than features of coercion, threats and forms of degradation. The most widely used arguments put forward are the 'it's a choice' and the 'better-than-nothing' argument, which hinge together (see next section B). The 'it's a choice' argument is articulated from a consequentialist perspective, which takes the following form. Under the condition that workers are not forced to accept sweatshop labour against their will, they choose, freely, to accept the conditions of their work and therefore engage in a voluntary agreement. Such choices are good indications of individual preferences, as they reflect the fact that individuals who work in sweatshops prefer to accept the work rather than decline it, and pursue other forms of work. In the absence of force, individuals choose the best alternative available to them. The individual liberty of sweatshop workers to make choices has priority over third party interference, because interferences are assumed to take away a preferred and therefore best option from individuals. Measures and actions against sweatshops are likely to cause workers harm and on that ground, opposing and interfering with sweatshop conditions is considered immoral.[47] This version of the 'it's a choice argument' thus turns on empirical evidence for the claim that external efforts to improve working conditions in sweatshops engender harmful consequences. The argument shifts to the extent that it could be shown that regulation or other actions would not cause harm, but would be able to produce and offer better alternatives to sweatshops workers.[48]

Before examining this point, another libertarian version of the 'it's a choice' argument should be discussed that is independent from the possible consequences of interference. In this version of the argument, the priority of liberty is based on principle, ie, on the idea that sweatshop workers' choices are autonomous choices that deserve respect. Interference with the autonomous choice for sweatshop work is wrong, not because it brings about harmful consequences, but because it shows a lack of respect for a person.[49] According to this line of reasoning, an individual's

[45] For an overview of these arguments, see Varley et al (n 8) Chapter 3; from a different (economic) perspective, see Powell and Zwolinski ibid.

[46] See for example: Zwolinski, M, 'Sweatshops, Choice, and Exploitation' (2007) 17 *Business Ethics Quarterly* 689–27; for a different view, see Miller (n 33) 97.

[47] Zwolinski, ibid, 691–95.

[48] Miller (n 33) 103–06.

[49] Zwolinski (n 46) 691–93.

choice to accept sweatshop working conditions is not very different from an individual's choice of religion. Namely, the claim is that the choice to work in a sweatshop likely involves a decision that is of central importance to a person. For instance, sweatshop work may represent securing survival or the provision of basic nutrition for children and family. As such, the choice to work in a sweatshop expresses personal identity, the ability to determine one's own life priorities, and an understanding of what it means to be a parent or member of a family. Opposing sweatshops is immoral, according to this view, because it is reflective of a lack of respect for sweatshop workers' autonomy, and an illegitimate interference with self-determination and individual life plans.[50]

Against both versions of the 'it's a choice' argument, stand arguments from coercion.[51] These arguments address, in the first place, the acceptance of sweatshop work, but also speak to the relation of coercive requirements on workers' productivity in the context of their job.[52] In the latter context, a claim of physical coercion points to the fact that sweatshop regimes include practices in which workers are physically forced to work, either through enclosing them on factory grounds or by means of physical abuse.[53] More often than not, however, the argument from coercion addresses the features of non-physical coercion that are associated with threats to which workers are exposed. Namely, critics of sweatshops point to the fact that workers often work overtime because supervisors threaten to fire them, or withhold their wage or impose penalties in case of non-compliance.[54] These threats constitute forms of psychological coercion that erode arguments based on voluntary acceptance, ie, various forms of the 'it's a choice argument'. From this perspective, the fact that workers yield and comply with demands under such threats provides no evidence of voluntary choice.

The 'it's a choice' argument is also refuted on the basis of its inability to answer the question of the moral status of sweatshops to begin with, beyond arguments that focus on practices in sweatshops that constitute physical or non-physical coercion. Can individual choices, regardless of the conditions in which they are made, disprove claims of immorality? Sweatshop critics have argued that immorality cannot be established without taking into account the conditions in which workers' choices are formed. In other words, they have argued that the ability to choose and the availability of alternative options, inform what it means to voluntarily accept sweatshop working conditions. Their arguments are discussed

[50] Zwolinski (n 46) 691–93, Zwolinksi states: 'But when the subject matter of the choice is of central importance to the agent's identity or core projects, it is plausible to suppose that autonomous choices do generate strong claims to liberty. And it is hard to deny that the choices made by potential sweatshop workers are of central importance in just this way' (p 692).

[51] Powell and Zwolinski (n 44) 463–66.

[52] For reasons previously mentioned, cases in which the acceptance of sweatshop work is subject to coercion, debt labour, etc are kept separate in this discussion.

[53] These sweatshop features are focused on for instance by Arnold and Bowie (n 16) 229. Neither version of the 'it's a choice' argument addresses situations in which sweatshops coincide with modern forms of slavery, such as debt bondage.

[54] Arnold and Bowie (n 16) 229–31.

in sections E and F below on exploitation and background conditions, which address the distinction between formal and substantive notions of choice. Before turning to these arguments, the following sections address several other frequently used arguments in defence of the moral legitimate status of sweatshops; we will start with the 'better than nothing' argument.

B. The 'Better Than Nothing' Argument

The 'it's a choice' argument, set out in the previous section, is often combined with the claim that sweatshops represent the best available alternatives to the workforce in those circumstances.[55] Namely, the argument builds on the idea that in the absence of force, individuals choose the best alternative available to them. Defenders of sweatshops view the fact that sweatshop workers do not have valuable alternatives as an argument in favour of sweatshops, or rather, as an argument against intervention. While the 'it's a choice' argument focuses on the existence of individuals' will to work in sweatshops in the absence of force, the 'better than nothing' argument places emphasis on the availability of sweatshop work in the absence of valuable alternatives. The 'better than nothing' argument is not a free-standing justification for opposing all efforts to improve the conditions of sweatshops, but is dependent on the assumption that those efforts to improve working conditions will be counterproductive (as such it is closely associated with the impossibility argument, see the next section). Interventions, even when directed at, and successful in, achieving improvements in working conditions, are claimed to, in effect, take away a preferred and therefore better alternative from the world's poor.[56] The claim is based on the idea that if conditions in sweatshops were to be improved, corporations would not use the labour forces in developing countries as much as they would otherwise.[57] The argument puts forward the idea that first, low cost labour countries have a competitive advantage over other countries and second, that this position can only be maintained as long as production costs remain lower than elsewhere. The improvement of working conditions (for instance higher wages, and safer and healthier working conditions) comes with higher costs, and rising production costs will result in the loss of developing countries' competitive advantage. As a result, corporations would move the production of their goods elsewhere, leaving current sweatshop workers without their preferred option.[58] Moreover, increases in wages and other improvements in working conditions thwart employment opportunities for others in developing countries,

[55] Powell, B, and D Skarbek, 'Sweatshops and Third World Living Standards: Are the Jobs Worth the Sweat?' (2006) XXVII *Journal of Labor Research* 263–73 conclude that apparel workers earn higher wages compared to others in their economy.

[56] Krugman, P, 'In Praise of Cheap Labor' *Slate* www.slate.com/articles/business/the_dismal_science/1997/03/in_praise_of_cheap_labor.html, accessed 10 September 2015; Zwolinski (n 46) 693–94; Varley et al (n 8) 47–48.

[57] Powell (n 33) 1037.

[58] Varley et al (n 8) 48; Krugman (n 56).

as the demand for goods is diminished with increases in production costs. The 'better than nothing' argument thus views sweatshop work in its most favourable light: as the best available alternative to individuals in their context. In other words, from this viewpoint sweatshops are good and desirable, as they generate economic growth and lift people out of poverty.[59]

However, the 'better than nothing' argument is contested on the basis of the empirical assumptions on which it depends. Two counter arguments challenge the 'better than nothing' argument. First, some argue that improvements in working conditions and increased wages in the past have not cancelled incentives for corporations to outsource their production activities in the developing world since production costs remain substantially lower than elsewhere.[60] In other words, the 'better than nothing' argument fails to the extent that there is room for improvement in working conditions, and an accompanying rise in costs, without undermining the continued existence of competitive advantage. Second, some argue that higher production costs that result from raising wages and improving working conditions generally, need not affect demand and result in unemployment. Much depends on the way goods are branded. To the extent that consumer demand exists for products that are branded as 'responsible' or 'sustainable', demand may in fact increase as working conditions and overall production conditions improve.[61] In such cases, the accompanying rise in production costs need not thwart employment opportunities for people. In fact, research suggests that consumers would be willing to pay higher prices for goods produced under socially responsible conditions.[62]

C. The Impossibility Argument

Closely related to the 'better than nothing' argument is the impossibility argument. Both arguments claim that sweatshops represent the best available options to people. The 'better than nothing' argument functions as an argument against interventions that take away valuable options from individuals as a result of the rising costs associated with improved working conditions. However, the impossibility argument claims the absence of an alternative to sweatshops altogether. That is to say, the argument claims the impossibility of improvement in sweatshop conditions. If the existence of sweatshops is a necessary fact of globalised production, sweatshops cannot be immoral, as morality cannot demand what is impossible.[63] In one form, the argument is based on the idea that sweatshops form

[59] Powell and Zwolinski (n 44) 451; Powell (n 33) 1041.

[60] Rothstein, R, 'Defending Sweatshops' (2005) *Dissent* 41–47; Varley et al (n 8) 50.

[61] Klein (n 6).

[62] Auger, P et al, 'What Will Consumers Pay for Social Product Features' (2003) 42 *Journal of Business Ethics* 281–304; Arnold and Hartman (n 8) 695.

[63] Meyers, CD, 'Moral Duty, Individual Responsibility, and Sweatshop Exploitation' (2007) 38 *Journal of Social Philosophy* 620–626, 624; Meyers, C, 'Wrongful Beneficence: Exploitation and Third World Sweatshops' (2004) 35 *Journal of Social Philosophy* 219–333, 329–30.

a part of a 'natural' progression, and represent a necessary and inevitable step on the road to prosperity. This 'step on the road to prosperity' argument holds that all nations (necessarily) go through a phase of deplorable working conditions as they strive towards prosperity. A sweatshop phase is considered essential, because it is the only source that gives developing countries a competitive edge over developed nations. Support for this view is often found in the historical development of developed countries that went through a similar period in which sweatshops existed before wages increased and working conditions improved.[64] In response to this first variation of the impossibility argument, others point to the fact that historically, improvements in working conditions often resulted from political pressure, not as a 'natural' result of market forces.[65] Some have argued that wages sometimes fall even when productivity is rising, contrary to economic models.[66] The assumption that developing nations move towards prosperity, because productivity itself will necessarily lead to improved working conditions over time is not supported empirically.[67] Notably, critics of sweatshops point to the fact that the benefits that workers obtain from sweatshop arrangements are insufficient to pull them and their family members (including future generations) out of poverty. In contexts in which sweatshop conditions do not progress as a result of productivity, the 'step on the road to prosperity' argument fails to be compelling. Moreover, in any case, the argument of a 'step on the road to prosperity' does not show that alternative forms of development are impossible.

In a second form, the impossibility argument does not rely on an account of natural progression and development, but rather refers to the economic impossibility for corporations to make shifts away from sweatshop production.[68] Corporations who currently produce their goods in sweatshops would lose their source of competitive advantage, if sweatshop conditions were to improve (ie, production costs were to rise) and thereby would be unable to survive over time. The second variant of the impossibility argument points to the market dynamics that link demand conditions and supply factors within the garment industry to sweatshop conditions. The argument claims that within the garment industry, the competitive forces leave corporations with limited space to engage alternative production strategies that would provide sufficient flexibility to succeed over time. This claim does not however, contest the objectionable status of sweatshops, but rather, indicates a possible issue with regard to competitive forces that determine the success and survival of corporations.

[64] Krugman (n 56); Kristof, ND and S Wudunn, 'Two Cheers for Sweatshops' *The New York Times Online Edition* www.nytimes.com/2000/09/24/magazine/two-cheers-for-sweatshops.html?pagewanted=all&src=pm, accessed 10 September 2015; Kristof, ND, 'Where Sweatshops Are a Dream' *The New York Times Online Edition* www.nytimes.com/2009/01/15/opinion/15kristof.html, accessed 10 September 2015.

[65] Rothstein (n 60); Varley et al (n 8) 51.

[66] Miller (n 33) 104; Varley et al (n 8) 51.

[67] Rothstein (n 60); Varley et al (n 8) 49–51.

[68] Meyers (2007) (n 63) 624–25.

D. The Argument from Relativism

Other arguments that are put forward in the debate on global sweatshops are based on various forms of relativism. The arguments from relativism generally express the view that individuals or groups of persons hold different beliefs about morality and that these beliefs can only be considered and evaluated within the context in which they are held.[69] Relativism problematises the debate on the moral status of sweatshops as a whole, to the extent that participants take as points of departure standards of morality that are articulated outside the context in which a sweatshop is situated. The argument from relativism as it relates to sweatshops primarily takes shape in terms of cultural relativism as a counter argument against those who consider sweatshops to be immoral. According to arguments from cultural relativism, it is considered illegitimate to assess sweatshops located in foreign nations on the basis of moral standards defined externally to the culture in which they are embedded.[70] Those foreign moral standards have no claim to authority over the norms and standards that are produced by conventions that are culturally embedded, and on a global level both sets of standards should be regarded as having equal standing. Moreover, international standards that make some claim to representing (more) universal, neutral, and objective criteria for evaluating diverging and competing local standards also lack authority. From the perspective of cultural relativism, claims of universality and objectivity fail given the descriptive truth of diversity among standards of morality and the normative standard that these diverging standards should have equal standing. The argument from cultural relativism thus functions against arguments that support and view sweatshops to be immoral—whether evaluated on the basis of other (local) moral standards or on the basis of internationally articulated principles. The argument from cultural relativism holds that sweatshop working conditions reflect standards that are considered morally acceptable within the cultural context in which they are situated. Moreover, because diverging moral standards are all equally valid, there is no set of standards available that has a legitimate claim of authority over these local standards.

There are two arguments that counter this cultural relativist view. In the first place, the debate yields an argument against the descriptive claim that sweatshop working conditions reflect standards that are considered morally acceptable within the cultural context in which they are situated. The standards, according to which the immoral status of sweatshops is assessed, need not be (exclusively) 'external' to the culture in which they are embedded. It is in particular the voices from within, that is, from those who work in sweatshops that inform moral concern.[71]

[69] For instance, as discussed by Ercel, K, 'Orientalization of Exploitation' (2006) 18 *Rethinking Marxism: A Journal of Economics, Culture & Society* 289–306, 294–95.

[70] Ibid; Varley et al (n 8) 20–22.

[71] The methodology underlying sweatshop studies includes notably qualitative interviews with (ex) sweatshop workers. See for examples of excerpts Bonacich and Appelbaum (n 6) 192; Armbruster-Sandoval (n 18) 62.

Sweatshops can exist and continue to exist within cultural contexts in which they are nonetheless morally condemned. What is more, the norms that are produced within the cultural contexts in which sweatshops are embedded may well have contributed and be supportive of the international standards that are used to evaluate the moral status of sweatshops. Said differently, the internationally developed, universally articulated standards of decent working conditions[72] need not represent externally formulated standards that are imposed from a high-handed position. Instead, these standards may be reflective of the moral standards that are part of the cultural contexts in which sweatshops are embedded. In the second place, the claim that sweatshops are in some sense an expression of a culture, which demands respect, is countered by claims that sweatshops are manifestations of the exact opposite. Namely, critics of globalisation argue that the domination of capitalist market culture encroaches on the integrity of other cultures, by requiring their engagement in commodification as a form of cooperation. From this perspective, sweatshops are manifestations of capitalism imposed as a foreign element on other cultures.[73] This second counter argument confronts not only the idea that sweatshops need not be considered morally acceptable within the cultural context in which they are situated, but also the idea that sweatshops are not culturally embedded phenomena.

E. The Exploitation Argument

The arguments that support the moral acceptance of sweatshops (sections A to D above) encounter a large number of critical perspectives and counter arguments that address the morally objectionable nature of sweatshops. The most prevalent arguments of this sort consider sweatshop conditions to represent practices that are wrongfully exploitative.[74] Various forms of the exploitation argument engage both the 'it's a choice' argument, as well as the 'better than nothing' argument, in either claiming their irrelevance with regards to the moral status of sweatshops or in claiming a mistaken understanding of *choice*, as merely the absence of force and deception. In relation to the irrelevance of the 'it's a choice' argument and the 'better than nothing' argument, critics claim that consent to or benefit from an arrangement does not necessarily transform an otherwise immoral status. In this

[72] Indicated by their articulation in the Fundamental Conventions of the International Labour Office.

[73] Sample, RJ, *Exploitation. What It Is and Why It's Wrong* (Rowman & Littlefield Publishers, 2003) 161–62.

[74] There are several forms in which this argument is made. For instance, wrongful exploitation may be based on the idea of harm, insufficient benefit, unfairness, or the infringement of a minimum standard. For an overview, see Zwolinksi (n 46) 704–11, who argues that even though other features of sweatshops may be exploitative, low wages are not. Also: Meyers (2004) (n 63), who argues that wrongful exploitation may occur even if the person exploited benefits from it and even if that person prefers the exploitation over other alternatives. Of interest is the fact that in the Commission's proposal for a Common European Sales Law (CESL) (2011), plural conceptions of exploitation have been included in Article 51, for instance excessive benefit and unfair advantage, but also the background conditions of the transaction. See next section on the 'unjust background conditions' argument.

context, the exploitation argument is generally framed in terms of unfairness or degradation.

In the first variation, exploitation points to the ways in which practices are predicated on unfairness which is constituted by one party taking advantage of the deprivation of another and securing a benefit that is considered disproportionate in relation to their contribution.[75] On the basis of this argument, sweatshops are immoral because of the distribution of advantages that are generated in part by those who work in sweatshops. The argument points to the fact that the advantages produced by sweatshop workers are disproportionately favourable to corporate actors and those who are in the position to buy the finished goods made in sweatshops. This focus on disproportionate advantage is mirrored by a focus on insufficient benefit received by sweatshop workers. Exploitation arguments based on unfairness are countered on the basis that they fail to show why disproportionate benefit from an arrangement is a matter of moral concern, particularly if the arrangement is entered into voluntarily.[76] Moreover, the claim that sweatshop workers receive insufficient benefit is criticised for underestimating the benefit that sweatshop jobs represent to those who are in desperate need of work to meet basic needs.

A second variation of the exploitation argument is based on a notion of exploitation that focuses on a lack of respect for sweatshop workers. This argument points to the ways in which sweatshop conditions infringe on human dignity, by treating workers as mere means to the ends of others, rather than as ends themselves. As illustrations, examples are brought to the fore of compromises in workers' safety for the sake of productivity, and to aspects of coercion such as the refusal to allow workers to seek medical attention during working hours.[77] Sweatshop conditions are morally objectionable, in this view, because they are degrading to the people who work in sweatshops. An alternative form of the exploitation argument that relies on denigration and a lack of respect is articulated with reference to basic needs.[78] This argument develops to substantiate the claim that the low wage and long working hours characteristic of sweatshops, independent of threats, coercion and other degrading practices, represent objectionable exploitation. Namely, low wages and long working hours represent a form of 'needs exploitation', which refers to an arrangement in which one takes advantage while disregarding the basic needs of the other.[79] In the context of sweatshops, the notion of needs exploitation is empirically supported by the fact that workers are often unable to fulfil their basic needs while working up to an 80 hour working week.[80]

[75] Meyers (2004) (n 63) 324–27.

[76] Snyder, JC, 'Needs Exploitation' (2008) 11 *Ethic Theory Moral Practice* 389–405, 391.

[77] Arnold and Bowie (n 16) 230–31. They argue from a Kantian perspective that sweatshops are immoral as they are representative of a lack of respect for those who work in them.

[78] Snyder (n 76) focuses on the fact that the basic needs of the individuals working in sweatshops are disregarded and therefore they are not respected as persons.

[79] Snyder (n 76); see also Sample (n 73) 159–60.

[80] This argument is used in particular to substantiate the claim that workers should receive a living wage. See for example Snyder (n 76), who argues that wage levels that fall below a decent minimum are for that reason morally problematic.

The exploitation arguments need not necessarily claim the irrelevance of choice. Instead, these arguments may take into account the influence of the conditions that characterise the lives of those who accept sweatshop jobs, ie, the context in which individuals make choices. In such form, arguments based on exploitation rebut the claim that sweatshop workers voluntarily agree to sweatshop conditions, merely because they are not physically forced or deceived. These arguments point to a mistaken understanding of *choice*, as it is used by those who invoke the 'it's a choice argument' and the 'better than nothing' argument. Instead, these arguments hold that the sort of choices that have morally transformative effects, are substantive choices, for which the mere absence of force and deception is insufficient. Unfavourable life circumstances may coerce an individual to agree to what would otherwise have been unacceptable.[81] In this light, the fact that sweatshops are—as claimed under the better than nothing argument—the only alternative aside from starvation, substantiate the wrongfully exploitative status of sweatshops rather than their moral legitimacy. This argument draws attention to the fact that the morally objectionable character of sweatshops cannot be properly understood by isolating the exchange which sweatshop workers engage in, from the overall circumstances of their lives. The unjust background conditions in which sweatshops are embedded represent a freestanding source of moral concern, which are paramount to the debate on the moral status of sweatshops.

F. The (Unjust) Background Conditions Argument

There are at least two ways in which the life circumstances are said to matter for the moral status of sweatshops. Firstly, sweatshop workers' life circumstances are relevant in a notion of choice that goes beyond the absence of force or deceit and thereby contribute to an understanding of why a particular exchange is morally objectionable. Secondly, the moral status of sweatshops can be predicated on the unjust background conditions that caused the circumstances that shape sweatshop workers' lives.

The first argument does not focus on the reasons behind the circumstances that have shaped individual lives. The mere fact that there is a lack of alternative options of a certain quality (eg beyond starvation and death) for sweatshop workers substantiates the claim that there is a defect in consent, or at least that the acceptance does not perform its 'moral magic'.[82] Namely, under conditions of severe deprivation and inequality, people accept conditions that they would otherwise never

[81] Sandel, M, 'What Money Can't Buy: The Moral Limits of Markets' (1998) *The Tanner Lectures on Human Values* 94.

[82] Zwolinski (n 46) 691–95 argues that individuals' choices for sweatshop work can transform otherwise morally problematic aspects of sweatshops, since their choices are expressions of autonomy and preference. For a different view, see: Chartier, G, 'Sweatshops, Labor Rights, and Competitive Advantage' (2008) 10 *Oregan Review of International Law* 149–88, 161–62; Miller (n 33) 97; Sandel (n 81) 94–95.

have agreed to.[83] According to this line of reasoning, the morally relevant comparison to make is between sweatshop conditions and conditions to which people would have agreed under fair background conditions, eg in the absence of pressing necessity. People with excellent life chances do not, in fact, choose sweatshop work. In addition, sweatshops are not generally considered as just another category of job among a range of alternative occupations. These arguments aim to show that there is a morally significant difference between choices made under conditions of urgent need, and those made under conditions of substantive freedom, ie, in a context in which there are valuable alternatives available.[84]

The second argument points to the reasons why some people do not have alternative options beyond sweatshop work. In this context it is of relevance to draw attention to the fact that individuals who lack alternative options are not distributed randomly among societies, or among groups of individuals at varying starting positions in life. Rather, sweatshop workers are located predominantly in developing countries, or, are members of a particular vulnerable and marginalised group, such as (illegal) immigrants.[85] The arguments concerning the unjust background conditions follow an inquiry into the context in which vulnerability, and comparatively, favourable bargaining positions of those who gain advantage from vulnerability, are shaped. The claim that the moral status of sweatshops is predicated on unjust background conditions, appeals to the idea that sweatshops are indicative of structural injustice, ie, that sweatshops only prevail within an unjust context.[86] This argument has been made in reference to both previous and current ongoing injustices, which are claimed to contribute to disadvantage on one side, and advantage on the other. Previous injustices that are brought to the fore include the seizure of natural resources and land under periods of colonialism, conditions of slavery and war.[87] Current features are also referred to as aggravating and sustaining the current measure of inequality between the lives of individuals in different nations and regions. This is exemplified by institutional structures supportive of terms of trade that protect the interests of those who are already well-off or the suppression of unions and labour protection at the request of corporate actors.[88] All these features are said to create a context of structural injustice and inequality that enables and sustains the existence of sweatshops over time.[89] It is not the very

[83] Meyers (2004) (n 63) 325.

[84] This line of reasoning, which focuses on the importance of substantive choice and freedom, shows significant overlap with the type of reasoning based on capabilities frameworks.

[85] Bonacich and Appelbaum (n 6) 169–75.

[86] Young, IM, 'Responsibility and Global Labor Justice' (2004) 12 *The Journal of Political Philosophy* 365–88, 378; Snyder (n 76) 393. For an overview of different versions of the argument, see Zwolinski (n 8) 8–10.

[87] See for example Sample (n 73) 162; Snyder (n 76) 392; for a different view, see Zwolinski (n 8) 21–22.

[88] Sample (n 73) 162–63; Zwolinski (n 8) 21–23; Young (n 86) 369–70; Snyder (n 76) 392.

[89] In some instances, this argument targets specific actors. For example, multinational enterprises are faulted for bargaining and lobbying for advantages, such as lower tax rates and diminished standards of labour protection in return for investments.

idea that these background conditions are unjust that is contested, or the question whether they matter for the moral status of sweatshops, rather, the question of how these conditions transform the moral status of sweatshops is the subject of ongoing debate.

IV. Sweatshops as Contractual Externalities?

The previous sections show that sweatshops are a topic of critical scrutiny and of academic debate regarding their moral status, and many of these arguments and critical perspectives have been voiced in popular media. As such, these arguments begin to illustrate why sweatshops may evoke questions of contractual immorality and invalidity. In this final section, this chapter now turns to the question of how sweatshops can be considered as negative externalities of consumer transactions for sweatshop products. The chapter will conclude by bringing in the book's normative framework developed in the previous chapter and will detail why sweatshop conditions are problematic from a capabilities perspective.

A. Sweatshops and Slavery as Subjects of Moral Debate

Sweatshops and forms of slavery are often bracketed together as examples of fundamental rights violations in corporate supply chains and as examples of deplorable production conditions that illustrate costs imposed on others, ie, externalities. However, the contrasts between sweatshops and slavery as subjects of moral debate and as examples of externalities provide an important illustration of this book's focus on questions regarding contractual immorality and injustice.

In the debate on the moral status of sweatshops, the latter are distinguished from modern forms of slavery on the basis of consent. Sweatshop workers who are subject to the sweatshop practices described above are said to have the freedom to leave their jobs whereas slaves do not. As such, sweatshop work is set apart from modern forms of slavery where total control is exercised over a person by means of force for the purpose of economic exploitation.[90] Where past forms of slavery entailed 'legal' ownership of persons, modern forms of slavery are recognised as all forced or compulsory labour, defined by the International Labour Organization (ILO) as 'all work or service which is exacted from any person under the menace of any penalty and for which the said person has not offered himself voluntarily'.[91]

[90] Bales, K, *Disposable People. New Slavery in the Global Economy* (University of California Press, 2004) 5–6.

[91] Apple Supplier Responsibility 2011 Progress Report (n 5), Forced Labour Convention, C29, 28 June 1930, Art 2.

Modern forms of slavery occur in today's world as part of supply chains of goods that are sold all around the world.[92] In the first place, modern forms of slavery can also be said to occur within the context of sweatshops. Namely, studies on sweatshops also describe the most common form of compulsory labour today, namely debt bondage or bonded labour.[93] Debt bondage occurs where workers have incurred debt and agree to repay their debt through labour.[94] For instance, a worker may incur a debt in order to pay for transportation by a contractor or agent to a factory location. The debt often escalates as excessive payments are required for housing and food, and high interest rates compound with the initial amount. Required payments exceed the low wages received by workers, which leads them to be enduringly unable to pay off their debts. In these circumstances workers find themselves trapped and tied indefinitely to their contractors.[95] In the second place, and apart from the context of sweatshops, reports also show that some goods sold in Europe are made by slaves, for instance by child slaves on cacao plantations in the Ivory Coast, the largest world producer of cacao and main supplier to the world's chocolate industry.[96] Chocolate production depends on labour intensive cacao production and children are trafficked from neighbouring countries into the Ivory Coast to work on cacao farms.

A categorical distinction is often maintained between slavery and sweatshops with respect to the question regarding moral status, whereas the former is universally, morally condemned, the latter is subject to controversy and debate. However, in light of modern conceptions of forced labour, forms of slavery may also overlap, as factual descriptions of sweatshops illustrate. What is more, both represent examples of deplorable forms of production that exist in supply chains of goods sold all over the world. Thus, for the purposes of this book, one could equally apply the question of contract law regarding the validity of consumer contracts for sweatshop goods to the example of transactions for goods made by slaves (including child slaves). The hypothetical case study of sweatshops that serves as a test case in the subsequent chapters (see Chapter 4), could thus be replaced by an example that details various forms of slavery in global supply chains. However, this book deals with the former, more controversial example, because it brings to the fore more readily the potentially salient elements regarding questions of contractual immorality and its potential frontiers. By doing so, the book engages in the debate on the moral status of sweatshops that stands in contrast to the universal condemnation of slavery. The abolition of slavery and its universal illegality was established after debate regarding its moral status, and only after that the idea

[92] Bales (n 90) 22–24.

[93] Bonacich and Appelbaum (n 6) Chapter 6; ILO, 'Labour Practices in the Footwear, Leather Textiles and Clothing Industry (2000) section 2.4.

[94] ILO, 'The Cost of Coercion: Global Report under the Follow-up to the ILO Declaration on Fundamental Principles and Rights at Work' (2009).

[95] Varley et al (n 8) 70–72. Bales (n 90) 9.

[96] International Programme on the Elimination of Child Labour (IPEC), 'Rooting Out Child Labour from Cocoa Farms'—Paper No 1 (2007), available at: www.ilo.org/ipecinfo/product/viewProduct.do?productId=6444, last assessed 21 October 2016.

took hold, by now ubiquitously shared, that slavery is immoral. Unlike sweatshops, slavery has moved beyond debates in which its (economic) benefits are put to the fore as a contribution to a defence for permissibility.[97]

B. Sweatshops and Slavery as Externalities?

The potential difficulties of a categorical distinction between various forms of forced labour and sweatshops are taken as a point of departure in the following discussion on contractual externalities. The distinction is further based on a formal conception of consent, which points to the absence of physical force or coercion, in order to capture the dominant, economic understanding of negative externalities. This view will be contrasted with this book's capabilities perspective on the question of whether sweatshop conditions should be understood as negative externalities of consumer contracts.

The link between sweatshop conditions and transactions for sweatshop goods has been described in economic terms: the former are identified as *negative externalities* of the latter.[98] The term externality is described in economics as a direct effect (either positive or negative) of an actor's action on the welfare of another actor, without the effect being incorporated in the market price.[99] Externalities can cause efficiency problems and represent market failures, since the price paid for a good does not reflect the costs that are necessary for the production thereof.[100] Environmental damage caused in the course of production is the archetypical example of a negative externality. If the costs associated with environmental damage are not transmitted as production costs throughout the supply chain, these costs are externalised and incurred by others who are affected by the environmental damage, but remain nevertheless uncompensated. Similarly, sweatshop conditions are identified as costs incurred by those who work in sweatshops for which they remain uncompensated. As such, sweatshop conditions are not transmitted as production costs throughout the supply chain. In particular, those who engage in transactions for goods made in sweatshops need not pay the price for safe production conditions, decent wages or overtime compensation. Instead such costs are imposed on those who produce them through substandard working conditions.

[97] Even though arguments could be articulated for the economic efficiency of slavery, for instance: Gray, LC, 'Economic Efficiency and Competitive Advantage of Slavery under the Plantation System' (1930) 4 *Agricultural History* 31–47. 'Obviously, this question involved neither the ethical aspects of slavery (…). Unfortunately, however, the consideration of the economic aspects of slavery as a competitive institution have been largely mixed up with these broader considerations (…)' (p 33).

[98] For instance: Lipschutz, RD, 'Sweating it Out: NGO Campaigns and Trade Union Empowerment' (2004) 14 *Development in Practice* 197–209, 197.

[99] Varian, HR, *Microeconomic Analysis* (WW Norton & Company, 2006) Chapter 24; Katz, ML and HS Rosen, *Microeconomics*, 2nd edn (Irwin, 2009) Chapter 17; Baye, MR, *Managerial Economic and Business Stategy*, 4th International edn (McGraw-Hill, 2002) 508–10.

[100] Baye, ibid.

This line of reasoning imports into the economic definition of externalities, normative standards about what a 'decent' wage would be or what 'substandard' conditions are. However, in a strict definition of externalities, such normativity is to be found in the choices made by individuals themselves. That is to say, whatever wage or working conditions one accepts as compensation is to be taken for granted; the market establishes what is adequate compensation, as opposed to a level of wage or working conditions labelled 'decent' or 'substandard' respectively. Consequently, whatever the sweatshop workers accept as compensation is equivalent to the costs incorporated within the total production costs. Those who work in sweatshops define for themselves what adequate compensation is—expressed by their voluntary acceptance—and thus they do not incur any residual costs. In short, from an economic perspective sweatshop conditions are not negative externalities of the activities of others and do not represent market failure because workers can adjust their conduct. It is for this reason that modern forms of slavery in supply chains *can* and should be considered as negative externalities, since voluntary acceptance is absent and slaves are not compensated for the costs they incur in the course of production. It follows from this view that the price of goods made by slaves does not reflect all production costs, whereas the price of goods made in sweatshops does.[101] Therefore, in terms of efficiency and market functioning, modern forms of slavery are deemed problematic, whereas sweatshops are not.

Taken on their own, however, the morally problematic aspects of lowering working conditions to sweatshop conditions need not be insignificant to consider the negative externalities of transactions for goods made in sweatshops. Namely, if one considers sweatshop conditions as acceptable this may be seen as reflective of lowering standards regarding the respect for human life, which is in turn associated with the social costs of increased criminality and violence, ie, the deterioration of social life.[102] The erosion of standards of respect for human life is described as a possible negative externality, and can be seen as an externality of transactions for goods, which are made under sweatshop conditions in supply chains. In such a case it is not the sweatshop conditions that represent external costs of transactions, but rather the negative effects on society, namely the lowered standards of respect for human life and associated social costs.

C. Contractual Externalities: A Capabilities Perspective

As articulated in the previous chapter, sweatshop conditions and the context in which they are embedded do not escape critical scrutiny from a capabilities perspective. To the extent that sweatshops are not identified as problematic on the basis of workers' acceptance of sweatshop conditions, this view is incompatible

[101] In other words, slavery qualifies as a form of negative externalities revealing market failure, whereas sweatshops do not.

[102] Shavell, S, *Foundations of Economic Analysis of Law* (Belknap Harvard, 2004) 322.

with a capabilities perspective of which the focus is on the individuals' substantive ability to choose. In asking what individuals are able to be and do in their lives, the capabilities approach points to the absence of valuable alternatives in the lives of those who work in sweatshops.[103] From a capabilities perspective, the arguments brought forward to substantiate the moral legitimacy of sweatshops (see section III) do not have a transformative effect on the concerns that come to the fore in terms of basic capabilities pertaining to minimum justice. Namely, in a context of absent valuable alternatives and exit options, individuals do not have the basic capabilities, ie, the substantive freedom to choose.

Thus, firstly the 'it's a choice' argument fails for being based on a formal conception of choice that neglects the consideration of the impediments in the broader context that constrain individuals' abilities to choose.[104] Instead, the capabilities perspective aligns with arguments that rely on substantive notions of choice, and that assign significance to the context and background conditions in which individuals make choices. Secondly, the 'better-than-nothing' argument does not engage the normative claim based on minimum justice that translates into fundamental entitlements of basic capabilities for individuals. The normative benchmark of minimum justice does not adjust to the options that are currently considered to be the best available alternatives. The best available option may still lack the qualities that minimum justice requires. Thirdly, the impossibility argument is not compelling from a capabilities perspective, primarily because considerations regarding global redistribution, normatively supported by a capabilities approach to minimum justice, would counter the impossibility of improvement. Moreover, where the impossibility argument identifies corporate economic impossibility, the argument becomes irrelevant within the capabilities framework, as the survival of a corporation does not represent a fundamental entitlement based on minimum justice.[105] And lastly, a capabilities perspective counters the argument from relativism by defending the universal status of basic capabilities.[106] The capabilities perspective detailed in the previous chapter builds on the idea that there are certain areas of individual freedom that are important to people, regardless of the cultures in which they are embedded. While one may debate about the appropriate

[103] People with excellent life chances do not work in sweatshops. In today's world many people travel for professional and other reasons, but well-off people do not pursue sweatshop job opportunities. Even as opportunities to spend some time abroad for students during a gap-year, for instance, sweatshops do not appear to be among a range of valuable options, as for instance agricultural labour is (eg, apple picking). Sweatshops as valuable research opportunities appear to be the exception, ie, the experience of working in a sweatshop provides valuable experiential knowledge. See: Fries, M, 'Stressforscher im Sweatshop' *Zeit Online* www.zeit.de/studium/uni-leben/2011-02/interview-bangladesch, accessed 10 September 2012.

[104] Nussbaum, M, *Frontiers of Justice* (Harvard University Press, 2006) 286–91; Nussbaum, M, 'The Supreme Court 2006 Term Foreword: Constitutions and Capabilities: "Perception" against Lofty Formalism' (2007) 121 *Harvard Law Review* 21–24.

[105] Similarly, Nussbaum (2006) ibid, 394.

[106] This universalist spirit is captured in the question: 'Why should we follow the local ideas, rather than the best ideas we can find?' Nussbaum, M, *Women and Human Development: The Capabilities Approach* (Cambridge University Press, 2000) 49.

threshold level of these basic capabilities as they would be defined locally, sweatshop conditions appear widely regarded as incompatible with any threshold level that takes account of the conditions necessary for human flourishing.

From a capabilities perspective, a sweatshop's objectionability is found in the absence of the social preconditions necessary for individuals to be able to make substantive choices in important areas of human functioning, ie, the basic capabilities. In that context, sweatshop conditions impair workers abilities 'to work as human beings, exercising practical reason and entering into meaningful relationships of mutual recognition with other workers'.[107] Sweatshop conditions do not escape critical scrutiny on the basis of the capabilities perspective detailed in Chapter 2, because they cannot be separated from the background conditions in which sweatshop workers accept them. A capabilities perspective treats sweatshop conditions and the overall (global) context in which they are embedded as inseparable for its normative judgements.[108] Critical scrutiny thus extends to the sweatshop conditions, and to the overall context that sustains them, which includes parts of domestic basic structures of society. Of particular concern for this book are the ways in which contract law regulates market exchanges, in particular consumer transactions that create advantages to those in affluent regions of the world, which are only possible in light of the costs (impairment of basic capabilities) borne by others in less affluent regions. From a capabilities perspective, there are normative reasons why sweatshops should be taken into account within the realm of relevant costs of transactions for goods made in sweatshops. As such, this represents a perspective on sweatshops from which they should be counted as problematic contractual externalities.[109]

In the context detailed at the beginning of this chapter, the terms of consumer transactions for goods made in sweatshops have capability impairing implications. The clothing market dynamics require corporations to be flexible in their ability to fulfil orders that meet volatile demand. Demand not only follows seasonal fluctuations, but also trends that are highly unpredictable. Retailers that aim to serve consumers with the latest fashion trends and pursue fast fashion strategies, produce many collections throughout the year. These corporations seek to serve consumers with clothing items that are inexpensive such that consumers are able to replenish

[107] As articulated on Nussbaum's list in Chapter 2 (Control over one's environment, point B), which reflects the central importance of the architectonic capability of practical reason and the capability of affiliation.

[108] Arguably, such direct scrutiny of sweatshop conditions would not be captured within a capabilities framework as articulated by Sen, due to the absence of a list of specific capabilities. On this point: Bagchi, AK, 'Freedom and Development as End of Alienation?' (2000) 35 *Economic and Political Weekly* 4408–20, 4418; also more generally Alexander, JM, 'Ending the Liberal Hegemony: Republican Freedom and Amartya Sen's Theory of Capabilities' (2010) 9 *Contemporary Political Theory* 5–24. By contrast, Nussbaum explicitly scrutinises substandard working conditions that enable profit making in a global context. See for instance: Nussbaum (2006a) (n 104) 277.

[109] For an alternative view of the sorts of externalities that are legitimately addressed within the realm of contract law, see: Bagchi, A, 'Other People's Contracts' (Fordham University School of Law, 2015), available at http://papers.ssrn.com/sol3/papers.cfm?abstract_id=2586136, assessed 21 October 2016.

their wardrobes as fashion trends shift. Retailers that meet consumer demands for such 'fast fashion' pursue flexible and inexpensive means of production. As this chapter details, sweatshop conditions serve to meet the type of fast and unpredictable demand that is part of this market dynamic. In this context, consumer transaction terms are causally linked to sweatshop conditions. Consumer demand for cheap and fashionable products that are immediately available as trends arise stand in direct relation to supply factors that are able to produce and make such products available on the market. In particular, the low prices paid for products that adhere to the latest fashion trends require inexpensive production conditions with short lead times, ie, the sorts of production conditions that characterise and produce sweatshops. The transactions that are sought by consumers of fast fashion cannot be made available as quickly, or realised at the same price levels, if not for sweatshop conditions. The availability of contracting options, and the price as a central contract term, are thus two important factors that directly link consumer contracts to sweatshop conditions.

D. Raising the Question of Contractual Immorality in Europe

The question of contractual invalidity and immorality in Europe (discussed in the subsequent chapters) follows both from the existence of the debate on the moral status of sweatshops in the public space, as well as from the identification of sweatshops as costs imposed on others (externalities) elsewhere through market activities. To start with the latter, the concept of externalities represents a potential normative justification for denying the binding force of an agreement, ie, the existence of a valid contract.[110] The previous sections showed that the identification of the costs that are taken into account as externalities depends on the underlying normativity that is captured in the application of the notion of voluntary choice. The economic interpretation of externalities would likely distinguish between forms of forced labour (slavery) and sweatshop conditions identifying only the former as problematic in that context. Conversely, a capabilities perspective would include the critical assessment of both.

In addition, and beyond the concept of externalities, the question of contractual immorality and invalidity also arises in light of the focus on sweatshops as a subject of public scrutiny and sweatshops as a topic of debate in academia. First, to the extent that contractual immorality reflects public morality, developments in the latter are of relevance to questions of contract law. Second, as the attention for deplorable production conditions of goods sold on the market in Europe increases as a subject of critical scrutiny, the awareness of market participants also increases. The question remains to what extent these developments are relevant under rules of contract law in Europe.

[110] See for instance: Study Group on a European Civil Code and Research Group on EC Private Law (ed), Draft Common Frame of Reference (Sellier, 2009) 62–63; Collins, H, *The Law of Contract*, 4th edn (Cambridge University Press, 2003) 102–03.

4

The Potential Frontiers of Contract Justice: A Sweatshop Case Study

The previous chapter discussed the main arguments regarding the moral status of sweatshops, illustrating the claim that sweatshops are a subject of moral concern. These concerns are also widely expressed and reflected in the popular media, where the perspectives of those who oppose sweatshops, generally captured by the view of sweatshops as morally problematic means of production, are dominant. Yet, even if these observations would be sufficient to establish the idea that sweatshops are commonly held to be morally objectionable in society, it does not follow that contract laws should respond in any particular way to contracts for sweatshop goods. Contract laws have their own internal normative structure and offer their own account of how they assess the immorality of contractual relations. However, within this book's normative capabilities framework, we can see why contract laws should not support consumer transactions for sweatshop goods *as* contracts. Namely, if sweatshops are morally problematic externalities of consumer transactions for sweatshop goods, the necessary implications of these transactions include the impairment of the basic capabilities of others. Taken together, the observations of moral disapproval in society and the normative capabilities based argument for contractual immorality prompt the question of how contract laws treat contracts for sweatshop goods. Do contract laws reflect the moral disapproval of sweatshops and thereby cohere with the capabilities standard of minimum contract justice?

The subsequent chapter provides an answer to this question on the basis of several European legal systems. This chapter develops the test case of a consumer contract for clothes made in a sweatshop elsewhere, in order to facilitate a case based analysis of the various contract laws in place. It presents the hypothesis that such transactions are invalid for immorality under rules of contract law in European legal systems. This hypothesis is informed by this book's normative framework: the capabilities based perspective on minimum contract justice. There are, however, several contractual objections to the normative argument for, and the hypothesis of, contractual invalidity for immorality. Specifically, as a hypothesis about current rules of contract law in Europe, it encounters several objections which claim to sever, in relevant ways, the link or association between the moral concerns evoked by sweatshops located elsewhere and the transactions in Europe for sweatshop produced goods. In other words, even if we accept and agree with those who oppose sweatshops for moral reasons, the internal accounts of contractual immorality may not offer a basis for including information regarding sweatshop production in the evaluation of contractual validity. The objections may offer some explanation for why contract laws' accounts of contractual immorality potentially diverge from the normative demands of a capabilities view of minimum contract justice.

This chapter will present four main objections as potential frontiers of the argument for minimum contract justice. These objections include: 1) consumer ignorance of sweatshop production condition of the products bought; 2) the principle of relativity or privity of contract; 3) the distant location of sweatshops; or 4) a separation between moral and legal norms as a bar to contractual invalidity for immorality. While the present chapter will discuss the hypothesis and the potential objections, the subsequent chapter will deal with the positive question of whether contracts, mutually beneficial to contracting parties, are invalid for immorality under the current rules of contract law in Europe, if the exchanged clothes are made under sweatshop conditions. The legal analysis takes a case based comparative approach. The last section of this chapter will briefly present that methodology, and conclude with the presentation of the test case, as well as some of its potential limitations.

I. Contractual Immorality and its Potential Frontiers

Consumer contracts, mutually beneficial to contracting parties, are invalid for immorality under the current rules of contract law in Europe, if the exchanged clothes are made under sweatshop conditions. That is the hypothesis that the present and subsequent chapter will examine. The articulation of this hypothesis follows in the first place from the book's capabilities based perspective on minimum contract justice. From this perspective the hypothesis seeks to test how, if at all, minimum contract justice is reflected in legal doctrine and the internal normative structure of actual contract laws in Europe. The hypothesis is also informed by the fact that sweatshop conditions in supply chains of goods bought and sold on the market are matters of current public and moral concern. This issue has attracted increasing attention and scrutiny, suggesting a changing awareness of a situation that has existed over time, but for which the conditions of modern life make information more easily accessible. Because information about sweatshop conditions (and production conditions more broadly) is becoming increasingly accessible and available over time, sweatshop conditions can be considered to represent a new case that confronts contract law. This development corresponds to similar attention for related issues pertaining to corporate responsibility, sustainable production and fair trade, which may also reflect changes in (moral) standards that occur over time. As such, the hypothesis also seeks to connect to developments in awareness of sweatshop conditions, in the expression of moral concern, and in the broader attempts to curb corporate conduct towards sustainable and fair practices. Furthermore, the hypothesis is strengthened by the suggestion that transactions of this sort could and would be immoral and invalid under the applicable contract law rules in at least one European legal system, ie, the Dutch legal system.[1]

Nevertheless, there are several objections against the hypothesis that transactions for clothes made in sweatshops are invalid for immorality under the rules of contract law in Europe.[2] These objections claim to sever, in relevant ways, the link or association between the moral concerns evoked by sweatshops elsewhere and the transactions in Europe for the exchange of clothes made in sweatshops. They thereby inform—on different grounds—the view that contracts mutually beneficial to contracting parties for the exchange of sweatshop clothes are not immoral and invalid under rules of contract law in Europe. The following sections present an inventory of the four main objections.

A. Beyond the Frontiers of Knowledge

The first objection invokes a lack of contracting parties' knowledge as a limit to contractual invalidity for immorality and can be brought forward against the hypothesis that transactions for clothes made in sweatshops are immoral and invalid under the rules of contract law in Europe. Specifically, this objection may put forward the idea that 1) consumers do not know, and/or cannot know, how the clothes they buy are made; and/or 2) retailers do not know, and/or cannot know, how the clothes they sell are made. There are thus at least two ways in which this objection could be spelled out. The first refers to the actual lack of knowledge of parties: contracting parties who do not know how the products that they exchange are made should not be confronted with the invalidity of their transaction on immorality grounds that relate to the production conditions. This objection invokes *actual* ignorance as an objection, regardless of the underlying reasons for ignorance. While actual ignorance may offer a defence to contractual immorality in some cases, general information regarding sweatshop conditions is becoming increasingly available, such that this interpretation of the objection is unlikely to affect a typical case. Moreover, the availability of information may also inform a normative judgement that parties should have been aware of the production conditions or even an accusation of bad faith that the parties must have known, even if they deny such awareness.

The second way in which lack of knowledge can raise an objection to the hypothesis seems more compelling. Instead of appealing to actual ignorance in the former sense, the objection focuses on the idea that contracting parties *cannot*

[1] Hesselink, MW, 'Capacity and Capability in European Contract Law' (2005) 13 *European Review of Private Law* 506.

[2] As is the case for the remainder of this book, references to the rules of contract law in Europe are only based on the legal systems included in this chapter.

have knowledge of the specific production conditions under which the clothes they buy and sell are made. This objection may be substantiated by referring to the distance—either geographically or in terms of the number of transactions—between the consumer contract (eg, the retail location) and the immoral production conditions that give rise to the question of contractual validity. If contracting parties cannot be cognizant of the conditions under which the clothes they sell and buy are made, the normative judgement that parties should have been aware of the production conditions bears no fruit. Moreover, if contracting parties' knowledge is impossible, transactions for clothes made in sweatshops cannot be distinguished from transactions for clothes that are produced under decent working conditions. As such, either all transactions would be suspect in terms of contractual immorality and invalidity, or on the contrary, none would be suspect. While the inability of contracting parties to make relevant distinctions between products on the market is compelling as an objection to the hypothesis of contractual invalidity for immorality, its empirical basis is weakened by the increase of available information and product branding regarding production conditions.

For instance, to the extent that popular media sources draw attention to sweatshop conditions, both as a general issue of concern, as well as in relation to specific brands, stores, and goods, an assumption of awareness among contracting parties is not implausible. Moreover, in that context, the terms of specific transactions may, at least, raise doubts as to the production conditions of a good. In particular, the price of a good can signal suspicion to consumers regarding sweatshop conditions in a supply chain, especially if this contract term has been publicly scrutinised in relation to deplorable production conditions. Consumers' pursuit of low priced goods presupposes decisions made in supply chains that drive costs down. An extremely low priced good may, or perhaps should, therefore raise suspicion, as it indicates low cost production. Extremely low prices may raise red flags for consumers regarding the production conditions of these goods, especially in combination with previous media attention for goods sold on similar terms.[3]

In light of the objection regarding contracting parties' knowledge, this book raises the question of contractual immorality and invalidity in relation to those cases for which the knowledge of contracting parties is not disputed; ie, knowledge is included in the design of the test case (see section II, C). In the legal analysis some attention will be given to requirements of contracting parties' knowledge. Namely, to the extent that features of distance (eg, geographical distance or the number of transactions) between those who engage in transactions in Europe and those who make goods in sweatshops dissolve the degree of certainty that one can have concerning the conditions of production, the objection of knowledge raises

[3] Information regarding deplorable production conditions may represent 'inconvenient facts' for consumers see, Hiscox, MJ, et al, 'Consumer Demand for Fair Trade: New Evidence from a Field Experiment Using eBay Auctions of Fresh Roasted Coffee' (2011) https://papers.ssrn.com/sol3/papers.cfm?abstract_id=1811783, accessed 21 October 2016.

the question to what extent knowledge makes any difference for questions of contractual immorality and invalidity under the rules of contract law in Europe.

B. Beyond the Frontiers of Contract Law: Third Parties

The second objection to the hypothesis relates to the bi-lateral character of contractual relationships, and its centrality for rules of contract law. Contract law governs the legal aspects of relationships that private parties, ie, the contracting parties, voluntarily engage in. Notions of freedom of contract, the binding nature of contract, and the relativity or privity of contract are central to contract law. Freedom of contract and relativity are often referred to in the same sentence, as representing different expressions or sides of party autonomy. The principle of relativity of contract, or privity of contract, refers to the idea that contracts are (generally) only binding for the contracting parties, that is to say, they only confer rights and impose obligations on the parties who have voluntarily committed themselves through their contractual relation.[4] The principle expresses contract law's central focus on the 'internal', often bi-lateral, and relational aspect of transactions. Rules of contract law are centrally concerned with the effects of contracts on those who have given their assent. In line with the central theme of the book, the hypothesis regarding contractual immorality in the sweatshop case, however, focuses on third party effects of contractual relationships, that is, the external implications, or negative externalities, of market conduct. This focus on the external implications of a consumer contract for sweatshop goods may bring to mind the idea that the question regarding its morality and validity falls beyond contract law's scope of consideration. From this perspective, the fact that a good is made in a sweatshop seems to be unrelated to questions concerning the legal status of the contract, and the rights and obligations it confers on the contracting parties.

However, the principle of relativity or privity of *contract* does not exclude the relevance of the external effect of contracts on third parties within the realm of *contract law* altogether. The hypothesis of contractual immorality and invalidity as put forward in this chapter, does not raise questions regarding the consequences of contracts for the legal positions of third parties, ie, whether the contract would result in legal obligations or rights for third parties. Rather, the question goes in the opposite direction, namely, to what extent the external implications of a contract may influence whether or not the contract indeed confers rights or imposes obligations on the contracting parties to begin with. Said differently, the hypothesis concerns the extent to which legal systems support and help realise market pursuits of private parties in light of the external implications of those pursuits. The hypothesis is directed at the legal position of private parties engaged in

[4] See on relativity/privity: Du Perron, CE, 'Contract and Third Parties' in A Hartkamp et al (eds), *Towards a European Civil Code*, 2nd edn (Kluwer Law International, 1998) and Du Perron, CE, *Overeenkomst en derden* (Kluwer Rechtswetenschappelijke Publicaties, 1999).

exchange—those who autonomously wished to engage in a legally binding relationship—rather than at the legal positions of others as a result of such exchange. Thus, the objection regarding the bi-lateral character of contractual relations, in principle, does not appear to undermine the hypothesis.

However, the idea that the sweatshop conditions are irrelevant to the legal status of the transaction between consumer and retailer, may still inform an alternative, potentially more effective objection to the hypothesis of immorality and invalidity. Namely, all contracts have (negative) external effects on others, for instance, because they exclude others from engaging in the exchange.[5] Contractual relations imply exclusion as a matter of demarcation precisely because of relativity or privity of contract, which can be considered a negative implication on those who are excluded. However, not all (negative) implications of contracts on others result in a hypothesis of invalidity. In this form, the objection raises a relevant question for contractual immorality and invalidity, namely: which external effects are relevant for the evaluation of the status of the contract itself; which external effects are acceptable, and which are not? The legal analysis will address this question and its relevance for the hypothesis.

C. Beyond the Frontiers of Europe: Geography

The third objection to the hypothesis invokes the distance between the contract and the sweatshop as a possible bar to contractual invalidity. In the context of this book, the location of the sweatshop is presented as remote from the transaction and located beyond the frontiers of Europe in a low labour cost country.[6] The purpose of focusing on sweatshop locations in developing countries serves to incorporate aspects of global inequality of (dis)advantage and its salience for the questions concerning the standard of justice reflected in contract law in Europe.

However, the remoteness of the sweatshop location from the transaction gives rise to the objection that, because of geographical distance, the transaction lacks sufficient connection to the morally objectionable source to be immoral and invalid. Why geographical distance would, independently, dissolve concerns of morality is not immediately evident. The objection can be understood in at least two ways. First, this objection can be interpreted to express the claim of uncertain knowledge, thereby coinciding with the first objection that sweatshop conditions fall beyond the frontier of contracting parties' knowledge (see above). Second, this objection can be interpreted as invoking the involvement of different communities, which translates into an objection regarding the applicable (social, moral and legal) standards. In the latter interpretation, the objection of geographical distance

[5] Shavell, S, *Foundations of Economic Analysis of Law* (Belknap Harvard, 2004) 320.

[6] The existence of sweatshops, and more generally deplorable production conditions, located in Europe is of course not denied. See for instance the case on exploitation in the asparagus harvest in the Netherlands: *Gerechtshof's-Hertogenbosch*, 6 July 2012, LJN BX0599 *(Asparagus exploitation)*.

addresses the potential divergence between standards applicable in the community of contracting parties and those applicable in the community where the sweatshop is located. It raises the question as to which standards are to be applied when assessing the morality and validity of the contract. The significance of this objection relies on the weak assumption that there is actual divergence in moral standards regarding sweatshops in the relevant communities. However, if sweatshop conditions would be deemed morally unacceptable by the standard applicable in the community of the consumer and retailer, but acceptable in the community where the sweatshop is located (or vice versa), the question as to which standards are to be applied makes a real difference for the hypothesis of contractual invalidity. The legal analysis will consider the relevance of the objection of geographical distance for the hypothesis, and will seek to answer the question: upon which standards are the norms of contractual immorality and invalidity based?

D. Beyond the Frontiers of Discipline: The Legal and Moral Realms

The fourth and last objection to the hypothesis invokes the separation between the legal and moral realm, and questions the relevance of the moral objections to sweatshops for the legal question of contractual invalidity. The previous chapter explored different arguments in the debate on the morally objectionable nature of sweatshops. The sophisticated arguments regarding the immorality of sweatshop production that are put forward in that context, find parallels in popular media. However, as this chapter (and the book more broadly) focuses on legal questions, one may wonder about the relevance of moral theory and moral concerns expressed publicly, within the legal realm. The objection points to the idea that the legal and moral orders remain independent normative orders, which, although they may interact and overlap, do not coincide. On the one hand, law may be immoral, and on the other hand, considerations of morality need not resonate with any legal significance. In short, the hypothesis regarding the invalidity of a consumer contract for a sweatshop good may be countered by the idea that moral objectionability does not equal legal objectionability. Insofar as the hypothesis would neglect the significance of this distinction within legal systems, the objection could have an undermining effect. However, the hypothesis invokes the question of contractual immorality as a basis for contractual invalidity, and to the extent that legal orders recognise the concept of contractual immorality, the latter is a legal concept to be interpreted within the legal realm. Indeed, no legal system in Europe supports transactions, which are considered to be immoral in this way.[7] All legal systems incorporate the rule that contractual immorality may lead to contractual invalidity. The question remains as to what extent the

[7] Kötz, *Illegality of Contracts in The Max Planck Encyclopedia of European Private Law Vol I* (Oxford University Press, 2012) 847; Kötz, H and A Flessner, *European Contract Law. Volume One: Formation, Validity, and Content of Contracts. Contract and Third Parties* (Clarendon Press, 1997) Chapter 9.

arguments put forward through moral theory, or in public debate, are relevant to the legal norms that determine contractual immorality and invalidity. How do legal systems determine the legal standards that govern the morality of a contract? This question will be addressed in the legal analysis in the subsequent chapter.

Together, the frontiers of knowledge, contract law, Europe, and discipline, represent four objections to the hypothesis of contractual invalidity for immorality that are assessed in the legal analysis of the various legal orders presented in the subsequent chapter. That chapter answers the question whether consumer contracts for sweatshop goods are invalid for immorality under various legal systems in Europe through a case based comparative approach. The last section of this chapter will briefly present the methodology, and conclude by presenting the test case central to the inquiry.

II. Methodology

In order to test the hypothesis of contractual invalidity for immorality of consumer contracts for clothes produced in sweatshops, this book undertakes a legal comparison and adopts a case based methodology. For this purpose, the current chapter designs a hypothetical case regarding a transaction for clothes produced in a sweatshop, and the following chapter will examine how the considered legal systems would address this same case.

This methodology is similar to one methodological pillar of the Trento Common Core Project. This methodology combines functionalism with a case based (factual) comparative methodology and compares 'the way in which the national systems of the different member States deal with the same practical cases relating to some of the main topics in some of the main areas of private law'.[8] The subsequent chapter adopts this methodological pillar and compares the way in which several European legal systems deal with the hypothetical sweatshop test case. The chapter asks specifically how, if at all, the case could encounter the moral limits demarcated within various contract laws, and explores if the hypothesis of contractual immorality encounters any of the four potential frontiers of contractual immorality, as discussed in the previous sections, within the selected legal systems.

A. A Functional Method

The adopted methodological pillar combines functionalism with a case based (factual) comparative approach. A functional method refers to the idea that legal

[8] Cartwright, J and MW Hesselink (eds), *Precontractual Liability in European Private Law* (The Common Core of European Private Law) (Cambridge University Press, 2008) 3; Bussani, M and U Mattei, 'The Common Core Approach to European Private Law' (1997) 3 *Columbia Journal of European Law* 339–56.

rules can be compared with regard to their similar functions, for example, where they address the same societal problem or conflict of interest and, in the present context: where legal systems address the same practical case.[9] This book's sweatshop test case puts forward a question regarding the balance of the interests of the contracting parties in relation to those of others elsewhere and society as a whole. On the one hand, legal systems value the freedom of contracting parties to decide what, with whom, and on which terms to engage in exchange: freedom of contract is a foundational principle of contract law. On the other hand, legal systems are also founded on other basic or fundamental values, and thereupon set minimum standards to which individuals must adhere, if they want their contracts to be recognised by law. Freedom of contract is informed by those minimum standards. Not all private endeavours pursued through exchange relationships qualify for public support, or are endorsed and supported through state power, ie, not all private transactions are recognised *as* contractual relationships. Contract laws take account of the ways in which private endeavours impact others and society as a whole, when assessing whether a transaction meets the minimum standards applicable to *contractual* conduct. In order to identify the legal concepts that should be the focus of the analysis, we must ask how, if at all, contract laws balance the interests of contracting parties to contract with the interests of others who may encounter the adverse effects of those transactions.

All of the legal systems that will be evaluated impose substantive limitations on the freedom of contracting parties. Contracts that are considered to be substantively objectionable within a legal system may not obtain the effects that contracting parties pursue and intend to accomplish through engaging in a contractual relationship. If a contract infringes the basic, foundational principles on which the legal system is founded, it is held invalid, ie, it is not recognised as a binding contract, and therefore cannot be enforced with the support of state power. The case based method and comparative legal analysis therefore focuses on the rules of contractual validity, and in particular, the legal concepts that reflect substantive limitations on contracts. In different legal systems, these concepts are referred to in terms of *good morals* and *public policy*. A considerable part of the substantive restrictions imposed on contractual freedom seek primarily to protect weaker contracting parties, for example based on inequality of bargaining power.[10] However, limitations on contractual freedom are also imposed with a view to the interests of others or society as a whole. Contractual immorality not only seeks to protect vulnerable contracting parties against exploitation through contract, but also functions to protect others and society as a whole against the detrimental, external effects of transactions. In those cases, the circumstances under which the contracting

[9] Zweigert, K and H Kötz, *An Introduction to Comparative Law*, 3rd revised edn (Oxford University Press, 1998).

[10] In such cases it can of course also be said that the protection of the interests of society at large plays a role.

parties entered into the contract are normally unobjectionable, ie, there are no defects of consent and the parties have the intention to be bound to the contract.

B. Purpose and Potential Criticisms

In order to assess the hypothesis of contractual immorality in relation to the sweatshop test case, the legal analysis in the subsequent chapter explores the demarcations of contractual validity that are informed by these other-regarding motives. The analysis is based primarily on the traditional sources of private law, namely statutes, case law and legal scholarship. In particular, the discussion of the law has focused on the authoritative representations thereof, in different legal systems. In these ways, the book's functional, case based legal method differs from methodology of the Trento Common Core Project. The latter has the ambitious aim to develop a reliable legal cartography of private law in Europe.[11] In this pursuit, the project combines the case based methodology with another methodological pillar, namely the theory of legal formants. This theory reflects the idea that 'the living law' is created from a diversity of formants, eg, statutes, scholarship, case law, custom and usage, which function as sources of law and need not generate a homogeneous answer as to what the law is.[12] The Common Core Project incorporates this theory by reflecting on several levels of formants on which national reporters participating in the Project respond to by questionnaire. This book has not adopted this pillar of the common core methodology. The substantive reason for deviation is found in the diverging purpose for analysis: the purpose for adopting the functional, case based method in this book is to test a hypothesis. Is the transaction described in the sweatshop case invalid for reasons of immorality in the various legal systems? This legal method for comparison is embedded in the book's broader methodology in which an external perspective, ie, a capabilities perspective on minimum contract justice, is central. This external, normative perspective informs the formulation of the case and the identification of the functional question. This book does not aim to develop and contribute to a legal cartography of contract law, but to evaluate how legal systems perform in light of the normative standard of minimum contract justice. The primary ambition is not to generate an accurate view of various contract laws with regard to contractual immorality, but to contribute to our ideas of the appropriate role of contract law within a minimum just society. The book aspires to contribute to a better understanding of where the demarcation between acceptable and unacceptable transactions ought to be drawn in such a society: what does minimum justice require of our contract laws when it comes to contracts for goods made in sweatshops?

[11] Bussani and Mattei (n 8).

[12] Sacco, R, 'Legal Formants: A Dynamic Approach to Comparative Law (Installment I of II)' (1991) 39 *The American Journal of Comparative Law* 343–401.

By adopting only one pillar of the common core method, this book's legal methodology is exposed to potential criticisms. The most important criticism relates to the functional element and the case based method of the approach. Functionalism, in particular, encounters strong opposition in debates concerning comparative law more generally.[13] The most significant issues in relation to the methodological design in this book, relates to the fact that the functional question and case formulation have not been articulated by a representative group of national reporters. This invokes the criticism that the results of the legal analysis may be entirely dependent on the author's pronunciations. While the criticism would be compelling within a project that aims to contribute to a legal cartography, this book's purpose justifies the methodological deviation. Namely, the book's broader methodology offers a capabilities perspective on minimum contract justice to frame the legal analysis. The legal methodology is embedded in this broader, normative methodology in which a capabilities perspective on minimum justice is central and leading for the formulation of the case and the identification of the functional question. In effect, this response pushes the traditional criticism to functionalism back to a different methodological level and informs a basic criticism. Namely, the external perspective imposes on *all* legal systems a 'function', which may be foreign to or reductive of them. While this criticism may be compelling from an internal perspective of contract law, it is an ineffective counter to the current project, which aims to further an understanding of what minimum justice requires of contract law. The current project does not aim to investigate the functions that contract laws perform, but rather the functions that contract laws should perform. That question requires us to take up a perspective that is by definition external, and examines contract law as an appropriate locus for the pursuit of minimum justice. If the traditional criticism to functionalism were to convert into the idea that contract laws should not pursue social justice aims, the criticism would coincide with a resistance to contract law's distributive function. This matter is discussed in more detail in Chapter 2, which engages the idea that contract law should not pursue social justice aims.

C. Case design

In order to present the comparative legal analysis in the following chapter, let us first briefly explore the case upon which the analysis is based and some matters of scope and criticism that it may encounter. The analyses of the legal systems are performed on the basis of the same factual representation of a case, which

[13] Michaels, R, 'The Functional Method of Comparative Law' in M Reimann and R Zimmermann (eds), *The Oxford Handbook of Comparative Law* (Oxford University Press, 2006). For a more elaborate discussion and further references, see: Cartwright and Hesselink (n 8) Chapter 1.

represents a mutually beneficial transaction, for the sale of a good on the internal market of Europe, which has been made under sweatshop conditions:

A European consumer buys a good in a European retail store. The parties intend to enter into a contract that concerns a straightforward and everyday transaction: clothes purchased for money. No special circumstances pertain, which would affect the legal capacity of contracting parties or the formation of the contract. The exchange is mutually beneficial to contracting parties; consumer and retailer enter the contract in the absence of any circumstances that compromise their consent. The clothes that are exchanged between consumer and retailer were made under production conditions that constitute a sweatshop, as described in Chapter 3. Both parties are aware that the clothes were made in such a sweatshop, for example because this fact has been brought to their attention through the media. This knowledge does not constitute a reason for the contracting parties to refrain from entering the contract in the first place, nor does it interfere with their pursuit to have the contract enforced by the court, in the event of a dispute.

The case design is informed by the scope of the inquiry in this book. This results, on the one hand, in the exclusion of some issues that may appear to be relevant *prima facie*. On the other hand, the case includes some elements that raise questions or criticism on two levels: the first pertaining to the degree of realism of the case, the second to its ability to test the hypothesis of contractual immorality. Both matters will be discussed in the following sections, starting with issues that fall beyond the scope of this book's inquiry.

i. Matters of Scope

The case design aims to bring to the fore particular reasons for contractual invalidity in the legal systems discussed, namely, those that engage in the negative effects of contracts on others, ie, on non-contracting parties. First, outside the scope of the legal analysis lie questions that focus on the contractual aspects pertaining to positions of the contracting parties, ie, the 'internal', bi-lateral, relational aspect of the transaction. For example, questions may arise concerning aspects relating to restitution following invalidity, or, apart from contractual validity, questions of contractual breach.[14] Questions of contractual breach come into consideration, for instance, if the consumer claims that the good is not what she could reasonably have expected, namely a good that is made under decent production conditions.[15] Such issues of legal non-conformity fall outside the scope of this book, because these issues focus the attention on consumer preferences and the interests of

[14] Questions regarding the process of unwinding a contract are matters relating to restitution or unjust enrichment and fall outside the scope of this book. Basedow, J et al (eds), *The Max Planck Encyclopedia of European Private Law Volume II* (Oxford University Press, 2012); Van Kooten, HJ, *Restitutierechtelijke aspecten van ongeoorloofde overeenkomsten* (Kluwer, 2002).

[15] See references in Chapter 1, section I, n 3.

contracting parties, as opposed to the positions of non-contracting, disadvantaged individuals elsewhere.

Second, the emphasis on the position of already disadvantaged third parties, namely those who work in sweatshops, may induce an inclination to focus on their interests and their fate more generally. That is to say, the context in which the questions are raised in this book may be read as an attempt to offer relief and solutions to the existence of sweatshops and the positions in which disadvantaged third parties find themselves. Consequently, the topic provokes the question of how the interests of third parties can be addressed and sweatshops combated, in an efficient and effective way. For such purposes, however, contract law is not the first instrument that comes to mind and this book does not intend to inflate its relevance with regard to these matters.

Third, within the realm of private law more broadly, questions of liability may seem more central when thinking about the ways in which third parties are affected by the engagements of others. The focal points of these questions are the rectification of harm, the rights of those affected, and the obligations of the wrongdoers. These matters are separate from the subject of this book.[16] The starting point of the questions raised in this book is not the position of individuals who work in sweatshops, or the question as to how the production conditions that characterise sweatshops can best be addressed or improved. This book focuses on the position of the contractual relations between European private actors that negatively affect third parties, within the European legal order and the values it reflects, ie, the validity of contract is framed as reflective of a minimum standard of social justice to which a society adheres.

Fourth, since this book is concerned with the ways in which the rules of contract law in Europe are reflective of a minimum standard of justice, the case design exemplifies solely a transaction that is governed by contract law in Europe. Thus, although other transactions associated with the same deplorable production conditions may be perceived to be *prima facie* more relevant or objectionable, these transactions fall outside the scope of consideration. For instance, contracts in the supply chain between contractor and subcontractor, or between sweatshop workers and subcontractors governed by other legal orders, are not considered. The case is submitted to each legal system for evaluation, on the assumption that the contract is governed by that system. Questions of applicable law in cross-border cases are not considered. The transaction between consumer and retailer is chosen as the subject of inquiry, because the hypothesis of contractual invalidity represents in some sense the most difficult for this case. For example, the objection of knowledge concerning supply chain conditions most strongly affects the position

[16] To the extent that a contract obliges one party to commit a tort in relation to a third party, the contract can consequently be deemed invalid under rules of contract law in Europe. See on this matter for instance Van den Brink, V, *De Rechtshandeling in strijd met de goede zeden* (Boom Juridische Uitgevers, 2002) 217.

of the consumer, over other participants in the supply chain. It is possible that other contracts in the supply chain are similarly governed by rules of contract law in Europe, to which the lines of reasoning put forward in this chapter may be extended (for instance between a retailer and supplier).

Fifth, associated with the attention concerning the validity of other transactions, the case may also give rise to questions regarding the legal relevance of a link between different transactions. In particular, the question of contractual invalidity may be considered dependent on the relationship between the consumer contract and other contracts in the supply chain. Namely, legal systems may, under certain circumstances and to certain degrees, consider the validity of a contract dependent upon the validity of contracts to which it is somehow linked.[17] For instance, under French law, the invalidity of one contract may affect the legal status of another contract if they form a unity (*ensemble de contrats indivisibles)*, ie, if they share the same purpose. If one of the contracts in the unit is held invalid and shared purpose can no longer be pursued by the other contracts, then its *causa* ceases to exist.[18] Under Dutch law, a contract that has the effect of building on an existent juridical relation is voidable on the basis of Article 6:229 BW (*voortbouwende overeenkomst*). This Article reflects the distinction between the existence and lawfulness of *causa* under 'old' Dutch law, where 6:229 incorporates the absence of *causa*.[19] The underlying aim of considering the link between such contracts as relevant for their legal status lies in the protection of contracting parties.[20] The topic falls outside the scope of this book since the latter focuses on the invalidity of contracts which are mutually beneficial, and invalid because of their negative implications for others. Moreover, the issue of linked contracts is primarily relevant to complex commercial realities. Although subcontracting systems in some cases may reflect complex relations between contracts, this would not include the contract between consumer and retailer. For example, the contract between consumer and retailer cannot be said to build on a pre-existing relationship (required to constitute a '*voortbouwende overeenkomst*').

Sixth, a matter of scope of a different order is the question of compatibility between a judicial decision of contractual invalidity for reasons of immorality on the basis of the conditions of production on the one hand, and free trade rules on the other hand. This question may be expressed as a challenge of 'protectionism in disguise', ie, the claim that if transactions for goods made in sweatshops elsewhere

[17] Validity here refers to the legal status of a contract, including not only the question of whether or not it is void, but also, and primarily, whether or not it is voidable.

[18] Ghestin, J, *Cause de l'engagement et validité du contrat* (Libraire Générale de Droit et de Jurisprudence, 2006) nr 383; see also, comments by Ghestin to *Avant-Projet de Reforme du Droit des Obligations (Projet Catala)*, Article 1125.

For example: Cass Civ 1e, 3 July 1996, Bull Civ I, nr 286 (D 1997, 499, ann P Reigne). Video club case: The cause was absent, because the purpose could no longer be achieved.

[19] Asser/Hartkamp & Sieburgh 6-III (2010) nr 299.

[20] Ibid, nr 300.

were held immoral and invalid this may be viewed as undermining the competitive advantage of low-cost labour countries and to creating benefits for domestic actors.[21] This question of compatibility would, however, not arise as an issue for the question of immorality and invalidity regarding the horizontal, contractual relationship between the transacting parties and therefore falls beyond the scope of discussion.

ii. Criticism: Realistic Representation and Testability?

The case is meant to represent a regularly occurring transaction in the market, and at least realistic and representative for some transactions that occur on the market. Against the claim that the case design has a realistic factual basis, stands the claim that some features of the case suggest that it is an improbable, marginal or otherwise irrelevant case. The claim may, in particular, be directed at the occurrence of sweatshops in supply chains of clothes bought and sold by European citizens and/or to the awareness of contracting parties thereof. Regarding the latter point, it may be argued that exchanges of clothes for money occur, in general, in ignorance of the conditions in the supply chain, at least on the side of the consumer. This claim is not only directly informed by the idea that information about production conditions is not readily available, but also by the stronger belief that consumers would not buy clothes if they knew that they were made in sweatshops. Along the same line of thought is the assumption that consumers would choose to return the clothes they bought if, after entering the contract, they obtained knowledge of deplorable production conditions.[22]

In other words, the belief is that consumers generally have (reasonable) assumptions about the responsible production conditions of goods they buy on the market, such that if they were to obtain contradictory information, they would pursue

[21] A striking parallel can be found between this issue and the debate about a distinction between product- and process-based regulation (ie, the so-called 'process-product' distinction) in the World Trade Organization (WTO)/ General Agreement on Tariffs and Trade (GATT) context. Process-based regulation refers to measures that are grounded, not in features of goods themselves—as is the case in product-based restrictions—but in the process or production method by which they are produced (therefore also known as: process and production method (PPM)-based regulation). Previously, such PPM measures were deemed irremediably illegitimate, wrongful barriers to trade. However, they may now be justifiable under Article XX GATT, which concerns the general exceptions to the prohibition of trade restrictive measures and permits countries to adopt measures that are, among others, 'necessary to protect public morals'. See on PPM measures in the WTO context, Kysar, DA, 'Preferences for Processes: The Process/Product Distinction and the Regulation of Consumer Choice' (2004) 118 *Harvard Law Review* 526–642 and expanding the issue from the WTO context to EU law, Davies, G, '"Process and Product Method"-based Trade Restrictions in the EU' in C Barnard (ed), *Cambridge Yearbook of European Legal Studies* (Hart Publishing, 2008). See on the general exceptions under Article XX GATT: Venzke, I, 'Making General Exceptions: The Spell of Precedents in Developing Article XX GATT into Standards for Domestic Regulatory Policy' (2011) 12 *German Law Journal* 1111–40.

[22] For such cases, non-conformity questions are pertinent. See references in Chapter 1, section I, n 3.

claims of non-conformity. These beliefs suggest that consumers would not consent to a contract for goods made in sweatshops, such that the designed test case is subject to the criticism that it does not occur, or does not occur often enough to be of any significance. The same holds for those who argue that sweatshop production is itself a rare occurrence, such that the quantity of sweatshop products on the market is insignificant. In short, both claims suggest that the case is marginal or irrelevant.

The question as to which set of assumptions is most representative (quantitatively) is an empirical matter. This book does not set out to provide a decisive answer on this matter, but rather present a case that can be generative for questions of justice as they apply to contract law. In order to fulfil this function, the test case should present a plausible case, ie, we need to be able to have reasonable confidence that there are cases in which consumers buy clothes with the knowledge that they are made under deplorable production conditions, ie, that they are made in sweatshops. There are at least two different factors that provide a basis for such reasonable confidence in the assumption of consumer awareness of sweatshop conditions. First, the fact that there have been numerous occasions where the media has extensively reported on the deplorable production conditions in the supply chains of particular companies or brands supports the idea that some consumers who continue to buy those goods must be aware of sweatshop conditions in the supply chain. Second, the fact that fast fashion goods are extremely popular even though they are frequently linked to deplorable production conditions. Media reports often connect fast fashion, low cost goods to deplorable production conditions, which suggest that certain terms of consumer contracts, notably the price and short delivery times, raise doubt over the production conditions of clothes. Since information on the issues is readily available through renowned and popular media, it is plausible that a significant number of consumers are aware of the issue.

Conversely, then, a claim can be made that the case design represents too many cases. Again, the plausibility of this claim depends on empirical data, on which this book provides no decisive answer. However, even if it is plausible that both the occurrence of sweatshop conditions is ubiquitous for all or most clothes bought and sold, as well as consumer knowledge thereof, this does not undermine the case design. The suggestion that the case design could somehow represent *all* transactions on the market—an exaggeration of the previous claim—does not erode the relevance of the case for this book. The inclusion of many or most market transactions does not pose a problem for questioning the minimum standard of justice in contract law. Moreover, the (in)frequency of transactions does not refute moral concern. However, the claim does raise the question of whether or not frequency of behaviour could be considered as an indicator for underlying values, and as a decisive factor for determining the values that inform the norms determining contractual invalidity. In addition, the inclusion of too many cases could be problematic on different grounds, for instance, the invalidity of many transactions on the market could be deemed problematic for economic activity and market functioning.

Another pragmatic response to the case design is to ask how the issue will be raised in court. Under the assumption that the contract is mutually beneficial to contracting parties who, in addition, are aware of the fact that the clothes exchanged are made in a sweatshop, it seems unrealistic that they would raise the issue of immorality and invalidity before a court. This question informs the claim that the question is only of theoretical relevance, and lacks interest in practice, because contracting parties will have no interest in the question's answer. However, in this respect, the contract is not distinct from many other contracts that are immoral and invalid. And even where neither contracting party raises the issue, a court often can and even must raise the issue of its own motion. No court will enforce a contract that is contrary to *good morals* or *public policy*, even if the parties do not raise that matter themselves.[23] The different roles that judges play, and the variances observed between common law and civil law procedures, have no bearing in this context, if the relevant facts of a case are presented to the court. For the objection to be effective, and render the significance of the question of contractual immorality and invalidity for the case design entirely bare, it would have to be shown that it is impossible for a court (currently and in the future) to have to consider a case similar to the sweatshop case; or, substantively, that the circumstances, as formulated, are in *all* cases evidently irrelevant for the court to consider. The practical significance of the case and the argument from minimum contract justice follows from the fact that it is plausible that a court will have to consider this question. The subsequent chapter will show how the various legal systems deal with questions of contractual invalidity for immorality, and address to what extent the various objections raised in this chapter, as potential frontiers to the argument for minimum contract, are successful.

[23] Asser/Hartkamp & Sieburgh 6-III (n 19) nr 312; Ellenberger, J, *Palandt Bürgerliches Gesetzbuch* (69. Auflage edn, Verlag CH Beck, 2010), nr 21; Fabre-Magnan, M, *Droit de Obligations. 1-Contrat et engagement unilatéral* (Presses Universitaires de France, 2012) 465–66; Prentice, DD, 'Illegality and Public Policy' in H Beale and AS Burrows (eds), *Chitty on Contracts Volume 1 General Principles* (Sweet & Maxwell, 2008) nr 16-204–06.

5

Contractual Immorality in Europe

Is a contract, mutually beneficial to contracting parties, invalid for immorality under current rules of contract law in Europe, if the parties exchange money for clothes that are made under sweatshop conditions? That is the question that this chapter will address. Since the courts in the jurisdictions under examination have not previously dealt with such a case, and, since it is not a case that easily fits with established categories of case law, the assessment considers the likelihood of immorality and invalidity under current rules of contract law in Europe. Therefore, the results of the investigation should be interpreted as largely conjectural. The sections that follow deal with the assessments under instruments of European contract law, and contract laws in the Netherlands, Germany, France and England respectively, on the basis of the hypothetical sweatshop case described in the previous chapter and briefly recapped here.

The hypothetical test case consists of the following facts: A consumer buys clothes in a retail store. The contract concerns a straightforward and commonplace transaction: an exchange of money for clothes. No special circumstances, which would affect the legal capacity of the contracting parties or the formation of the contract, pertain. The exchange is mutually beneficial to the contracting parties; the consumer and the retailer entered the contract in the absence of any circumstances that might compromise their consent. The clothes that are exchanged between the consumer and the retailer are made under production conditions that constitute a sweatshop, as described in Chapter 3. Both parties are aware that the clothes purchased have been made in a sweatshop. This knowledge does not constitute a reason for the contracting parties to refrain from entering the contract in the first place or from pursuing the enforcement of the contract in the event of a dispute. Is the contract immoral and on that ground invalid?

I. European Instruments of Contract Law

There is no European instrument of general contract law in place at the present time that would govern issues of contractual invalidity for immorality. However, it is not inconceivable that in the future such an instrument will be created. The developments in the field of European contract law reveal diverging stances towards the articulation of a European norm concerning contractual invalidity on the basis of immorality. In Part I of the Principles of European Contract Law (PECL)—an academic project published in 2000—Chapter 4 on validity, for instance, stated that it did not deal with contractual invalidity arising out of immorality.[1] To quote,

> because of the great variety among the legal systems of Member States as to which contracts are regarded as unenforceable on these grounds (…) further investigation is needed to determine whether it is feasible to draft European Principles on these subjects.

Part III of the PECL, as published in 2003, however, included contractual immorality in a chapter on 'illegality'. This chapter opens with Article 15:101, which states: 'A contract is of no effect to the extent that it is contrary to principles recognized as fundamental in the laws of the Member States of the European Union'.[2] With this articulation, the drafters explicitly intended to avoid diverging national conceptions of immorality, referring instead to fundamental principles found across the European Union. The Draft Common Frame of Reference (DCFR) took over this rule in Chapter 7 of its Book II. Article 301 therein states: 'A contract is void to the extent that: a) it infringes a principle recognized as fundamental in the laws of the Member States of the European Union; and b) nullity is required to give effect to that principle'.[3] The comments to this Article in the DCFR were taken over in full from the comments to Article 15:101 PECL, without major amendments. In contrast, developments towards enacting a Common European Sales Law (CESL) revealed the absence of the articulation of a common European standard concerning contractual morality.[4] Contractual immorality was excluded from the scope of the CESL proposal and the applicable national rules would govern this aspect of the contract even if parties were to opt into the CESL. The exclusion of a CESL based control of contractual morality was criticised for missing the opportunity to provide a basis for developing further a common conception of European values[5] and for revealing a lacuna in the CESL's reflection of a 'European model of just conduct'.[6] As it stands, the CESL will not be pursued in its current form, and is modified to serve the Digital Single Market Strategy and enhance online consumer sales in the internal market.[7] The most recent proposal for a legal instrument

[1] Article 4:101, PECL (I–II) (1999).

[2] PECL (III) (2003).

[3] DCFR (2009).

[4] European Commission, *Proposal for a Regulation of the European Parliament and of the Council on a Common European Sales Law* COM (2011a) 635 Final (CESL Proposal) nr 27, 19–20.

[5] Mak, C, 'Europe-Building through Private Law: Lessons from Constitutional Theory' (2012) 8 *European Review of Contract Law* 339–40.

[6] Hesselink, M, 'The Case for a Common European Sales Law in an Age of Rising Nationalism' (2012) 3 *European Review of Contract Law* 359–61.

[7] See *Annex 2 to the Commission Work Programme 2015*, COM (2014) 910 final, 12 nr 60. In addition, see the most recent proposal by the European Commission for a Directive *On Certain Aspects Concerning Contracts for the Online and other Distance Sales of Goods*, COM (2015) 635 final, which has subsumed parts of the original proposal for a CESL.

targets e-commerce only, and has provided no relevant substantive change regarding the rules on contractual immorality.

Thus, as it stands, there is no legal instrument that offers a European answer to our hypothetical sweatshop case and the question of the contract's immorality and invalidity. The proposal on CESL refers to the diverging national rules of contract law in the Member States and explicitly excludes a substantive norm for contractual immorality leading to invalidity that is shared by all Member States.[8] On the basis of the proposed CESL, the minimum requirements for interaction on a European level remains dependent on the applicable national rules, and internal market transactions remain governed by diverging national regimes in this respect.[9]

The DCFR, thus, represents the most recent suggestion for a European rule on contractual invalidity due to immorality (in contrast to the CESL) in the wording of infringements of fundamental principles. The question arises as to what is meant by such principles recognised as fundamental in the laws of the Member States.[10] On the one hand, the comments to the Article suggest guidance from European sources, such as the European Convention on Human Rights (ECHR),[11] and the Treaty on European Union and EU Charter on Fundamental Rights.[12] In this sense, the DCFR seems to put forth a European Union Law based articulation of fundamental principles. The comments, for instance, state that the national concepts (such as good morals and public policy) would have no direct effect under this Article. On the other hand, however, the wording of the Article does not refer to principles recognised as fundamental in the European Union, but to those recognised as fundamental in the laws of its Member States. The comments moreover suggest that a comparative study of national concepts could be helpful for the 'identification and elucidation' of the principles referred to in Article II 7: 301. Overall, the DCFR seems to provide a potential basis for developing a more autonomous European notion of contractual immorality. The autonomy of this notion seems to be supported, in addition, by the comments that refer to the

[8] See CESL Proposal (n 4) 6.

[9] Which national rules are applicable to B2C contracts depend on Art 6 Regulation (EC) No 593/2008 of the European Parliament and of the Council of 17 June 2008 on the law applicable to contractual obligations (Rome I) [2008] OJ L177/6–16, which lead to the application of the law of the consumer.

[10] See Hesselink, M, *CFR & Social Justice* (Sellier European Law Publishers, 2008) 7.2; Mak, C, 'Constitutional Aspects of a European Civil Code' in AS Hartkamp et al (eds), *Towards a European Civil Code* (Wolters Kluwer, 2011) 347–48.

[11] European Convention for the Protection of Human Rights and Fundamental Freedoms (ECHR) (Rome, 4 November 1950).

[12] Treaty of Lisbon amending the Treaty on European Union and the Treaty establishing the European Community [2007] OJ C306/01. The comments explicitly mentioned are the prohibition of slavery and forced labour (Article 3 ECHR); the freedom to choose an occupation and the right to engage in work (Article 15 European Union Charter on Fundamental Rights) and the right of collective bargaining and action (Article 28 European Union Charter on Fundamental Rights).

irrelevance of the intentions and knowledge of the parties under the Article.[13] As we will see, the knowledge of the contracting party is not irrelevant to the question of immorality and invalidity, in the national legal systems discussed in this chapter. As such the DCFR diverts from what seems to be a common—albeit not uniformly applied—requirement in contract law in Europe for contractual immorality and invalidity.

Comparatively, then, the DCFR may provide, on the one hand, a more favourable basis for our hypothetical sweatshop case than the other legal systems discussed in this chapter. For instance, since contractual invalidity on the basis of the DCFR would seem not to depend on a particularly close involvement or association of the contracting parties, as not even their awareness of the facts underlying the immorality is required. Strictly, this has no direct relevance to the hypothetical sweatshop case, as knowledge is assumed. However, the absence in the DCFR of the requirement of contracting parties' knowledge suggests that the underlying rationale of Article II 7:301 is found emphatically in safeguarding the interests of third persons or society at large,[14] rather than those of the contracting parties.[15] In this sense the DCFR Article may provide a promising alternative to articles in national legal systems that do not place a similar emphasis on the protective potential of contractual immorality and invalidity for others (ie, non-contracting parties) and society as a whole. In fact, the stated irrelevance of the contracting parties' intentions and knowledge in the DCFR removes objections to the hypothesis of contractual immorality and invalidity that are directed at the impossibility or uncertainty relating to parties' knowledge through arguments of distance. For this reason, the fact that the immorality in our hypothetical sweatshop case is associated with the interest of others elsewhere, may play less of a role than it could potentially in national legal systems. Moreover, as already stated above, the fundamental documents of the European Union (the EU Treaty, the EU Charter on Fundamental Rights and the ECHR) are mentioned as primary guiding sources for contractual immorality, in the context of the DCFR. With this guidance, a more universal character of contractual immorality would be able to develop under a DCFR through further constitutionalisation of contract law, which can express European values regarding contractual conduct externally. If so, such a conception would also have the potential to take more easily into account, the interests of others living elsewhere, who may be impacted negatively by contractual relations governed by contract law in Europe. For now, though, the assessment of contractual invalidity and immorality must be done on the basis of national regimes of contract law and consequently on diverging national understandings of contractual immorality discussed below.

[13] DCFR (2009) Book II, Chapter 7, Article 301, comment under C.

[14] As suggested in the sections on the principles of the DCFR under nr 5. Ibid 64–65.

[15] This line of reasoning corresponds to criticism expressed by French legal scholars to the former requirement of both parties' knowledge of the facts underlying the immorality, which the *Cour de cassation* reversed in 1998 to requiring only the knowledge of one of the parties. See section IV below.

II. The Netherlands

Party autonomy is a descriptive point of departure for the rules of contract law in the Netherlands and is often accompanied in the same sentence with a reference to contractual freedom. The latter refers to the idea that parties are, in principal, free to arrange their relations by means of contracts, including the freedom to decide whether or not to transact; to freely choose contractual counter parties; and to give shape to the content, consequence and conditions of the transaction.[16] Contractual freedom may, however, conflict with other principles, such as the idea that contractual relations must be socially acceptable.[17] This principle holds that contractual validity presumes the contract's compatibility with the society's fundamental values, and is reflected in Dutch law by Article 3:40 (1) *Burgerlijk Wetboek* (BW), which states that: 'Een rechtshandeling die door inhoud of strekking in strijd is met de goede zeden of de openbare orde, is nietig'.[18] Here, the legislator incorporated the concept of good morals, an open norm, leaving it to the courts to determine its substantive content with reference to the facts of a particular case.[19] As such, the courts and case law are of particular importance to questions concerning contractual immorality. If a court holds a contract immoral, the contract is invalid whether or not the contracting parties raise the question before the court.[20] The *ex officio* application corresponds to the underlying idea that the invalidity of an immoral contract lies in the objectionability of the availability of state power for the enforcement, which can be described in

[16] Asser/Hartkamp & Sieburgh 6-III (ed), *Mr Asser's Handleiding tot beoefening van het Nederlandse recht. 6. Algemeen overeenkomstenrecht* (2010) nr 41; Loth, MA, *Dwingend en aanvullend recht* (Monografieën Nieuw BW A-19, Kluwer, 2009) nr 14.

[17] Asser/Hartkamp & Sieburgh, ibid, nr 43.

The principle of 'maatschappelijke aanvaardbaarheid' is translated here as social acceptability.

[18] Translation in Warendorf, H et al, *The Civil Code of the Netherlands* (Kluwer Law International, 2009) Article 3:40, subsection 1, 447: 'A juridical act which by its content or necessary implication is contrary to good morals or public policy, is a nullity'.

[19] In case law, good morals and public policy are not often distinguished. For the hypothetical case, further discussion on public policy is immaterial as public policy is only independently mentioned in cases involving the infringement of a legislative provision. As an exception see: *Hoge Raad*, 11 May 2001, NJ 2002,364 *(OZF/AZL en AZL/Erven Moerman)* where the *Hoge Raad* (HR) (Supreme Court of the Netherlands) referred only to public policy ('zo fundamentele beginselen van de rechtsorde' translated as 'fundamental principles of the legal order') r.o. 4.4. In the case note, Hijma observed that this is a divergence from the practice to refer to good morals and public policy together. See case note from Hijma under nr 2. See on the distinction: van Kooten, HJ, 'Burgerlijk Wetboek 3, Artikel 40' in *Groene Serie Vermogensrecht* (2012), nr 7.2; Asser/Hartkamp & Sieburgh (n 16) nr 330 and 345; Van Zeben, CJ et al, *Parlementaire Geschiedenis van het Nieuw Burgerlijk Wetboek, Boek 3, Vermogensrecht in het Algemeen* (Kluwer, 1981) nr 191–92; Reehuis, WHM and EE Slob, *Parlementaire Geschiedenis van het Nieuw Burgerlijk Wetboek, Invoering boeken 3,5 en 6, Boek 3, Vermogensrecht in het Algemeen* (Kluwer, 1990) 1138–42.

[20] Article 25 *Wetboek van Burgerlijke Rechtsvordering* (Dutch Civil Procedure Code). On the *ex officio* application of 3:40 (1) see further: Asser/Hartkamp & Sieburgh (n 16) nr 312; Loth (n 16) nr 19; Van den Brink, V, *De Rechtshandeling in strijd met de goede zeden* (Boom Juridische Uitgevers, 2002) 35.

terms of 'the offence it would cause if the agreement would be realized by means of the law'.[21]

A. Contractual Immorality: Content and Necessary Implications

Thus, notwithstanding contractual freedom, a mutually beneficial contract can be considered immoral under Dutch law on the basis of either its content, or its necessary implications, in which case the contract is invalid.[22] In our hypothetical sweatshop case, there are no facts that support the immorality of the contract's content. The contractual obligations of the consumer and the retailer in the hypothetical case are neither independently immoral nor in relation to each other (ie, the exchange of clothes for money) and therefore the contract's content is not objectionable.[23] Namely, what the parties have obliged themselves to exchange, ie, the performances to which the parties have agreed, does not involve the performance of an immoral act: neither the obligation to pay money for clothes nor the obligation to supply clothes for money raises any issue of morality. Nor do the contractual obligations in relation to each other form an immoral exchange. An example of such a case involves for instance a case in which money is exchanged for things that are external to the market, ie, things that cannot be exchanged for money, such as human organs.

The answer is not so obvious in relation to the question of the contract's possible immorality regarding its 'necessary implications'. In fact, there are reasons to suggest that the contract's invalidity could and should follow, if a court considers the sweatshop conditions a form of objectionable exploitation. These reasons relate to the fact that the necessary implications of a contract refer not only to the motives of contracting parties, but also to the contract's foreseeable consequences.[24] The facts of our hypothetical case do not call into question the morality of the parties' motives, and may be assumed to be similar in nature to the typical reasons parties have for buying or selling clothes (eg, to be clothed; to follow the latest trends; to generate income and profit). This would only be different, if the hypothetical case would be designed to include the specific, and rather unusual, intentions of parties to engage in the exchange specifically in order to exploit others elsewhere by having them produce clothes in sweatshops. The factual basis would then be very much unlike common market transactions, and more similar to the typical, yet unrealistic, illustration of a case in which parties exchange money for an ordinary kitchen knife, with regard to which the buyer expresses the intention to harm a

[21] As articulated by Advocate General Langemeijer in the opinion to *HR* 16 November 1956, NJ 1957,1 *(De Vries/Van Kroon)*, 7; see also Van den Brink, ibid, 35–36.

[22] Similar to any other type of juridical act.

[23] On immoral content see: Asser/Hartkamp & Sieburgh (n 16) nr 333; also Van Zeben et al (n 19) 190.

[24] Asser/Hartkamp & Sieburgh (n 16) nr 333; Van Zeben et al (n 19) 190.

third person.[25] The contract's invalidity in our hypothetical sweatshop case could be based, instead, on the immorality of the contract's foreseeable consequences for others elsewhere.

B. The Exploitation of Third Parties

In the *Sibelo/Lamet* case the *Hoge Raad* referred explicitly to the fact that a contract is immoral and invalid, if its foreseeable consequences constitute facilitation of the exploitation of third parties.[26] Although the case itself did not bring to the fore facts that provided sufficient support for such a decision, this may be different in our hypothetical case.

In the *Sibelo/Lamet* case, Lamet had agreed to buy a sex club, Club 13, from Sibelo for the price of 35,000 Dutch guilders. The price was primarily determined by the sex club's goodwill, which was based on the potential profit Club 13 could generate. In turn, this profit was significantly based on the fact that Lamet would receive payments for the use of two rooms by prostitutes. The Court of Appeal declared the contract void, because the transaction entailed the exchange of money for the possibility to deliberately bring about or advance prostitution.[27] Although the *Hoge Raad* overruled the decision on the basis of the considerable changes in popular opinion regarding prostitution, it made explicit reference in the judgment to the contract's possible invalidity on the basis of its immoral foreseeable consequences. Notably, the *Hoge Raad* stated that the contract could have been invalid on the basis of an infringement of *good morals*, if it paved the way for or advanced the exploitation of prostitutes or abuses of other kinds.[28]

Taking this decision into account, the invalidity of the contract in our hypothetical sweatshop case is not implausible. Namely, the contract's foreseeable consequences could be considered immoral, if the facts of the case show that it advances the exploitation of workers in sweatshops. If the courts consider the exploitation of workers in sweatshops immoral, the contract should be held invalid. Thus, even though both consumer and retailer may be in agreement concerning the existence of mutual contractual obligations between them, in the event of a dispute, a court may find the contract to be immoral due to its necessary implications for third parties and refuse to lend its support for its enforcement. Under Dutch law, the fact that the sweatshop workers are third parties to the contract that is assessed does not preclude the application of Article 3:40 BW. The interests of third parties

[25] This is the classic illustration of a contract that is invalid due to its immoral implications. See: Van Zeben et al (n 19) 190; also Van den Brink, V, 'Artikel 3:40 onder het mes?' (2012) 44 *Nederlands Tijdschrift Burgerlijk Recht*.

[26] *Hoge Raad* 2 February 1990, NJ 1991, 265 *(Sibelo/Lamet; Club 13)*.

[27] At the time, the intention to drop the so-called brothel prohibition in the Dutch Criminal Code was at a far advanced stage, yet the Court of Appeal held that the contract's invalidity followed from the enforcement of that prohibition. Ibid, ro 2.2.

[28] Ibid, ro 3.3. The facts of the case in question, however, did not substantiate that this was the case.

are not beyond the frontiers of consideration for questions of contract law and a court can consider a contract invalid under Article 3:40 (1) BW, on the basis of its immoral foreseeable consequences for third parties.

Indeed, for questions of contract law, the interests of third parties can be of significant weight even beyond concerns of contractual immorality. For instance, in the *Negende van Oma* case the *Hoge Raad* considered whether or not the municipality of Vlaardingen was contractually obliged to place a work of art on an apartment building.[29] The residents of the apartment building were elderly people, and third parties regarding the contract between Vlaardingen and the artist. They felt denigrated and stigmatised by the word 'Oma' (which means 'grandma'), which would be placed on their building, and consequently objected. The Court of Appeal considered their objections so weighty that, in accordance with good faith they should prevail over the interest of the artist, a contracting party, in having the work displayed. In this case, the *Hoge Raad* confirmed that the interests of third parties were to be considered when determining the existence of rights and obligations between contracting parties.

C. What is Foreseeable?

Under Dutch law the parties' knowledge in our hypothetical sweatshop case proves to be a crucial requirement for the contract's immorality and invalidity. Namely, in order for the contract to be considered immoral and invalid, it is required that both contracting parties were aware of the contract's immoral implications. The *Hoge Raad* articulated this requirement in *Burgman/Aviolanda*, in which it overruled the decision of the Court of Appeal in view of the latter's decision that the good faith of one party was irrelevant for the contract's invalidity.[30] Although this case concerned the infringement of a statutory prohibition, the knowledge requirements regarding the contract's necessary implications can generally be regarded as applicable to foreseeable consequences that are immoral yet not prohibited.[31] In *Burgman/Aviolanda* the *Hoge Raad* held that the contract could be invalid due to its necessary implications only if *both* parties pursued, or were aware that the performance of the contract would lead to, the infringement of a

[29] *Hoge Raad* 20 May 1995, NJ 1995, 691 *(De Negende van OMA)*.

[30] *Hoge Raad* 11 May 1951, NJ 1952, 128 *(Burgman/Aviolanda)*. Aviolanda, a manufacturer of airplane parts, was to manufacture 250,000 hair combs for Burgman, which fell outside its normal operational activity. Under Dutch law, Aviolanda was only permitted to do so, if she obtained a licence. Aviolanda was not granted such a licence and therefore could not lawfully manufacture the goods ordered by Burgman. Burgman claimed the termination of the contract as well as damages on the ground that Aviolanda had failed to perform its obligations under the contract. Before the Court of Appeal, Aviolanda brought forward the defence that the contract was invalid on the basis of Articles 1356 (4) and 1371 of the old BW (now 3:40 BW), which required a lawful cause. In turn, Burgman had argued that she was unaware of the fact that the required licence had not been obtained, and of the fact that Aviolanda was not permitted to produce the combs.

[31] See *Sibelo/Lamet; Club 13* (n 26) section 5.1.2.

prohibition.[32] For cases that concern a violation of *good morals* not relating to a statutory prohibition—such as the contract in our hypothetical sweatshop case—the contract's invalidity depends on the question of whether both contracting parties were aware of the implications of the contract's performance.

Although, in relation to our hypothetical sweatshop case, the contracting parties had knowledge regarding the sweatshop's conditions under which the product was made, it should be noted that it has been the subject of debate whether or not the foreseeability of the contract's necessary implications entails a normative and objectified standard, ie, that the parties *should* have been aware. Most authors hold that in order for a contract to be considered immoral and on that ground invalid under Dutch law, it suffices that parties should have been aware of the contract's immoral implications.[33] Until recently, however, the *Hoge Raad* had not been explicit on the matter. In previous case law, notably in the *Verkerk/van der Veen* case, the *Hoge Raad* put this question aside.[34] In this case note, Brunner reflected further on the issue, stating that:

> The appraisal that someone should have been aware or must have been aware is not merely a normative attribution of not-knowing, but also and primarily a rule of evidence for the factual judgement as to whether he knew or with great certainty suspected what he states not to have known.[35]

In Brunner's phrasing, a distinction can be found between the strictly normative statement that 1) someone *should have been aware* and the presumption of facts, 2) that someone *must have been aware* of the contract's implications.[36] However, the potential importance of this distinction appears to have been superseded by more recent case law, in which the *Hoge Raad* has held that the fact that parties should have been aware of the contract's immoral implications suffices for contractual invalidity.[37]

As noted previously, this is not of decisive importance for the contract in our hypothetical sweatshop case. However, for situations in which the parties do not expressly state that they know that the clothes purchased are made in a sweatshop, it remains to be seen what facts, or their combined concurrence, will be sufficient for the claim that the contracting parties must have known of the

[32] *Burgman/Aviolanda* (n 30).

[33] See for instance in Asser/Hartkamp & Sieburgh (n 16) nr 325; van Kooten in Groene Serie Vermogensrecht (n 19), Art 3:40 Strijd met goede zeden, openbare orde of wet, nr 7.6; van Schaick, A in D Busch, et al (eds), *The Principles of European Contract Law (Part III) and Dutch Law* (Kluwer Law International, 2006) Chapter 15, 246.

[34] The *Hoge Raad* left the question unanswered in *Hoge Raad,* 28 June 1991, NJ 1992, 787 *(Verkerk/Van der Veen)*, ro 3.2.

[35] Case note Brunner, nr 2. 'Het oordeel dat iemand iets behoorde te weten of moest weten, is niet slechts een normatieve toekenning van niet-weten, maar ook en vooral een bewijsregel voor het feitelijk oordeel dat hij wist of met grote waarschijnlijkheid vermoedde wat hij zegt niet geweten te hebben.'

[36] The distinction may be of importance. Namely, for the latter statement, the burden of proof is relevant, since the question whether someone actually has knowledge is relevant, whereas for the former (normative) statement, a party's factual ignorance is not.

[37] See *Hoge Raad,* 28 October 2011, RvdW 2011, 1314 *(Ponzi-scheme)*; and *Hoge Raad,* 1 June 2012, RvdW 2012, 765 *(Esmilo/Mediq)*, notably the Opinion by Advocate General Wissink, nr 3.27.

contract's consequences. It seems highly unlikely that a court would consider the mere fact of a product's low price sufficient for such claim.[38]

D. How to Concretise Good Morals?

So far under Dutch law, we have seen no principled obstacles for the immorality and invalidity of the contract in our hypothetical sweatshop case: neither the parties' knowledge requirements nor the fact that the necessary implications concern third parties constitutes an obstacle. However, the statements of the *Hoge Raad* in *Sibelo/Lamet* concern the exploitation of third parties in the Netherlands and our hypothetical case may be assessed differently, because the sweatshops are located beyond the national borders. And thus the question remains whether or not a court would deem the exploitation of individuals in sweatshops located elsewhere immoral and the contract on that ground invalid. In other words, is the necessary reliance by contracts governed by Dutch law on sweatshops located in other countries considered as contrary to *good morals*?

Since *good morals* is a rather open textured concept, its content cannot be described through an abstract definition.[39] The absence of clear guidelines for interpretation complicates the articulation of its substance in light of a new case, such as the hypothetical sweatshop case. Generally, the concept of *good morals* is described in reference to the sources that can and cannot be used as direct reference points. For the hypothetical case it is of relevance to note that alongside ideologies and religious doctrines,[40] ethical theories have no direct impact on the legal standard of *good morals*.[41] Such sources can influence the legal standard of good morals only indirectly through common social opinion, prevalent in Dutch society (see below). Thus, although the moral arguments regarding the moral status of sweatshops, described in Chapter 3, cannot *directly* inform the standard of contractual immorality, they can be relevant insofar as they are endorsed, as a matter of common social opinion in Dutch society. It is, however, more difficult to work out how one can establish what 'common social opinion' is for any particular case.

Common social opinion is described predominantly to consist of those moral viewpoints that enjoy the largest degree of consensus in a society. According to Van den Brink, this formula is understood implicitly as referring to majority opinion.[42]

[38] Compare the *Ponzi-scheme*, ibid, case. The case concerned a loan agreement from which one party (an investor) received excessive interest, which was generated by the borrower through a so-called ponzi-scheme (a fraudulent investment scheme). The apparent disproportionate interest rate did not suffice for the claim that the investor must have been aware of the ponzi-scheme, nor for the claim that the interest rate should have motivated the investor to conduct further research into the practices of the borrower.

[39] See Van den Brink (n 20), particularly 122 and further, with references.

[40] Asser/Hartkamp & Sieburgh (n 16) nr 331. Van den Brink (n 20) 128–29.

[41] Van den Brink (n 20) Chapter 5.

[42] Van den Brink (n 20) 127–128 and 194, 209. Van den Brink's monograph of 2002 is the most recent comprehensive study on the Dutch concept of good morals.

Although Van den Brink seems to agree with this interpretation of *good morals*, he describes common social opinion in different terms, referring to a *minimum* degree of consensus in social opinion regarding morality.[43] Regardless of these divergences, it remains rather obscure as to how one can fathom the degree of consensus (whether majoritarian or minimum) that exists regarding moral views. This is particularly true in relation to new concrete cases, such as the sweatshop case.[44] The degree of consensus regarding moral viewpoints is moreover subject to divergence and evolution over time and place,[45] and current Dutch society seems to be increasingly pluralistic in this regard.[46] Thus, in this context the hypothetical sweatshop case may not only exemplify a 'new' case with regards to the facts, but also as a case that brings to the fore possible changes in moral viewpoints. Of course both developments are mutually interdependent.

The moral views that are at stake in cases of contractual immorality are those deemed fundamental to the social fabric of society.[47] These views are often described as those that are part of common social opinion regarding basic decency ('het maatschappelijke oordeel omtrent hetgeen behoort') as related to Dutch society.[48] Since the degree of consensus in social opinion with regard to our hypothetical sweatshop case is not prima facie evident, the content of *good morals* is to be found in the fundamental values that are encompassed within the legal system.[49] When considering the potential infringement of good morals or public policy under Article 3:40 (1) BW, the *Hoge Raad* also uses the language of 'fundamental principles' within the legal order.[50] In this context, courts are likely to rely on objective sources, ie, treaties, legislation, case law and general principles of law, which express a society's common social opinion over time.[51] Although special importance is to be given to written sources of law that refer to fundamental rights, Dutch courts have only rarely referred to such sources directly.[52] An example is provided by the *Mensendieck* case in which the *Hoge Raad* considered whether a contractual clause that prohibited a contracting party from teaching a

[43] Van den Brink (n 20) 194.

[44] Van den Brink (n 20) 122–32.

[45] Loth (n 16) nr 16; *Sibelo/Lamet; Club 13* (n 26); *Hoge Raad,* 7 September 1990, NJ 1991, 266 *(Catoochi)*.

[46] Nevertheless, in Asser/Hartkamp & Sieburgh (n 16) nr 330, the assumption is made that an overall consensus can (still) be found as to what is considered decent in most cases.
See also the discussion by Van den Brink (n 20) 129–30.

[47] Van den Brink (n 20) 194.

[48] Asser/Hartkamp & Sieburgh (n 16) nr 330–31; van Kooten in Groene Serie Vermogensrecht (n 19) aant 7.2.

[49] Van den Brink (n 20) 212.

[50] See n 19 and recently in *Esmilo/Mediq* (n 37) ro 4.4. This case involved a contract requiring a performance contrary to a statute. The *Hoge Raad* confirmed that under Article 3:40 (1) BW, a court must consider whether such a contract is, amongst others, contrary to the fundamental principles of the legal order, constituting an infringement of good morals or public policy.

[51] Van den Brink (n 20) 209–12 and Asser/Hartkamp & Sieburgh (n 16) nr 331.

[52] Mak, C, *Fundamental Rights in European Contract Law* (Private Law in European Context Series, Wolters Kluwer, 2008) 93; Van den Brink (n 20) 43.

paramedical therapeutic method, the Mensendieck method, infringed the party's right to education (ECHR, First Protocol, Article 2).[53] Although the *Hoge Raad* held that the contract did not infringe the party's fundamental right, the case is an example of the Court's consideration of fundamental rights in articulating the concept of *good morals*. Another example of the effect of fundamental rights on private relations came to the fore in the *Valkenhorst* case in which the *Hoge Raad* recognised a general personality right, which granted a child the right to ascertain the identity of her biological parents.[54] The child's (fundamental) right offset the private obligation that Valkenhorst held to keep such information secret in relation to the mother. This case suggests that the fundamental rights of third parties may have an effect on the private obligations that contracting parties possess with regard to each other.

As such, fundamental rights may be of special importance for the articulation of contractual immorality in the sweatshop case. The ECHR contains explicit articles on the prohibition of slavery and forced labour (Article 4) and the right to freedom of assembly and association, which includes the right to form trade unions (Article 11). Similarly, such fundamental rights are articulated in the fundamental conventions of the International Labour Organisation, to which the Netherlands is a party.[55] To the extent that Dutch courts take account of the interest of third parties in determining whether or not a contract is immoral and invalid, they may do so in light of fundamental rights. There is no principled reason why the geographical location of those third parties would thwart such consideration, particularly where it concerns universal fundamental rights.

Nevertheless, there is no case law in which a court articulated contractual immorality explicitly in reference to fundamental rights of third parties who were not engaged in the dispute in question. Thus, the explicit consideration of contractual immorality in light of fundamental rights in our hypothetical case seems unlikely.[56] The absence thereof, however, does not preclude the relevance of values in Dutch society expressed through universally endorsed fundamental rights.

Moreover, there is no indication that the fact that the sweatshop is located elsewhere (beyond the geographic borders of the Netherlands) should be of decisive relevance for the evaluation of the contract on the basis of 3:40 BW. The concept of good morals should be established on the basis of the norms that are prevalent in

[53] A student member of the Mensendieck Union ('Nederlandsche Mensendieck Bond') had failed to comply with the requirements of the Union to become a certified mensendieck physiotherapist teacher, and consequently, she was prohibited from teaching mensendieck lessons on the basis of the contract. The student however, presented herself as a mensendieck teacher by, first assisting her mother who was a certified mensendieck teacher, and later starting her own practice. The Mensendieck Union then obtained an injunction to stop the student teaching mensensdieck exercises in her practice. *Hoge Raad*, 31 October 1969, NJ 1970, 57 *(Mensendieck I)*; *Hoge Raad*, 18 June 1971, NJ 1971, 407 *(Mensendieck II)*.

[54] *Hoge Raad*, 15 April 1994, NJ 1994, 608 *(Valkenhorst II)* ro 3.2.

[55] See discussion in section on German law below.

[56] One may more reasonably expect such references in cases that entail an alleged infringement of a contracting party's fundamental right, eg *Mensendieck I* and *Mensendieck II* (n 53). See also Mak (n 52) 30–31 and 83–86; Van den Brink (n 20) 211.

the community in which the norms are applied.[57] And in terms of the values fundamental to Dutch society, neither objective sources (universal fundamental rights) nor expressions in public opinion suggest that sweatshops located beyond national borders are exonerated from scrutiny, merely because of their distant location.

What is considered to be immoral in the hypothetical sweatshop case depends both on (developments in) common social opinion and the values of society that have been expressed in objective sources. Whether or not the contract will be held invalid depends on how a court will weigh the interest of society in eschewing transactions, for products made by means of third party exploitation, recognised and enforced with support of state power, against the interests of contracting parties in realising such a transaction through law. Where sweatshops are the subject of (increasing) moral scrutiny, society may come to view the enforcement of contracts for products made in sweatshops through law, as offensive.

E. Concluding Remarks: Contractual Invalidity on the Basis of Third Party Exploitation

A court may hold the contract in the hypothetical case invalid for immorality under Dutch law. This could be the case if a court considers the performance of the contract to advance the exploitation of third parties, ie, those who work in sweatshops, and for that reason the court could declare the contract immoral and invalid. In other words, a court could consider the advancement of third party exploitation in sweatshops to be an immoral necessary implication of the contract, ie, an immoral foreseeable consequence, and therefore invalid. The contracting parties' awareness is a decisive factor in the analysis. In the event that parties would not confirm that they were aware that the clothes exchanged were made in a sweatshop, other factual circumstances of the case would be the determining factor as to whether or not a court would hold that the parties should have been aware. The standard of good morals may be articulated in light of the fact that the exploitation relates to the infringement of fundamental rights, but would depend ultimately on whether the court would regard the moral views that are at stake in the case as fundamental to Dutch society.

III. Germany

Freedom of contract in Germany is regarded as the expression of private autonomy and the fundamental right to give shape to and develop one's personality.[58]

[57] See: Van den Brink (n 20) 130–31.

[58] Grundgesetz für die Bundesrepublik Deutschland: Article 2 subsection (1): Jeder hat das Recht auf die freie Entfaltung seiner Persönlichkeit, soweit er nicht die Rechte anderer verletzt und nicht

In principle, private parties are free to engage in market transactions, such as the exchange of money for clothes, as they see fit. However, this freedom is not absolute, and demarcated by, not only the rights of others, but also by the ethical norms fundamental to the German legal order.[59] The German legislator ensured the protection of the fundamental values of the legal order from infringement by private agreements, by including the concept of good morals in the German *Bürgerliches Gesetzbuch* (BGB).[60] Article 138 I BGB holds that contracts (more broadly: juridical acts) which infringe good morals, are invalid: '*Ein Rechtsgeschäft, das gegen die guten Sitten verstößt, ist nichtig*.'[61] Thus, although the contracting parties are in principle free to exchange money for clothes, this freedom may be curtailed if the exchange is deemed contrary to the ethical norms that form the foundations of the German legal order, in short, if the contract is considered immoral.

The German concept of good morals is articulated as a general clause and its content is to be established by courts in light of the circumstances of a particular case.[62] A German court must determine *ex officio* whether a contract is immoral and invalid.[63] Over time, scholars developed different categories (*Fallgruppen*) of immoral contracts as they emerged in case law.[64] Case law thus plays an important role for questions concerning contractual immorality.[65] Of particular interest for the sweatshop case is the distinction between contracts deemed immoral in light of the interests of contracting parties and contracts that have been deemed immoral and invalid in light of general or third party interests.[66]

gegen die verfassungsmäßige Ordnung oder das Sittengesetz verstößt. Armbrüster, 'Münchener Kommentar zum Bürgerlichen Gesetzbuch (BGB) 6 Auflage 2012' (Beck Juristischer Verlag, 2012), rn 20; Köhler, H, *BGB Allgemeiner Teil*, 33 Auflage edn (Verlag CH Beck, 2009) 32 et seq.

[59] Ellenberger, J, *Palandt Bürgerliches Gesetzbuch*, 69 Auflage edn (Verlag CH Beck, 2010) rn 1; Armbrüster, ibid, rn 1.

[60] Next to the purpose of §138 to protect these fundamental values on which the legal system is built, an additional aim is found in the *deterrence* of those who wish to pursue immoral aims through their contracts. The legal order does not facilitate such contracts, which are considered to reflect an abuse of party autonomy (freedom of contract). §138 is considered a significant contribution to the protection of values, even though the legal order has alternative ways in which to uphold its fundamental values from abuse of private autonomy (regulation in the area of public law offers alternatives) see: Armbrüster (n 58) rn 1–2.

[61] A juridical act, which is contrary to good morals, is void. Although the Article does not explicate it, it also includes juridical acts, ie, contracts, that are against 'ordre public'. Ellenberger (n 59) rn 3.

[62] Ellenberger (n 59) rn 1; Armbrüster (n 58) rn 1; Teubner, G, *Standards und Direktiven in Generalklauseln* (Athenäum Verlag, 1971).

[63] Ellenberger (n 59) rn 21; also Armbrüster (n 58) rn 9 and rn 155.

[64] There is no uniform system of categorisation and categories generally overlap and exclude many individual cases, which do not fit neatly within any category.

[65] The important role of the judiciary is reflected in the *Delegationsfunktion* of the general clause good morals, as identified by Teubner. The *Delegationsfunktion* refers to the fact that the legislator delegated the concretisation of the concept of good morals for specific cases to the judiciary. Teubner (n 62), Part IV *Erörterung der Funktionen*. Current commentaries to the BGB still make reference to the three functions Teubner identified. See for example: Armbrüster (n 58) rn 3.

[66] Ellenberger (n 59) 132 distinguishes *Fallgruppen* on the basis of immorality against counter parties and immorality against general and third party interests. Palandt distinguishes different *Fallgruppen* on the basis of this distinction.

A. *Das Gesamtcharakter*: The Interests of Third Parties and Society

In principle, the contract in our hypothetical sweatshop case can be held invalid under German law, in spite of the fact that the question of contractual immorality is not raised because the contracting parties' interests are at stake. On the basis of §138 I BGB, courts will look at a contract's '*Gesamtcharakter*' (meaning comprehensive character).[67] Important factors that constitute a contract's comprehensive character are: objective content, the motivations and purposes of the contracting parties, as well as the circumstances that have led to the conclusion of the contract.[68] Contractual immorality need not follow from any one of these features considered separately, but may be based on the way in which different aspects of a specific case contribute to its character. The contract's implications for third parties, or society as a whole, reflect one aspect of a contract's character and are thus to be taken into account in the assessment of a contract's validity.[69] It is thus relevant whether or not the terms of a contract, or the particular circumstances of a case, lead to the exploitation of others under German law.[70]

B. Knowledge Requirements

A court is likely to consider the knowledge of contracting parties in the sweatshop case to be of particular salience in asking the question of contractual immorality. Namely, for contractual immorality to have a bearing on the exchange between consumer and retailer, it is required that both parties know of the facts that underlie the immorality associated with general or third party interests.[71] Accordingly, in the sweatshop case, the parties' awareness of the fact that the clothes were made in a sweatshop is of decisive importance in order for a court to consider the

[67] Armbrüster (n 58) rn 9 (*Umstandssittenwidrigkeit)*; Ellenberger (n 59) rn 7–8 and 40 (*Gesamtcharakter*); Köhler (n 58) rn 22, 192 (*Gesamtwürdigung)*. The only exception is made where contracts are deemed contrary to good morals on the basis of their objective content (*Inhaltssittenwidrigkeit*).

[68] Armbrüster (n 58) rn 9; Ellenberger (n 59) rn 8; Köhler (n 58) 192.

[69] Ellenberger (n 59) rn 40 et seq.

[70] Similar to the case under Dutch law (section 5.1.2), the *Bundesgerichtshof* held that agreements for rent of a brothel were valid, unless the terms of the contract (eg, the high rent) would lead to the exploitation of the persons working there. See: *Bundesgerichtshof*, 1 January 1975 BGH NJW 1975, 638.

[71] Ellenberger (n 59) rn 8; BGH NJW 2005, 41, 2992 (see n 72). Also: *Bundesgerichtshof*, 6 December 1989 BGH NJW, 1990, 9, 568. The case involved a lease contract for a guesthouse, the price of which was based on a minimum required sale of beer. The Court of Appeal deemed the contract immoral because it was against the interests of others and society (in light of societal, health and social implications), as it was possible or even likely that the keeper would for instance sell alcohol to minors in order to meet the minimum amount of sales. The *Bundesgerichtshof* held that the agreement was not contrary to good morals since the case did not bring forward any facts that supported the claim that both parties indeed engaged in immoral activities, or were aware of those activities. '(…) die Vorschrift des §138 I BGB unter der Gesichtspunkt der Verletzung von Interessen der Allgemeinheit oder Dritten grundsätzlich nur anwendbar ist, wenn alle Beteiligten sittenwidrig handeln, also die Tatsachen kennen oder sichzumindest ihrer Kenntnis grob fahrlässig verschliessen, die die Sittenwidrigkeit des Rechtsgeschäfts begründen', 568.

contract's possible invalidity. But under German law, the contracting parties need not have been aware of the infringement itself or of the harm that is caused. For contractual immorality to have a bearing on the case, it suffices that the parties were consciously or grossly negligent as to obtaining knowledge of these facts.[72] Whether or not the contract in the sweatshop case will be considered immoral depends on how a court considers sweatshops in light of the fundamental ethical values that provide the basis for the German legal order.[73]

C. Good Morals: *die Gesamtbeurteilung*

Under German law, the legal norm of good morals reflects a minimum basis of shared ethical norms as a precondition for, and therefore fundamental to, German society.[74] The concretisation of good morals results from the interaction between ethical norms in the legal order and social order.[75] In the evaluation of the contract's morality in the sweatshop case, a court would take account of all the moral conceptions of the social and legal order that are relevant to its particular facts.[76] This means, in particular, that a court may take account of (changing) norms in the German social order regarding exchanges of money for clothes produced in sweatshops.[77]

It is likely that, consistent with case law involving contractual morality under German law, a court would make use of the so-called *Anstandsformel* in the wording of the assessment: '*das Anstandsgefühl aller billig und gerecht Denkenden*'.[78]

[72] Ellenberger (n 59) rn 8; BGH NJW 2005, 41, 2992. Köhler (n 58) 193 rn 23. Standard German case law holds that it is sufficient if the parties were consciously or grossly negligent with regard to the facts underlying the immoral character of the transaction. See for instance in the case of stolen goods *Bundesgerichtshof*, 9 October 1991 NJW 92, 310 *(Stolen goods)* or with regard to the inexperience of an older consumer *Bundesgerichtshof*, 29 June 2005, NJW 2005, 41 in which the Court refers to the fact that '(…) weder das Bewusstsein der Sittenwidrigkeit noch eine Schädigungsabsicht erforderlich [ist], es genügt vielmehr, wenn der Handelnde die Tatsachen kennt, aus denen die Sittenwidrigkeit folgt; dem steht es gleich, wenn sich jemand bewusst oder grob fahrlässig der Kenntnis erheblicher Tatsachen verschliesst', 2992.

[73] Ellenberger (n 59) rn 1; Armbrüster (n 58) rn 1; Beck'scher Online-Kommentar BGB/ Wendtland, §138, rn 2, Stand: 01.11.2011 Edition: 21.

[74] Mayer-Maly, T, 'Was Leisten die guten Sitten?' (1994) 194 *Archiv für die civilistische Praxis* 105–76, 171. Armbrüster (n 58) rn 11; Ellenberger (n 59) rn 5.

[75] Ellenberger (n 59) rn 2–3; Armbrüster (n 58) rn 11–12, 14–15; and Köhler (n 58) rn 19–20.

[76] Armbrüster (n 58) 1655, rn 20 and rn 13.

'*Die Gesamtbeurteilung*' reflects that the concept of good morals does not only reflect values that have absolute protection under the law, under those conditions contracts are not immoral, but illegal (§134 BGB).

[77] Next to the *Delegationsfunktion* (see n 65), Teubner identified the *Rezeptionsfunktion*, which refers to the legal significance given to norms and norm structures external to the legal order through good morals; and the *Transformationsfunktion*, which refers to recognition of the transformation of norms in society in the legal norm of good morals. Teubner (n 62) Part IV *Erörterung der Funktionen*.

[78] Ellenberger (n 59) rn 2; Köhler (n 58) 191; Armbrüster (n 58) rn 14. For a historical discussion, see Teubner (n 62) section 4.4; see for an example of a recent reference by the *Bundesgerichtshof: BGH NJW 2009*, 19, 1346, §10: 'Die Frage der Sittenwidrigkeit nach § 138 Absatz I BGB beurteilt sich danach, (…)dass es dem Anstandsgefühl aller billig und gerecht Denkenden widerspricht'.

Although *die Anstandsformel* is criticised and questioned for its lack of determinate guidance,[79] the legal formula excludes certain methodologies through which to define contractual morality. Notably, contractual morality cannot be based on widespread practices or beliefs, as they would emerge from public opinion polls or empirical research.[80] This methodological exclusion is of relevance to the sweatshop case because it shows that the transaction's empirical frequency, ie, the sale of clothes produced in a sweatshop for money, cannot on its own establish its normality and thereby rebut the immorality of the transaction and its invalidity under §138 I BGB.[81]

Moreover, although developments in moral convictions can and do take place in the social order, the legal order and in particular the German Constitution, is the primary source and point of reference for interpreting the legal norm of good morals.[82] This primacy follows not only from procedural reasons, ie, a judge is bound primarily by the law,[83] but also from substantive reasons, ie, the legal order is presumed to encompass the ethical values that have been, over time, fundamental for a society.[84] Therefore, the primacy of the legal order does not express its prevalence *over* the social order; rather, it is a reflection of the moral conceptions that have been, over time, of central importance to the social order itself.

In particular, in light of the fact that it is not *prima facie* evident that a contract for the sale of clothes produced in sweatshops is considered immoral and unacceptable in the German society, the German Constitution (GG) forms an important starting point for its assessment. The *Bundesverfassunggericht* referred to the GG as the primary source for the interpretation of general clauses in the BGB in its *Lüth* judgment; a seminal decision in the development of private law constitutionalisation in Europe. The Court held that it is primarily the values articulated and enacted by society in the Constitution that are to guide the concretisation of general clauses in civil law by courts, explicitly referring to the interpretation of the concept of good morals.[85] Courts should consider both the articulation of specific constitutional rights, as well as the overall purpose of the Constitution.[86]

[79] Discussed by Sack, R, 'Das Anstandsgefühl aller billig und gerecht Denkenden und die Moral als Bestimmungsfaktoren der guten Sitten' (1985) 14 *Neue Juristische Wochenschrift* 761–824; Ellenberger (n 59) rn 2; Köhler (n 58) 191, rn 19; Armbrüster (n 58) 1652, rn 15; for further references, see van den Brink (n 20) 146–47.

[80] Armbrüster (n 58) rn 14, suggested differently by Teubner.

[81] Armbrüster (n 58) rn 14.

[82] Ellenberger (n 59) rn 3.

[83] Köhler (n 58) rn 20 (reference to Art III, 20, III GG).

[84] See reference to *Lüth* (n 85).

[85] BverfGE 7, 198 (206) rn 29 =NJW 1958, 257. 'Dier Rechtsprechung bieten sich zur Realisierung dieses Einflusses vor allem die "Generalklauseln", die, wie §826 BGB, zur Beurteilung menschlichen Verhaltens auf ausser-zivilrechtliche, ja zunächst überhaupt ausserrechtliche Massstäbe, wie die "guten Sitten", verweisen. Denn bei der Entscheidung darüber, was diese sozialen Gebote jeweils im Einzelfall fordern, muss in erster Linie von der Gesamtheit der Wertvorstellungen ausgegangen werden, die das Volk in einem bestimmten Zeitpunkt seiner geistig-kulturellen Entwicklung erreicht und in seiner Verfassung fixiert hat.'

[86] Armbrüster (n 58) rn 20; Ellenberger (n 59) rn 3–5.

With regard to the sweatshop case, Articles 1 (human dignity); 2(1) (development of personality); 9 (freedom of association); 12 (the right to choose an occupation freely without threat or coercion) and 20 (the *Sozialstaatklausel*) GG are of particular relevance. The first article refers to the obligation of all forms of state power to respect and protect the human dignity of *all people*.[87] Similarly, Article 2(1) is interpreted to reflect the right of individuals to contract freely with others. This freedom is restricted, in the same article, by the rights of others and the GG's underlying moral order. Conversely, Articles 9 and 12 regarding freedom of assembly and occupation are not formulated as rights for all people, but rather as rights applicable to German citizens. Article 20 encompasses the so-called *Sozialstaatklausel* that characterises the fundamental form of the German state as a social state.[88] Furthermore, with regard to the assessment of the contract in the sweatshop case, the fundamental values as expressed on a European level, for example in the ECHR, may also play a role in the interpretation of good morals.[89] For example, the right to free association is recognised in the ECHR as a right for all in Article 11, and Article 4 refers to the prohibition of slavery and forced labour.[90]

In the context of the sweatshop case, a court is to consider whether or not the freedom of contracting parties is restricted by the rights of others and the moral values as expressed in these instruments. The standard of good morals in §138 is articulated on the basis of values that are found within German society and the German legal order.[91] In principle, the norms of the sweatshop's country of origin are immaterial.

D. German Interest: *Borax* and *Nigerian Cultural Heritage*

Although the norms articulated in foreign legal orders are, in principle, immaterial to the German concept of good morals, the fact that the sweatshop is located beyond German borders may not be entirely irrelevant. In the *Borax* case, the *Bundesgerichtshof* considered a contract's morality in light of the question of whether a German interest was at stake.[92] This case concerned a contract for the

[87] Grundgesetz für die Bundesrepublik Deutschland, Article 1:

(1) Die Würde des Menschen ist unantastbar. Sie zu achten und zu schützen ist Verpflichtung aller staatlichen Gewalt.

(2) Das Deutsche Volk bekennt sich darum zu unverletzlichen und unveräußerlichen Menschenrechten als Grundlage jeder menschlichen Gemeinschaft, des Friedens und der Gerechtigkeit in der Welt.

(3) Die nachfolgenden Grundrechte binden Gesetzgebung, vollziehende Gewalt und Rechtsprechung als unmittelbar geltendes Recht.

[88] Ellenberger (n 59) rn 3–5.

[89] Armbrüster (n 58) rn 16; Ellenberger (n 59) rn 2; Köhler (n 58) rn 19. For a comprehensive discussion of the way in which general clauses function as a gateway for the effects of fundamental rights in contract law, see Mak (n 52), and Busch, C and H Schulte-Nölke (eds), *Fundamental Rights and Private Law* (Sellier, 2011) represents a practical tool on the subject for judges.

[90] ECHR, Articles 4 and 11.

[91] Ellenberger (n 59) rn 3; Armbrüster (n 58) rn 16.

[92] *Bundesgerichtshof*, 21 December 1960, BGHZ 34,169/NJW 1961, 822 *(Borax)*.

sale of borax, a substance that is used in the process of generating nuclear power, among other uses. The contract between an American export company and a German importer infringed an American export prohibition targeting the market of Eastern bloc countries.[93] In evaluating the contract, the *Bundesgerichtshof* considered whether the purpose of the American legislation included an interest of vital importance to Germany. The *Bundesgerichtshof* asked whether a German interest was at stake in the potential export of borax to Eastern bloc countries, in which case the American prohibition would include the protection of a German interest and the contract would be contrary to good morals (§138). In the case at hand, the *Bundesgerichtshof* held that German interests were at stake, given the fact that the prohibition served the interests of the West as a whole, against the strengthening of Eastern bloc countries in times of war.[94]

The *Bundesgerichtshof* also addressed the question of German interest in another case regarding the morality of a contract.[95] The *Nigerian Cultural Heritage* case concerned an insurance contract for the transport of Nigerian objects of art overseas.[96] Several artefacts were lost en route from Nigeria to Germany, for which the transporter claimed insurance compensation. At the time, however, a Nigerian export prohibition was in place for Nigerian cultural heritage, and the insurer argued that the contract was invalid on the basis of §138, because it infringed the prohibition. The *Oberlandesgericht* (Hamburg Court of Appeal) disagreed, holding that the contract was not immoral and invalid on the basis of §138, principally because there was no German interest at stake. Subsequently, the *Oberlandesgericht* also denied immorality in light of the Nigerian interest to protect its cultural heritage. Yet it suggested that in the case where a Nigerian interest regarding public health or the growth of the welfare state had been at stake, the judgment would differ.[97] The *Bundesgerichtshof* agreed with the *Oberlandesgericht* that the prohibition did not protect a *German* interest and could not be immoral and invalid for that reason.[98] However, the *Bundesgerichtshof* also considered whether the insured activity was contrary to good morals, in which case the contract would be without

[93] Namely, the seller, an American export company, required a licence to export borax, which would not have been issued if the borax was intended for the market of Eastern bloc countries. The licence was conditional upon the buyer's provision of a statement regarding the location of the borax and its final destination of use. If the buyer intended to sell the substance to a third party, a similar statement was required from the third party, replaceable by an explicit guarantee of the buyer that the borax would not be delivered directly or indirectly to countries in the Eastern bloc. In the case in question, the third party refused to provide the required statement, and the German importer refused to provide the explicit guarantee. Subsequently, the American exporter refused to proceed with the delivery.

[94] Armbrüster comments that it would have been more convincing if the Court had based the immorality on the maintenance of its internal order, in light of treaty obligations at the time that included the embargo the United States placed on East European countries at the time. See Armbrüster (n 58) rn 17: 'In derartigen Fällen ist vielmehr ausschlaggebend, dass auf Grund der Bündnisverpflichtungen der Bundesrepublik Deutschland eine Beziehung zur inländischen Ordnung besteht.'

[95] See also Armbrüster (n 58) rn 17.

[96] *Bundesgerichtshof*, 22 June 1972, BGHZ 59, 82/NJW 1972, 1575 *(Nigerian Cultural Heritage)* 85.

[97] Ibid 1576–77.

[98] Ibid 1576.

effect in light of Article 2 of the *Allgemeine Deutsche Seeversicherungsbedingungen* (ADS). This Article required that the insurance contract protected a permissible interest, ie, an interest that would not be deemed immoral under §138.[99] The *Bundesgerichtshof* held that the contract lacked a permissible interest (§2 ADS) and held that the contract was invalid, because the interests protected by the insurance were not insurable. Contrary to the *Oberlandesgericht*, the *Bundesgerichtshof* placed decisive weight on Nigeria's interest to maintain possession over cultural heritage and protect that heritage from foreign traders, referencing UNESCO (in particular the World Heritage Convention) and the fact that the protection of people's cultural heritage was generally endorsed.[100] Consequently, the *Bundesgerichtshof* considered the interest protected under the insurance impermissible and contrary to good morals.

Although both the *Borax* case and the *Nigerian Cultural Heritage* case differ from the contract in the sweatshop case as they involve the infringement of a statutory prohibition,[101] these cases suggest a possible distinction under German law between situations in which the alleged immoral activity facilitated by the contract affects a German interest and those in which it does not. In cases in which the activity does not affect a German interest, courts may question whether the (foreign) interests at stake are considered of such significance that infringement thereof is contrary to German values. For the sweatshop case, a court may consider international conventions regarding fundamental rights at work similar to the *Bundesgerichtshof*'s reference to the World Heritage Convention. In particular, it seems that the International Labour Organisation's (ILO) fundamental conventions and the general recognition of the importance of decent labour standards for all people could play an important role there.[102] As Germany is a member of the ILO and has ratified all the fundamental conventions established by that organisation, the fundamental principles endorsed therein could be viewed as specific formulations of values endorsed by the German legal order.

E. Concluding Remarks: Overcoming the Absence of a German Interest

Under German law, the contract in the sweatshop meets, in principle, all the requirements for contractual immorality on the basis of §138 BGB. There are no

[99] The impermissibility of the insured interest would be established if the insurer could not have entered the contract without it being invalid under §138 I BGB.

[100] At the time, Germany had ratified the World Heritage Convention, but it had not yet entered into force. *Convention concerning the protection of the world cultural and natural heritage*, 16 November 1972.

[101] Such contracts are generally not dealt with under §134, on the basis of which contracts can be deemed void if contrary to a statutory prohibition, but assessed on the basis of §138. See Armbrüster (n 58) §138 rn 17 and §134 rn 40.

[102] Fundamental conventions of the ILO, including fundamental rights are: freedom of association; elimination of all forms of forced or compulsory labour; effective abolition of child labour; elimination

principled obstacles that would block a judgement of the contract's invalidity for immorality. There are several elements in our hypothetical sweatshop case that are favourable for the likelihood of contractual immorality under German law. First, the contracting parties' knowledge regarding the production conditions under which the clothes are produced establishes that the contract could in principle be deemed immoral in light of the interests of third parties or society as a whole. Second, those production conditions seem, in principle, incompatible with the ethical norms fundamental to the German legal order, as expressed among others, in the German basic law and the fundamental ILO conventions. That said, however, there are also factors that count against the invalidity of the contract. Notably, the sweatshop location may have some bearing on the evaluation of whether the contract as a whole infringes the concept of good morals in §138. The question regarding the German interest involved in the *Borax* and *Nigerian Cultural Heritage* cases may be raised similarly in relation to the sweatshop case. In the absence of an infringement of a German interest in the sweatshop case, however, the contract may still be held to be immoral and invalid by a court if the ethical norms that are at stake are broadly endorsed. In light of the fundamental conventions of the ILO, it seems that a court would have a substantial basis to consider sweatshops reprehensible, regardless of their location.

IV. France

Similar to Dutch and German law, freedom of contract is a foundational principle in the French law of contract.[103] The idea that contracting parties are to be free to engage in and give shape to their contractual relations runs counter to the hypothesis of contractual immorality and invalidity in the designed sweatshop case. Under French law, the contract in the hypothetical sweatshop case may, however, encounter substantive limitations—equivalent to those found in Dutch and German law—through the requirements regarding the contract's *objet* and *cause*. For, in relation to the validity of a contract, Article 1108 of the French Code Civil (CC) requires '(…) un objet certain qui forme la matière de l'engagement' and 'une cause licite dans l'obligation'.[104] The requirements in relation to the contract's *objet* and *cause*, are found in Articles 1126–30 CC, and Articles 1131 and 1133 CC, respectively.

of discrimination in respect of employment and occupation. Also: *ILO Declaration on Fundamental Principles and Rights at Work and its Follow-up*, adopted 18 June 1998.

[103] Fabre-Magnan, M, *Droit de Obligations. 1-Contrat et engagement unilatéral* (Presses Universitaires de France, 2012) 57 et seq.

[104] Translation, Article 1108 CC: 'Four requisites are essential for the validity of an agreement: The consent of the party who binds himself; His capacity to contract; A definite object which forms the subject-matter of the undertaking; A lawful cause in the obligation.' This book refers to the Code Civil pre 1 October 2016, unless explicitly stated otherwise.

The contract's *objet* (subject matter) refers to the 'things' which the contracting parties commit to transfer to each other,[105] ie, in our hypothetical sweatshop case the retailer is obliged to deliver the clothes, and the consumer is obliged to pay the price. Since this exchange represents a regular transaction on the market, and the exchange concerns commodifiable goods (as required by Article 1128),[106] which are determinable (under Article 1129),[107] the contract's validity in the hypothetical case seems not to be questionable on the basis of the substantive requirements regarding the contract's subject matter.

The requirements for the validity of a contract, pertaining to the notion of *cause* are stated in Article 1131 CC 'L'obligation sans cause, ou sur une fausse cause, ou sur une cause illicite, ne peut avoir aucun effet'.[108] For our hypothetical sweatshop case, particularly the latter reference regarding a contract's '*cause illicite*' is of relevance (see next section).[109] This prerequisite for valid contractual relations reflects a control of contractual morality and its underlying rationale is found in the protection of the general interest (*l'intérêt général*).[110] Under French law, a court can determine (without the parties bringing the legal issue to the fore) whether or not a contract is invalid for immorality *ex officio*.[111]

Before continuing the discussion as to how requirements of contractual morality take shape under French law, and how they may affect the validity of the contract in the hypothetical case, it should be mentioned that, together with the concept of a contract's *objet*,[112] the concept of *cause* has long been subject to diverging

[105] Article 1126 CC states: 'Tout contrat a pour objet une chose qu'une partie s'oblige à donner, ou qu'une partie s'oblige à faire ou à ne pas faire', translated as: 'Any contract has for its object a thing which one party binds himself to transfer, or which one party binds himself to do or not to do.'

[106] The requirement of commodifiability reflects the fact that certain things may not be owned or alienated; under French law it is immoral (contrary to public order or good morals) to exchange certain things. Examples in this context include contracts for surrogate motherhood. See *Code Civil 2011 Paris Dalloz*, comments to Article 1128, 1289–93.

[107] Article 1128 states: 'Il n'y a que les choses qui sont dans le commerce qui puissent être l'objet des conventions'. Article 1129 states: 'Il faut que l'obligation ait pour objet une chose au moins déterminée quant à son espèce. La quotité de la chose peut être incertaine, pourvu qu'elle puisse être déterminée'. Translation: 'Only things which may be the subject matter of legal transactions between private individuals may be the object of agreements', and 'An obligation must have for its object a thing determined at least as to its kind. The quantity of the thing may be uncertain, provided it can be determined'.

[108] This Article is translated as: 'Obligations have no effect when the cause is absent, false or unlawful'.

[109] The concept of cause in relation to its required existence is generally understood to refer to the contractual counter-performance, which is sometimes also described in terms of the objective notion of cause. See n 120. Translated to the contract in the sweatshop case, this notion of cause refers to the delivery by the retailer of the clothes, and the transfer by the consumer of the money, as the contractual counter-performance (*cause l'obligation*) is dependent on the contractual structure, ie, sale. This notion of cause does not affect the validity of the contract in the sweatshop case.

[110] See for instance, Terré, F et al, *Droit Civil: Les Obligations* (Dalloz, 2009) nr 359. The requirement regarding the existence of cause reflects a protection of the parties' interests, ie, a party's obligation is to be sufficiently justified.

[111] Article 423 *Code de procedure civile*; see also Fabre-Magnan (n 103) 465–66.

[112] The contested issues are found in the multiplicity of the concept's interpretations and references: a discussion regarding the question to what the notion of *objet* refers to, ie, the obligation, performance and/or contract as a whole? On the one hand the requirement of lawfulness is referred to in terms of *l'objet de l'obligation*, to which, on the other hand, some authors add the idea that contracts are also to

approaches in the courts' case law and debate among legal scholars and is under debate in the context of proposals for the reform of the entire French law of obligations.[113] A forthcoming revision is, however, unlikely to affect the underlying rationale and function that a substantive control of contractual morality plays through the concept of cause.[114] Under each proposal for reform, French law will require the parties' compliance with standards of morality and will consider any contract—even when mutually beneficial – that undermines the general interest, to be invalid.[115]

A. *La Cause Illicite*

The contract in the hypothetical sweatshop case may encounter substantive limitations to the contracting parties' freedom on the basis of *cause illicite* (Article 1131 CC). This concept takes further shape in Article 6 CC: On ne peut déroger, par des conventions particulières, aux lois qui intéressent l'ordre public et les bonnes mœurs', and more specifically in Article 1133: 'La cause est illicite, quand elle est prohibée par la loi, quand elle est contraire aux bonnes mœurs ou à l'ordre

be assessed, independently (from commodifiability and the lawfulness of the cause) on the lawfulness of *l'objet du contrat*, ie, the contract's overall subject matter. This latter idea is contested among French authors; where some consider it redundant, as the lawfulness of the agreement is sufficiently covered by the other requirements, others find it useful to use as an explication of the contract's unlawfulness. For a brief overview, see for example, Ghestin, J, *Cause de l'engagement et validité du contrat* (Libraire Générale de Droit et de Jurisprudence, 2006) nr 1295. Terré et al (n 110) seem to be proponents of this idea, nr 265, 318.

[113] The proposals vary in retaining or replacing the concept of cause, for instance, the *Avant-Projet de Reforme du Droit des Obligations (Projet Catala)* (2007) maintains reference to cause, while the *Projet de la Chancellerie* (2008) replaces it with the concept of *intérêt*, while Terré, F, *Pour une Réforme du Droit des Contrats* (Dalloz, 2009) puts the concept aside entirely. For background information on the instigation and development of these projects, see: Cartwright, J et al (eds), *Reforming the French Law of Obligations. Comparative Reflections on the Avant-projet de réforme du droit des obligations et de la prescription ('the Avant-projet Catala')* (Hart Publishing, 2009) 15–20. The reform took place 1 October 2016, but does not affect the requirements regarding a lawful cause, see article 1128 Code Civil (new).

[114] The contested issues pertain particularly to the requirement of the existence of *cause*, and the alternative concept of *intérêt*, for instance have a role there, whereas the control of contractual morality is articulated in terms of '*La liceité du contrat*'. See Articles 88–89 in *Projet de la Chancellerie* (n 113). Moreover, the debate on the existence of cause was related to the case law of the *Cour de cassation*, notably the Chronopost and Video club cases (*Cour de cassation* Com, 22 October 1996, D 1997.121 and *Cour de cassation* Civ, 3 July 1996, Bull Civ I, nr 286) where the *Cour de cassation* annulled a clause and the contract respectively, for absence of *cause*, even though in both cases there was a cause in the definition that was up to then prevalent.

[115] *Avant-projet* (n 113) Articles 1124 and 1126-1: 'La convention est valable quand l'engagement a une cause réelle et licite qui le jusitifie' and 'L'engagement est sans justification, faute de cause licite, lorsqu'il est contracté, par l'une au moins des parties, dans un but contraire à l'ordre public, aux bonnes mœurs, ou, plus généralement, à une règle impérative'; *Projet de la Chancellerie* (n 113) Articles 88–89: *La licéité du contrat*; *Projet Terré* (2008) Article 59: 'Le contrat ne peut déroger à l'ordre public au bonnes mœurs, ni par son contenu ni par son but que ce dernier ait été connu, ou non, par toutes les parties. Il ne peut, pareillement, porter atteinte aux libertés et droits fondamentaux que dans la mesure indispensable à la protection d'un intérêt sérieux et légitime.'

public.'[116] In the context of contractual morality, the concept of *cause* refers to the determining, subjective reasons (*les mobiles déterminants*) for the existence of the contract, in particular the contracting parties' subjective reasons for entering the contract; their motives, desired effects and the purposes pursued through the contract.[117] In this sense any single contract is likely to have a variety of reasons that fall under the control of the concept *cause illicite*. Under French law if only one reason is immoral,[118] the contract will be held invalid.[119] For the question of the contract's immorality and invalidity in our hypothetical case depends on the following questions under French law: first, whether the fact that the clothes are produced in a sweatshop is a determining subjective reason (*mobile déterminant*) for the existence of the contract, and second, whether or not it will be considered immoral by the court.

B. *Un Mobile Déterminant?*

Legal scholars describe '*les mobiles déterminants*' in terms of the contracting parties' subjective reasons for entering into a contract, which includes their motives

[116] Article 6 CC, translation: 'Statutes relating to public policy and morals may not be derogated from by private agreements' and Article 1133 as: 'The cause is unlawful, if it is contrary to the law, good morals or public order'.

[117] See for instance in: Fabre-Magnan (n 103) 445 et seq; Terré et al (n 110) nr 366; also Ghestin (n 112) nr 1238; Mekki, M, *L'intérêt Général et le Contrat* (Paris, Libraire Générale de Droit et de Jurisprudence, 2004) nr 1247; for a brief overview see also the conclusion from the Conseiller rapporteur to the *Cour de cassation*, for instance: M Bizot, Arret n 519, 29 October 2004 under nr III. This notion of cause is different from the objective notion of cause that is meant in the context of the requirement of an existing cause (also in Article 1131 CC). The *Cour de cassation* distinguished between the different notions of cause in a decision on 12 July 1989. (First Civil Chamber *Cour de cassation* 12 July 1989, Bull Civ, I, nr 293). In this case, two parapsychologists had entered a contract for the sale of books and materials concerning occultism. The Court of Appeal held the contract invalid due to an unlawful cause. The buyer had intended to use the material for activities involving paranormal phenomena, which was prohibited by law at the time. This judgment was upheld by the *Cour de cassation*, where the seller had appealed on the basis of the fact that the contract's *cause* does not entail the buyer's (subjective) intended use of the material, but the objective contractual counter performance, ie, the delivery of the material by the seller. In its judgment, the *Cour de cassation* distinguished between the cause of the obligation, which was indeed the contractual counter performance, and the cause of the contract, which was also to be based on subjective motives of the parties: 'si la cause de l'obligation de l'acheteur réside bien dans le transfert de propriété et dans la livraison de la chose vendue, en revanche la cause du contrat de vente consiste dans le mobile déterminant'. The duality of the concept of cause and its specific interpretation is a source of disagreement among French legal scholars: see for instance, Rochefeld, J, 'A Future for la cause? Observations of a French Jurist' in Cartwright et al (n 113) 77–81, who argues that the *cause de l'obligation* refers to the real interests that contracting parties have in the contractual counter-performance, which departs from the more objective notion of cause, in which the reasons why contracting parties took on the obligations under the contract are explained in terms of the contractual counter-performances.

[118] Fabre-Magnan (n 103) 446.

[119] Fabre-Magnan (n 103) 461 et seq; Terré et al (n 110) nr 369. Under French law, immoral contracts are sanctioned with absolute nullity (*nullité absolue*), which refers to the fact that the invalidity affects the contract in absolute terms: its inexistence is of importance to society as a whole.

or the desired effects and purposes pursued through the contract.[120] The focus lies on the factors that contribute to the contracting parties' will to contract, which go beyond the mere counter-performance they receive. In a general sense, however, the determining reasons extend to a multiplicity of factors that may contribute to the conclusion of any particular contract and it may be difficult to determine whether or not one factor can be identified as decisive.[121] In relation to the context of the contract in our hypothetical sweatshop case, the phrase *cause* in terms of the parties' motives—the *desired* effect and purpose—suggests that the contract did not have an immoral *cause*. Namely, the contracting parties' motives, desired effect and purpose are not likely to have been *determined* by the fact that the clothes exchanged are produced in a sweatshop. In the hypothetical case, the contracting parties do not have the specific intention to sell or buy clothes produced in a sweatshop; rather, the case assumes their indifference to this fact. From this perspective, it seems that the sweatshop conditions under which the clothes are produced may not constitute a *mobile déterminant*, as to render the contract invalid because of an immoral cause under French law.

However, it could be argued that the interest and benefit that the contracting parties pursued under the contract are determined by the fact that the clothes were produced under sweatshop conditions. Moreover, one may point out that the sweatshop conditions are part of broader background conditions and contexts in which the contract has been formed. The contracting parties might not have entered into a contract, or might not have been able to even enter this contract, if not for the fact that the clothes were produced under sweatshop conditions. For instance, in a general sense (abstracted from the particular contract) a consumer might not have entered the contract if the price of the product was higher. If the terms of the contract are inextricably bound to the conditions of production, the latter may indeed be a determining reason why contracting parties decide to engage in the exchange. Although low price motivation is not by itself objectionable, it may become objectionable if the contracting party knew that the clothes were produced in a sweatshop. Generally, one may ask whether the contracting parties would have entered the contract if the clothes had not been produced under sweatshop conditions. Namely, one may argue that what is relevant for the hypothetical case relates to the question whether the contracting parties could have entered this contract—a transaction under the same terms—if not for the fact that the clothes were produced in a sweatshop. Or, it may be argued that the sweatshop conditions have to be considered as a determining reason for the contract's existence because the particular clothes that are sold would not have been available for sale to begin with, and, in any case, not under the terms of the contract, if not for their production in a sweatshop. In other words, there would not have been a contract, at least not this particular contract, if sweatshop workers had not produced the clothes.

[120] Fabre-Magnan (n 103) 446.

[121] Ghestin (n 112) nr 1249; Terré et al (n 110) nr 366.

C. Knowledge Requirements: Only One Party

The knowledge requirements that pertain to contractual immorality and invalidity under French law reveal the importance of the protection of general interest. Whereas in both the Netherlands and in Germany, contractual invalidity requires that both contracting parties were aware of the facts that engendered the contract's immorality, under French law the knowledge of one of the contracting parties suffices. In 1998, the *Cour de cassation*, contrary to prevalent requirements regarding knowledge in the case of contractual immorality and invalidity, confirmed this. The decisive case concerned a dispute between a divorced couple over an agreement concerning the conversion of a payable loan from the ex-wife to the ex-husband into an increase in alimony. It was clear from the facts of the case that the ex-wife had been unaware of any unlawful purpose under this agreement. However, the ex-husband had set up the agreement to obtain unlawful tax deductions. In spite of the ex-wife's uncontested ignorance, the Court deemed the agreement invalid, stating: 'Mais attendu qu'un contrat peut être annulé pour cause illicite ou immorale, même lorsque l'une des parties n'a pas eu connaissance du caractère illicite ou immoral du motif déterminant de la conclusion du contrat (…)'.[122] This case overturned the prevalent understanding that contractual immorality and invalidity required the knowledge of both contracting parties (similar to the current laws of both the Netherlands and Germany). That requirement had been criticised for undermining the protection of the general interest in the control of contractual morality for the sake of the private interests of unknowing contracting parties.[123]

Thus, for the hypothetical sweatshop case it seems that in light of the decision of the *Cour de casssation* (1998), under current French law, it would suffice that only one of the contracting parties had knowledge of the sweatshop conditions under which the clothes were produced, to render the contract invalid.

D. *L'intéret Général: l'Ordre Public et les Bonnes Mœurs*

If the conditions under which the clothes are produced are accepted as a factor that determined the existence of the contract (*mobile déterminant*) in our hypothetical case and at least one of the parties was aware thereof, the question arises whether or not a sweatshop would be deemed immoral under French law.

French law restricts contractual relations that undermine the general interest through the concepts of public order and good morals (*l'ordre public et les bonnes mœurs*). The *Cour de cassation* explicitly held that this control is not confined to

[122] *Cour de cassation* First Ch Civ 7 October 1998. Translation by the author: 'However, a contract may be invalidated on the basis of an unlawful or immoral cause, even if one party was unaware that the determining reasons underlying the contract's existence were unlawful or immoral'.

[123] Ghestin (n 112) nr 1243–47.

a mere control of legality, but extends to a wider notion of *l'ordre public.*[124] The content and application of this notion is under the discretion of the courts, as it changes over time.[125] In this sense, it is unlikely that the contract in our hypothetical case will be considered immoral and invalid, because it does not fit in with existing case law regarding contractual invalidity in light of a contract's '*cause illicite*'. Legal scholars distinguish between the narrow content given to the substantive limitations through the concept of good morals (mostly relating to infringements of sexual morality and personal relations),[126] and a wide conception of public order with subdivisions of an '*ordre public de direction*' and an '*ordre public de protection*'.[127] Under the latter subdivision, protection is offered to weaker contracting parties in light of the values that are part of the French social and economic order,[128] whereas the former commands respect for the fundamental values of French society in light of its traditional and political order.[129] A public order in which the protection of fundamental rights is central has been recognised by legal scholars ('*l'ordre public philanthropique*'),[130] but there is no French case law in which the interests of others have been articulated in light of fundamental rights. The contractual invalidity of our hypothetical case does not seem to be easily accommodated under current French law. Particularly, if, as Mekki suggests, the notion of general interest reflects the outcome of a particular hierarchy of both public and private interests,[131] it seems unlikely that in our hypothetical case, the interest of others elsewhere would take priority over other interests at stake, as to render the contract invalid under French law.

E. Concluding Remarks: The Centrality of General Interest

It is not likely that the contract in our hypothetical case will be held invalid for immorality under French law. The current implausibility thereof depends for the most part on the rare case law in which courts find a contract's cause '*illicite*'. The question of the substantive immorality would however become relevant if the court would find that the conditions under which the clothes are produced

[124] See for instance, Ghestin (n 112) nr 1237; Fabre-Magnan (n 103) 449 and *Cour de cassation* Civ 4 decembre 1929 *Terré, Les Grands arrêts de la jurisprudence civile Henri Capitant*, T1, 11e ed, 2000.

[125] *Terré*, ibid, comments nr 2 and 5 to *Cour de cassation* Civ 4 decembre 1929.

[126] Fabre-Magnan (n 103) 390.

[127] Fabre-Magnan (n 103) 389–390; see also in Fauvarque-Cosson, B and D Mazeaud, *European Contract Law Materials for a Common Frame of Reference* (Sellier. European Law Publishers, 2008) Chapter 4.

[128] In the discussion of contractual morality, the concept of human dignity is given shape in reference to contractual restrictions of a party's freedom, eg, through specific clauses that are thought to be too restrictive, such as celibacy, or through duration of an obligation. See for instance Mekki (n 117) nr 455 et seq.

[129] Fabre-Magnan (n 103) 390.

[130] For instance: Fenouillet, D, 'Les bonnes moeurs sont mortes! Vive l'ordre public philanthropique' in *Le droit privé francais à la fin du XXème siècle, Etudes offertes à Pierre Catala* (Litec, 2001).

[131] As suggested by Mekki (n 117).

constitute the contract's *cause*, ie, that it would fall under the contract's determining, subjective reasons (*mobile déterminant*). There seems to be, however, a fair case for the latter to be argued under French law. The hypothesis of contractual invalidity is not undermined by requirements of knowledge under French law. Even if the facts of the hypothetical case would be such as to deny the knowledge of one of the parties, this would not obstruct the contract's invalidity.

V. England

The question of contractual validity in the hypothetical sweatshop case—similar to the other legal systems discussed above—engages a part of contract law in England that presents a tension between the principle of freedom of contract and the law's disapproval of certain contractual arrangements.[132] Although Atiyah described the decline of freedom of contract during the twentieth century and even stated that, beyond the law courts, it '*ceased to be a living issue*',[133] it remains a fundamental principle that suggests prevailing restraint on interference with contractual relations.[134] Under the English law of contract, the relevant substantive limitations to the contractual freedom of the contracting parties are discussed under the heading of public policy and illegality.[135] It is noteworthy that under the heading of public policy, authors and courts alike do not always deal with the question of contractual invalidity in isolation from other legal questions, which, for instance, pertain to the legal consequences of invalidity (ie, questions of restitution).[136] Moreover, the question of contractual invalidity is often dealt with in the form of a question regarding the enforceability of a particular claim, by a particular party, or regarding the legitimacy of the use of public policy or illegality as a defence against such a claim. Both Prentice, and more recently the Law Commission, have suggested that contractual invalidity in relation to public policy should be understood in reference to the basic question: 'does public policy require that this claimant, in the circumstances which have occurred, should be refused relief to which he would otherwise have been entitled with respect to all or part of his claim?'[137] The present discussion of English law will focus on the question of

[132] Whittaker, S, 'Introductory' in H Beale and AS Burrows (eds), *Chitty on Contracts Volume 1 General Principles* (Sweet & Maxwell, 2008) nr 1-011 et seq and 1-021; Prentice, DD, 'Illegality and Public Policy' in Beale and Burrows, ibid, nr 16-004.

[133] Atiyah, PS, *The Rise and Fall of Freedom of Contract* (Clarendon, 1979) 717 et seq.

[134] Whittaker (n 132) nr 1-011 et seq; Prentice (n 132) nr 16-004.

[135] Prentice (n 132) nr 16-142, 16-163. Other authors also refer to 'unenforceable terms and contracts', Atiyah, PS and SA Smith, *Atiyah's Introduction to the Law of Contract* (Oxford University Press, 2005) Chapter 8.

[136] See also Atiyah and Smith, ibid, 209.

[137] Prentice (n 132) nr 16-001; also *The Law Commission, Consultation Paper No 189 2009, The Illegality Defence, A Consultative Report*, nr 3.143. The Law Commission has, over the last decade,

contractual invalidity, as necessitated by the scope of this book's inquiry and foregoes distinctions between the specificities of the circumstances under which the case might be brought to court.

A. Contracts Contrary to Public Policy

Under the heading of public policy, contracts are held invalid even though the parties themselves have voluntarily engaged in them. As a general rule, a contract is rendered void (invalid) if it is illegal or otherwise contrary to public policy and courts will not enforce the contract.[138] There are various rationales to support contractual invalidity in such cases, amongst which the protection of the interest of the general public, interests of others and the contracting parties themselves.[139] Other justifications are found in the idea that a court cannot be called on to support and advance illegal or immoral activities; that aiding a party's illegal or immoral activities would offend the dignity of the courts; and that contractual invalidity would have a deterring effect on illegal and immoral conduct.[140] The courts decide which transactions are against public policy.[141]

Different authors identify various configurations that may lead to invalidity, because the law disapproves of the contract.[142] In relation to our hypothetical sweatshop case, it is helpful to draw an initial distinction between contracts that are prohibited by statute per se (statutory illegality), and contracts that are objectionable (through formation), or become objectionable (through performance), because they are associated with *activities* that are either illegal, or deemed reprehensible and are therefore contrary to public policy. The former category (statutory illegality) is irrelevant to the discussion of our hypothetical case because the

scrutinised the area of law that deals with contracts that are unlawful or contrary to public policy. The Law Commission however excluded from consideration contracts involving conduct that is not strictly unlawful, but immoral or otherwise contrary to public policy, stating: 'We believe the courts remain the best arbiters of which transactions, while not involving unlawful conduct, should be regarded as contrary to public policy (…)', ibid., nr 1.11. Moreover, the Government has communicated that the proposed reform is not a 'pressing priority' in light of the 'severe economic situation'. See: Ministry of Justice, *Report on Implementation of the Law Commission Proposals* (March 2012) 3 and 15.

[138] Prentice (n 132) Chapter 16. However, although strictly speaking a void contract does not exist, as voidance implies the non-existence of the contract, sometimes 'void contracts' do have legal effects, especially in the case in which illegality constitutes the ground of voidance. See: Whittaker (n 132) nr 1-080.

[139] Atiyah and Smith (n 135) 208. Also, Deakin distinguishes two protective functions: the first concerns protection of the market against its own functioning, the second concerns protection of society (or certain social institutions) against the functioning of the market. Deakin, S and A Supiot (eds), *Capacitas: Contract Law and the Institutional Preconditions of a Market Economy* (Hart Publishing, 2009) 3.

[140] Atiyah and Smith (n 135) 213–214; McKendrick, E, *Contract Law* (Palgrave Macmillan, 2009) 260.

[141] This judicial task was also affirmed by the Law Commission, see references in n 137.

[142] Compare Prentice (n 132) nr 16-002-003; Atiyah and Smith (n 135) 209.

contract does not belong to a class or category of contracts prohibited by statute.[143] The latter category encompasses a vast range of cases, which can be further categorised on the basis of diverging grounds of public policy. Prentice, for instance, distinguishes between contracts that are associated with activities which are illegal; are injurious to good government; interfere with the proper workings of justice; are immoral; and contracts in restraint of trade.[144] In relation to the hypothetical case, there seems to be no close match between the existing heads of public policy that currently informs contractual invalidity. Under English law, immorality only applies to a narrow selection of contracts, mostly relating to sexual or marital matters.[145] In addition, cases dealing with exploitative agreements only include exploitation between the contracting parties, such as those dealt with under the restraint of trade. Under the restraint of trade heading, contracts that restrict personal liberties may be held to be unreasonable between the contracting parties or in relation to the public interest.[146] Contracts that deal with voluntary enslavement for instance, or contracts with features that 'savour of slavery' or 'savour of serfdom' are held invalid, because they are contrary to public policy.[147] It is thus clear that under English law it would be contrary to public policy to enforce contracts that resemble—elements of—slavery. However, there is no case law that suggests contractual invalidity for cases in which the features that 'savour of serfdom' are found in the contract's foreseeable consequence, let alone in circumstances where those features concern others elsewhere. Although the fact that a contract does not fall neatly under the existing heads of public policy, does not

[143] Prentice (n 132) nr 16-142 et seq.

[144] Prentice (n 132) nr 16-005.

[145] Atiyah and Smith (n 135) 212–14. Under immorality, for instance, a contract that facilitates prostitution is likely to be deemed invalid. In *Pearce v Brooks* [1866] LR 1 Exch 213, the Court held that a contract for hiring out a carriage was invalid, because it facilitated prostitution, which the Court qualified as an immoral purpose. Pearce had hired out a carriage to Brooks, who used it in the exercise of her profession (ie, prostitution). Since the Court held that Pearce had known about Brooks' profession, and the fact that she would use the carriage in exercising it, the contract was deemed invalid. Even though Pearce had denied knowledge, Judge Pollock CB held that 'If evidence is given which is sufficient to satisfy the jury of the fact of the immoral purpose, and of the plaintiffs' knowledge of it, and that the article was required and furnished to facilitate that object, it is sufficient, although the facts are not expressed with such plainness as would offend the sense of decency' (at 218).

[146] Prentice (n 132) nr 16-075 et seq. An example of an unreasonable restriction is an agreement under which a songwriter was obliged to offer his services exclusively for a period of five years to a publisher, while the latter was not obliged to publish or promote the work of the songwriter. The consideration only consisted thereof that the latter would receive royalties from published work. *A Schroeder Music Publishing Co Ltd v Macaulay* [1974] 1 WLR 1308.

[147] In *Horwood v Millar Timber and Trading Company Ltd* [1917] 1 KB 305, a case that dealt with a loan agreement that stipulated that the borrower, amongst others, could not relocate or sell his property without the consent of the lender, Lord Cozens Hardy MR, referred to the contract as to '*savour of serfdom*' (at 312). Lord Warrington LJ agreed with the invalidity of the contract, because 'Even in the most trivial incidents of life he cannot do as he pleases; he can only act in a way to which this money-lender will consent' (at 314). Lord Scrutton LJ, who was of the same opinion, stated that he could '(…) conceive nothing more dangerous to the interests of the public than (…) a system of money-lending like this (…)' (at 318).

rule out its invalidity, a conclusion as to contractual invalidity in the hypothetical sweatshop case lacks positive support.

However, changes can occur as to what courts consider as contrary to public policy. The role that the courts may play in prompting such a change has been controversial. In this respect, Prentice refers to the two sides of the debate representing a 'narrow' view and a 'broad' view.[148] Whereas the former denies the creation of new heads of public policy by courts, the latter accepts judicial law-making in the area of public policy. Although the doctrine of public policy is still perceived as conservative, the debate is now confined to creation of entirely new heads of public policy and it is the dominant opinion that courts can extend heads of public policy to cases constituting new situations and that public policy changes over time in accordance with developments in society's values.[149] Thus, although, as it stands, the contract in the hypothetical sweatshop case seems to steer clear of potential invalidity under English law, new developments may occur. For our hypothetical case, such a development may go in the direction of perceiving the contract for clothes made in a sweatshop as facilitating or assisting in activities that 'savour of slavery'. Therefore, although support for the hypothesis that the contract is invalid for immorality is thin under English law in light of the existing heads of public policy, given potential changes in public policy over time, it still is of interest to explore briefly the requirements regarding the contracting parties' knowledge for the hypothetical sweatshop case.

B. Knowledge of Both Contracting Parties

Under English law, the invalidity of a contract may follow from various connections between a contract's performance and activities deemed objectionable. For instance, a contract may require that a party engages in activities deemed objectionable; its performance may facilitate objectionable activities;[150] or it may be performed with objectionable means. With respect to these connections, it is not easy to discern clear-cut guidelines that can be used to determine the circumstances under which a particular contract will be held invalid by a court. However, in all cases where the contract is not objectionable prima facie, the contracting parties' knowledge regarding the objectionable activities (facts) is of decisive weight. Notably, in *Chitty on Contracts*, Prentice refers to four sets of circumstances under which contracts are not enforced[151] and both parties are prevented from suing on the contract entirely. Namely, if: 1) both knew that its performance necessarily

[148] Prentice (n 132) nr 16-004.

[149] Prentice (n 132) nr 16-004.

[150] See for instance, *Pearce v Brooks* (n 145) in which the contract was deemed invalid because the parties knew that it facilitated an immoral purpose, ie, prostitution.

[151] Which is distinct from the category of 'unenforceable contracts', which refers to contracts that are valid, yet 'one or both parties cannot be sued on the contract'. Whittaker (n 132) nr 1-084.

involved the commission of an act which, to their knowledge, is legally objectionable, that it is illegal or otherwise against public policy; 2) both knew that the contract is intended to be performed in a manner which to their knowledge is legally objectionable in that sense; 3) the purpose of the contract is legally objectionable and that purpose is shared by both parties; or 4) both participate in performing the contract in a manner which they know to be legally objectionable.[152]

It seems that the contract in the hypothetical case could fall under the first category: the necessary implication of the contract's performance entails the production of the clothes in a sweatshop and the contracting parties in our case are assumed to have been aware of that fact.[153] Moreover, if sweatshops would be considered to entail objectionable activities contrary to *public policy* according to courts, the contracting parties' awareness of these activities would be sufficient to render the contract invalid. Where the legal objectionability of the activities is based on a statute (eg, the activities are prohibited), contractual invalidity requires a higher degree of the parties' involvement in that reprehensible behaviour; mere knowledge does not suffice, but must either constitute intention or must be present in combination with participation.[154]

C. Concluding Remarks: Unlikely Invalidity in Light of Current Heads of Public Policy

The contract in our hypothetical case would not likely be held contrary to public policy under English law and thus the hypothesis of contractual invalidity seems weak. The existing heads of public policy do not appear to include the objectionability of the production of clothes in sweatshops elsewhere, which would render the contract void. Only if the contract would be considered contrary to public policy (as to performance), the knowledge of contracting parties would suffice for its invalidity. If legal objectionability would be based on unlawfulness, eg, relating to a statutory prohibition, the contract's invalidity would require a higher degree

[152] Prentice (n 132) nr 16-010.

[153] See 'Case Design', Chapter 4, section II, C.

[154] This would be different if the activities would be considered legally objectionable, because they are 'merely' prohibited, for instance, if it would become prohibited to import sweatshop goods. In such case, it is not only required that the parties were aware of the sweatshop production and the illegal import thereof, but that they participated therein. For instance, in *Ashmore, Benson, Pease & Co Ltd v AV Dawson Ltd* [1973] WLR 828, the Court held that parties could not sue on the contract, because they had participated in the illegal performance of it. Ashmore (…) and Dawson had agreed that the latter would transport two tube banks for the former, even though both were aware that Dawson did not have at his disposal suitable vehicles, which could legally transport them. The underlying motivation was the fact that this way the transport would be 'done cheaper' (Lord Denning MR at 833), ie, Ashmore contracted Dawson 'in order to economise on the job' (Lord Phillimore LJ at 834). Yet, the fact that the parties were aware that the transport could not take place legally was insufficient to bar the parties from suing, rather this was the case because the parties had also participated in the transport (ie, had observed the loading process).

of involvement, such as the parties' intention or participation in the activities disapproved of by the law. It seems unlikely that the contract in our hypothetical sweatshop case would be deemed invalid under English law, due to the contracting parties' knowledge of the contract's implication, ie, the production of clothes in sweatshops elsewhere.

VI. Comparative Conclusions

All the legal systems examined in the previous sections hold that the mutually beneficial character of a contract does not settle the question of contractual validity and build in space for the consideration of the interests of third parties or society as a whole. The case design aimed to test the hypothesis of immorality and invalidity and bring forward the potential decisive nature of the contracting parties' knowledge and the location of the sweatshop. These two factual aspects of the case represent two central pillars of objection against the hypothesis. Given the fact that the case has not been dealt with by a court—the contract has not yet been held immoral and invalid—the presented results are conjectural and the discussion is oriented towards the likelihood that courts will deem the contract in our hypothetical sweatshop case immoral and invalid.

From the previous sections we can see that the legal systems show considerable similarity in the underlying rationale and fundamental issues that come to the fore in our hypothetical case. Although private autonomy, expressed through the freedom to contract, represents a point of departure in contract laws in Europe, no jurisdiction assists in the realisation of a private transaction that is contrary to the society's values and in that sense inimical to the general interest. The contracts that are deemed contrary to a society's values are discussed under various national concepts such as immorality, illegality, public policy or public order, or good morals. These concepts express that in spite of the parties' potential interests in the contract's realisation through law, the courts can refuse to make such assistance available.

A. Knowledge

Under Dutch, German and English law it is of decisive importance for the contract's invalidity that *both* parties were aware that the clothes were produced in a sweatshop. If one of the parties were to deny such awareness (contrary to the design of the case study), it suffices that due to the circumstances of the case, the court would hold that this party should have been aware or must have been aware in the Netherlands and Germany. In this context, weight may be attached to media attention with regards to the sweatshop production of a specific product or corporation, and perhaps to the price of the product, although the latter would be an insufficient basis on its own. It is noteworthy that although knowledge is also a decisive requirement for contractual invalidity under French law, knowledge is only required by one of the parties corresponding to the case law of the *Cour de cassation* since 1998.

What is most striking is that the DCFR suggests the irrelevance of the parties' knowledge altogether. This approach is exceptional in the sense that it represents an approach that is uncommon among the national legal systems of Europe examined here. Under national rules of contract law, the absence of the knowledge of one (Netherlands, Germany, France) or both (France) of the contracting parties seems to sever, in relevant ways, the link or association between the moral concerns evoked by sweatshops elsewhere in the world and the transaction engaged in by contracting parties in Europe. The DCFR approach is of interest in light of the development in French law and the criticism expressed to the requirement of knowledge of both contracting parties' as it was overturned by the *Cour de cassation*. This requirement was criticised for undermining the protection of the general interest for the sake of the private interests of contracting parties. From this perspective the divergent knowledge requirements in national legal systems (both parties or one) and the DCFR (none/irrelevant), reveal divergences in the balance between the interests of the parties on the one hand, and the general interest or the interests of others on the other hand. In this sense, the suggested DCFR approach assigns relatively more weight to the latter, in comparison to the Netherlands, Germany and England where the interests of contracting parties appear to lead. In this context, the French requirements represent a middle ground position.

B. Sweatshop Location

The distance of the sweatshop's location from the contracting parties is a relevant feature of our hypothetical case in relation to the knowledge requirements discussed above, insofar as the former dissolves the degree of certainty that a party can have concerning the production conditions of the clothes sold. None of the legal systems, however, incorporate independent requirements regarding the geographical location of the objectionable aspect of a case, which would suggest that geographical distance does not dissolve immorality or sever the connection between the objectionable aspect of the case and the contractual behaviour. However, case law in Germany suggested that a question of German interest might arise in cases where the objectionable activities take place beyond national borders, affecting primarily the interests of others elsewhere in the world. Yet even in the case in which the *Bundesgerichtshof* discussed the question of German interest, and found no German interest at stake in relation to an objectionable activity, contractual immorality and invalidity still followed as a result of the infringement of fundamental values. Thus, the location of the sweatshop does not appear to be of decisive weight as an independent factor in any of the legal systems and as such provides no principled obstacle to the invalidity of the contract for immorality.

Moreover, the sweatshop's geographical location does not play a decisive role in any of the legal systems, to determine the substantive content of what is considered immoral. In all national legal systems, the content of contractual immorality relates to the underlying values of their own legal and social orders and it is the judiciary's task to interpret and concretise such fundamental values in specific cases. Moreover, the law develops in light of new cases that give rise to the opportunity to reflect changes in social and moral convictions occurring over time.

C. Concluding Remarks

With regard to the contract in our hypothetical case, this chapter shows that the hypothesis of contractual immorality and invalidity finds no principled obstacles in any of the jurisdictions. In spite of the absence thereof, the likelihood of the hypothetical contract's invalidity for immorality varies across the legal systems in light of the (absence of) obvious connections in the existing national case laws and the observations in legal scholarship regarding contractual morality in those national legal systems. The hypothesis of immorality and invalidity finds support in the existing case law regarding contractual invalidity in light of the contract's immoral foreseeable consequences under Dutch law. The *Hoge Raad*'s explicit reference to the exploitation of third parties provides support in this context. The decision as to how far the freedom to contract goes, and at what point the interests of third parties and society at large prevail, is a matter of balancing the conflicting interests. The developments in public opinion regarding sweatshops may play a decisive role. The same observation is to be made under German law where the contract's invalidity depends on whether the court would consider the contract's comprehensive character to be immoral, taking into account several aspects of the case including the question of the parties' knowledge of facts constituting the immorality. Compared to the Dutch approach, the German approach, which assesses the contract's comprehensive character, may leave more room for the consideration of the sweatshop's location. Under French law, the contract's invalidity depends on whether the production conditions of the clothes can be said to constitute the contract's 'cause' (*mobile déterminant*), and if so, whether it would be deemed 'illicite'. It seems that the contract's invalidity under French law would depend on whether the contracting parties could have entered the contract, if not for the sweatshop conditions. The knowledge requirements under French law—ie, that only one of the parties must possess the knowledge that the clothes were made in a sweatshop—however suggest that the interests of others and society as a whole may have comparatively more weight under French law than under Dutch or German law. The latter could provide additional support for the hypothesis of the contract's invalidity for immorality, but only marginally so. It seems least likely under English law that the hypothetical case will be held immoral and invalid. Although the contract's invalidity may follow in light of the necessary implications of its performance (the production of clothes under sweatshop conditions), the case is rather far removed from the established categories of transactions deemed contrary to public policy. The contract is, therefore, not likely to be held contrary to public policy unless the English courts are prepared to develop the law in this direction. As it stands, it seems unlikely that a European instrument of contract law would bring a change to these national outcomes. The latest proposal for a CESL is now up for modification in light of the Digital Single Market Strategy, but there is no indication that the modification would include a change of scope with regard to the exclusion of issues of contractual immorality and invalidity. Yet, the previous, academic proposal for a common frame of reference (DCFR) suggests a European approach, on the basis of which the contracting parties' knowledge, however, becomes irrelevant. The absence of knowledge requirements is, as we have seen, uncommon to the national jurisdictions included in the inquiry. Such a European approach would thus suggest a different balance of interests, placing comparatively more weight on the interests of others and society as a whole.

6

Conclusion

This book argues that a society that strives to be minimally just should not lend its power to the recognition and enforcement of contracts, the terms of which impair the basic capabilities of others elsewhere. Requirements of minimum justice bear on contract law, and have implications for how a society ought to define contractual relations. *Minimum contract justice* details some of these implications, sketching the defining structure of contractual relations in capability terms. It presents a capabilities perspective on minimum contract justice as it pertains to rules on contractual immorality and invalidity, and illustrates the implications through the example of a sweatshop test case. As such, it presents the question of contractual recognition of consumer transactions for sweatshop produced goods within the scope of social justice considerations. While predominantly presumed to count as 'normal' market transactions, minimum contract justice contests this view, and argues instead that consumer contracts for goods made in sweatshops do not meet the standards of permissible contractual conduct within a society that strives towards justice. In particular, contractual terms that necessarily involve production under deplorable conditions, should be deemed unacceptable under contractual regimes that serve as models for just market conduct. Alongside the book's normative case for minimum contract justice, the book also provides some insight into the way in which different contractual regimes in Europe would deal with the hypothetical case of a transaction for clothes made in a sweatshop. In tandem, the normative standard of minimum contract justice allows for a ranking of the outcomes of the inquiry into positive law. In this concluding chapter, minimum contract justice's viewpoint is brought together with the answers that various contract regimes provide to the question of contractual immorality and invalidity for the hypothetical case.

I. A Ranking of Contractual Regimes Based on Minimum Contract Justice

First, it is useful to recapitulate the book's understanding of the normative implications of a capabilities perspective on minimum justice within the realm of contract law, particularly as applied to contractual immorality and invalidity.

These implications derive from a conception of contract law that recognises its political function in establishing a just market order, and the role that rules of contractual validity play in constructing the institution of economic exchange recognised and supported by the state, ie, contract. Rules on contractual immorality and invalidity are part of the set of rules that outline the basic or defining structure of contract and they demarcate the realm of acceptable market conduct from unacceptable market conduct. As such, these rules reflect the minimum substantive standards for contractual conduct within that realm and are at the core of a legal regime that models just market conduct.

The normative implications of a capabilities perspective on minimum contract justice, as put forward in this book, identify unacceptable market relations as those that impair basic capabilities of the contracting parties themselves or of certain other (non-contracting) parties. The state should not make available its coercive power to realise such transactions, because this would run counter to the orientation of a decently just society. Namely, these transaction options are not expressions of valuable freedoms and are contrary to the political conception of the good that is ensconced in the idea of minimum contract justice informed by a capabilities perspective. This view does not exhaust claims of justice, but provides one illustration of what minimum justice requires of our society generally: its legal system should deny the recognition of transactions, as *contracts*, that impair the basic capabilities of others, whatever else a legal system may find unacceptable as market conduct under rules of contractual immorality and invalidity. The defining structure of contractual relations should reflect a society's commitment to the normative significance of basic capabilities.

From the perspective of minimum contract justice, so defined, there is no need for a complicated balancing of the contracting parties' interests against the interests of others in the hypothetical case of transactions of clothes made in sweatshops elsewhere. For the question of contractual immorality and invalidity, the interests of the contracting parties are not to be given decisive weight in the assessment. The predominant idea that consumers are weaker contracting parties in need of protection, often informs two assumptions about consumer contracts for sweatshop goods. First, consumers must have been misinformed or otherwise unaware that certain consumer goods are made under deplorable conditions. Second, consumers are unwilling to engage in exchange, if they know that the goods are made under deplorable conditions. The image of consumers as weaker contracting parties thus obscures the fact that consumers are able to make decisions, and may be willing to contract on terms that the state does not wish to endorse and support. Consumers are not entitled to the ability to buy products, or products at a certain price or within a certain time frame, that are made through the exploitation of others; and similarly, corporations are not entitled to the ability to obtain a profit from the production and sale of products made in sweatshops. By contrast, every human being is entitled to being able to work as a human being; an ability that is at stake for those who work in sweatshops. From a capabilities perspective, only the latter comes into view for considerations of minimum justice within a market order, and are thus subject to the requirements of minimum contract justice.

The capabilities perspective on minimum contract justice as articulated in this book concludes that legal systems, which are more likely to take account of the basic capabilities of others elsewhere in the assessment of contractual immorality and invalidity, do better in terms of shaping a just market order. Provided that contractual immorality allows for the consideration of the interests of others than those of the contracting parties, the assessment offers a response to the question of whose interests actually count and how they are considered in relation to the interests of contracting parties. This inquiry corresponds to two salient aspects of the hypothetical case represented in this book, which are identified as potential frontiers for minimum contract justice. First, the distance of the sweatshop in the hypothetical case raises the question as to whether or not the interests of others elsewhere in the world count in the assessment of contractual immorality at all. Second, the contracting parties' knowledge may be considered indicative of the weight attached to the interests of contracting parties. These factors play an important role in assessing the probability that the contract would be held immoral and invalid in a legal system in Europe, and thus offers an indication of how legal systems can be ranked in terms of minimum contract justice, in relation to the hypothetical case of transactions for clothes made in sweatshops elsewhere.

Although the distant location of the sweatshop does not appear to present a principled obstacle to the contract's immorality within any of the legal systems examined in this book, one should not easily assume that the contract will be held invalid, given the absence of strong connections between existing case law and the hypothetical case. Nevertheless, such connections are found in some legal systems more easily and convincingly than in others. In terms of minimum contract justice, the most favourable outcome of the test case is to be expected under Dutch law. Under this contract regime contractual invalidity follows from a contract's immoral foreseeable consequences. This includes a contract's immoral necessary implications, such as immoral conditions without which the contract could not have been performed. In this way, the exploitation of others elsewhere can qualify as a contract's immoral necessary implications. The independent importance of the contract's foreseeable consequences for the assessment of its immorality and consequent invalidity under Dutch law bodes well for the type of consideration that the basic capabilities of others should receive. If a court would consider the exploitation of others as a necessary implication of the contract in the hypothetical test case, those implications are sufficient for contractual invalidity. Under German contract law, a court is also likely to take account of the exploitation of others and consider deplorable production conditions as an implication of the contract. It is however less certain that this aspect of the case would be decisive for establishing the contract's comprehensive character as invalid for immorality under German law. The broader analysis leaves room for the conclusion that although the contract's implications may be deemed objectionable, the contract's comprehensive character would not be. The latter brings with it an uncertainty as to the conclusion of contractual immorality and invalidity in the hypothetical case, and thus leaves more room for a conclusion that runs counter to what is required by minimum contract justice.

However, the Dutch and the German approach are similar in that they strike a balance between the contracting parties' interests against those of others. This is reflected in the knowledge requirements for contractual immorality and invalidity. Both legal systems give decisive weight to the contracting parties' interests under circumstances in which they are considered unaware of the sweatshop conditions. This priority of the interests of contracting parties is not easily accounted for from the perspective of minimum contract justice. In this sense, French law is viewed more favourably, since it provides a balance requiring that only one of the parties is aware of the sweatshop conditions, thereby giving more weight to the interests of others. With regard to the hypothetical case, however, it remains uncertain whether the production conditions would be considered as the contract's *mobile determinant*, as the determining subjective reason for the transaction. Thus, it remains uncertain whether the outcome in the hypothetical case would be compatible with minimum contract justice as articulated in this book. The contract's invalidity seems least likely under English law, as it would depend on the willingness of the courts to develop the law more in this direction, which seems to go beyond the existing categories of immoral contracts. This does not appear likely given the controversial nature of developments in the case law that are not easily argued for under existing heads of public policy. The ranking of the national legal systems thus suggests diverse outcomes in terms of minimum contract justice as illustrated by the outcomes of the legal analysis.

Given the exclusion of rules regarding contractual immorality from its scope, the Common European Sales Law (CESL), a proposal for a European instrument of contract law, does not navigate between these diverse outcomes towards an outcome that is favoured as a matter of minimum contract justice. The Commission's Digital Single Market Strategy has not had an impact on the viewpoint that questions of contractual immorality reflect national, rather than a European outlook. As such, there is no (common) European legal rule that distinguishes between acceptable and unacceptable market conduct through a standard of contractual immorality. If a more comprehensive European instrument of contract law were to be developed and adopted in the future, the proposal for a Draft Common Frame of Reference (DCFR) would represent a preferred alternative from a perspective of minimum contract justice over the CESL and its successor. Minimum contract justice requires that priority is given to the importance of entitlements that pertain to minimum justice, ie, central capabilities, including those of others elsewhere, over other kinds of interests. If a uniform European standard of contractual immorality were to mature in compliance with this requirement, the contract in our hypothetical case would be held invalid under the respective European legal instrument. In short, consumer contracts for sweatshop goods would not be presumed to count as 'normal' market transactions, but would instead be regarded as examples of unacceptable market conduct. Moreover, if a uniform European standard of contractual immorality would be interpreted in conformity with the commentary on the DCFR, this would be favourable to the basic capabilities of others in the case of consumer contracts for sweatshop goods. Namely, with regard to the contracting parties' knowledge, the DCFR suggests that contractual immorality leads to invalidity even in the absence of the parties' knowledge regarding the sweatshop conditions under which the clothes were made. As such, the commentary suggests an approach to contractual immorality that is uncommon among national contractual regimes, as it pertains to the requirements of parties' knowledge. Though uncommon to the national regimes, this approach would be preferred from a viewpoint of minimum contract justice. Namely, it corresponds to the priority that minimum contract justice would give to the ability of individuals to work as human beings, ie, those who work in sweatshops, over the interests of contracting parties.

II. A Way Forward

This book suggests that a model for just market conduct should take account of the ways in which market transactions have an impact on the basic capabilities of others elsewhere in the world. If the necessary implications of transactional terms involve the impairment of the basic capabilities of others, legal systems should not recognise such transactions as contractual relations. Rules on contractual validity form the defining structure of contract and are subject to the requirements of minimum justice to which a society commits. This book, together with the conclusions regarding the likelihood of a transaction's invalidity for immorality in the examined legal systems in the case of consumer transactions for clothes made in sweatshops, offers three recommendations.

First, the book deals with an important issue for contract law theory, examining the legal recognitions of consumer transactions that impair the basic capabilities of others elsewhere. By treating this issue through a capabilities perspective, it offers a focus for the discussion of how theories of justice bear on this issue. To the extent that various legal theories include issues of social justice as legitimate concerns within the realm of contract, this book adds issues of global injustice to the range of justice considerations that ought to be included in discussions and questions of contract law. The increased and increasing interconnectedness between the lives people all over the world are able to live requires attentiveness to global justice concerns in the realm of contract law. It is no longer true that we are unaware of, or unable to decipher, the causal connections our market conduct has to the lives that others elsewhere are able to live. In particular, our consumption decisions are connected to the conditions under which our products are produced, and the terms of our transactions can have a severe negative impact on the lives of others elsewhere. The question of how we understand unacceptable externalities of market conduct in the case of sweatshop produced goods is an exercise in envisaging a contract law, and a just market order, that is attentive to those concerns. The fact that contract law is not the most effective and efficient instrument for contributing to a solution to global justice issues, does not require the absence of these kinds of questions in the realm of contract law. Contract law's minimum substantive standards for economic and social interactions cannot avoid reflecting a society's account of decency and justice towards others beyond national borders. If contract law fulfils the political function of constructing a just market order, the concern for the basic capabilities of others elsewhere should be, at least, a topic of debate in that context.

Second, the issue of contractual externalities beyond European geographical borders poses a challenge for the internal, common European market, and the idea that national legal systems should be the exclusive source for the minimum substantive standards for internal market relations. In leaving the question of what externalities are acceptable and unacceptable to the discretion of the Member States, the European Union cannot ensure that its internal market order will be compatible with a minimum standard of decency and justice. The EU should not be indifferent to the minimum standards that are applicable to conduct on its market. This position is entirely compatible with the idea that national contract regimes should not be replaced by a European regime altogether. National regimes and standards may be the appropriate sites of authority for domestic market conduct, yet it is not clear why the internal European market should be governed by a variety of national standards that each constructs a slightly different defining structure of contractual relations. In the case of externalities of transactions on the internal market especially, a European vision of minimum contract justice should be preferred over divergent national views. If the common, internal market is a European achievement, the ways in which transacting parties should behave towards each other and others ought to reflect the fundamental values and minimum standards espoused by the European Union. Moreover, by articulating concretely the implications of a capabilities perspective for the realm of contract law and specifically for the question of contractual invalidity in the case of transactions for clothes made in sweatshops, the book illustrates, in a slender fashion, an approach to making these issues accessible and debatable more broadly. If European standards will govern internal market conduct, such standards should be decided on in a European democratic forum.

Third, while contract may not be the most effective and efficient instrument through which to combat the problem of deplorable production conditions, this book offers an alternative avenue through which to pursue an activist agenda. As a legal strategy, bringing a contract case before the courts may support other attempts to advocate for and advance justice, and may offer an opportunity to improve contractual regimes in the direction suggested by minimum contract justice. This book offers the doctrinal argument through which to pursue minimum justice through contract. Namely, in order for contract laws to be compatible with the requirements of minimum contract justice, contractual immorality should be understood to encompass those cases in which transactions impair the basic capabilities of others. If courts are willing to develop the law in this direction, this book provides a moral argument engaging minimum contract justice, to support such a decision. For the courts to be able to develop the law in this direction, a test case could be brought forward, which is most likely to be successful under Dutch law, similar to our hypothetical case of a consumer contract regarding the sale of clothes produced in a sweatshop. This book offers the court not only a capabilities based argument of minimum contract justice, but also the legal points of departure through which it may motivate a decision of invalidity for immorality. For instance, the basic capabilities of others elsewhere could be taken into account in the assessment of contractual invalidity for immorality through reference to shared social norms. If sweatshops are contrary to widely shared social norms, these may inform the interpretation of contractual immorality. It may however, be more opportune to appeal to the social norms that have been ensconced within legal systems. In this context, it is particularly pertinent that this book's moral and doctrinal arguments dovetail well with the development of contract law constitutionalisation. Constitutionalisation allows fundamental rights argumentation to inform and inspire the interpretation of contract law's open norms, such as contractual immorality. The arguments of minimum contract justice could be compellingly formulated and translated into fundamental rights argumentation, which would amount to an extension of contract law constitutionalisation by suggesting that fundamental entitlements (ie, the basic capabilities) of others should be taken into account when assessing the market conduct of private actors. If contractual regimes developed in the direction that minimum contract justice proposes, the latter would gain explanatory power within the realm of contract theory. As it stands, minimum contract justice simply offers a normative, justificatory account for the invalidity of transactions that impair the basic capabilities of others elsewhere, such as consumer contracts for sweatshop goods.

BIBLIOGRAPHY

Alexander, JM, 'Ending the Liberal Hegemony: Republican Freedom and Amartya Sen's Theory of Capabilities' (2010) 9 Contemporary Political Theory 5–24

Anderson, E, 'What is the Point of Equality?' (1999) 109 *Ethics* 287–337

Appelbaum, RP et al, 'The End of Apparel Quotas: A Faster Race to the Bottom?' http://escholarship.org/uc/item/40f8w19g

Armbrüster, 'Münchener Kommentar zum Bürgerlichen Gesetzbuch (BGB) 6 Auflage 2012' (Beck Juristischer Verlag, 2012)

Armbruster-Sandoval, R, *Globalization and Cross-border Labor Solidarity in the Americas: the Anti-Sweatshop Movement and the Struggle for Social Justice* (Routledge, 2005)

Arneson, RJ, 'Perfectionism and Politics' (2000) 111 *Ethics* 37–63

Arnold, DG and NE Bowie, 'Sweatshops and Respect for Persons' (2003) 13 *Business Ethics Quarterly* 221–242

—— and LP Hartman, 'Worker Rights and Low Wage Industrialization: How to Avoid Sweatshops' (2006) 28 *Human Rights Quarterly* 676–700

Asser/Hartkamp & Sieburgh 6-III (ed), *Mr. Asser's Handleiding tot beoefening van het Nederlandse recht. 6. Algemeen overeenkomstenrecht* (Kluwer, 2010)

Atiyah, PS, *The Rise and Fall of Freedom of Contract* (Clarendon, 1979)

—— and SA Smith, *Atiyah's Introduction to the Law of Contract* (Oxford University Press, 2005)

Auger, P et al, 'What Will Consumers Pay for Social Product Features' (2003) 42 *Journal of Business Ethics* 281–304

Bagchi, AK, 'Freedom and Development as End of Alienation?' (2000) 35 *Economic and Political Weekly* 4408–20

Bagchi, A, 'Other People's Contracts' (2015) available at http://papers.ssrn.com/sol3/papers.cfm?abstract_id=2586136

Bales, K, *Disposable People. New Slavery in the Global Economy* (University of California Press, 2004)

Basedow, J et al (eds), *The Max Planck Encyclopedia of European Private Law Volume I* (Oxford University Press, 2012)

——, *The Max Planck Encyclopedia of European Private Law Volume II* (Oxford University Press, Oxford 2012)

Baye, MR, *Managerial Economic and Business Stategy*, 4th International Edition (McGraw-Hill, 2002)

Beck, U, *What is Globalization?* (Wiley, 2000)

Benvenisti, E, 'Sovereigns as Trustees of Humanity: On the Accountability of States to Foreign Stakeholders' (2013) 107 *The American Journal of International Law* 295–333

Betlem, G, 'Transnational Litigation against Multinational Corporations before Dutch Civil Courts' in M Kamminga and S Zia-Zarifi (eds), *Liability of Multinational Corporations under International Law* (Kluwer International Law, 2000)

Biondi, F, 'Is Martha Nussbaum really Political Liberal?' (2008) 94 *Archiv für Rechts- und Sozialphilosophie* 311–24

Bonacich, E and RP Appelbaum, *Behind the Label: Inequality in the Los Angeles Apparel Industry* (University of California Press, 2000)

Bonell, MJ, 'The New Provisions on Illegality in the UNIDROIT Principles 2010' (2011) 16 *Uniform Law Review* 517–36

Busch, C and H Schulte-Nölke (eds), *Fundamental Rights and Private Law* (Sellier, 2011)

Busch, D et al (eds), *The Principles of European Contract Law (Part III) and Dutch Law* (Kluwer Law International, 2006)

Bussani, M and U Mattei, 'The Common Core Approach to European Private Law' (1997) 3 *Columbia Journal of European Law* 339–56

Cahen, JLP, *Overeenkomst en derden*, 2nd edn (Monografieën Nieuw BW B-57, Kluwer, 2004)

Cartwright, J and MW Hesselink (eds), *Precontractual Liability in European Private Law* (The Common Core of European Private Law, Cambridge University Press, 2008)

Cartwright, J et al. (eds), Reforming the French Law of Obligations. Reflections on the Avant-projet de réfrome du droit des obligations et de la prescription ('the Avant-projet Catala') (Hart Publishing, 2009)

Castermans, AG, *De burger in het burgerlijk recht. Of de eigenschappen van perensap* (Boom Juridische Uitgevers, 2009)

—— and JA van der Weide, 'The Legal Liability of Dutch Parent Companies for Subsidiaries' Involvement in Violations of Fundamental, Internationally Recognized Rights' (Commissioned by the Ministry of Economic Affairs, 2009)

Chartier, G, 'Sweatshops, Labor Rights, and Competitive Advantage' (2008) 10 *Oregon Review of International Law* 149–88

Clapham, A, 'The Question of Jurisdiction under International Criminal Law over Legal Persons: Lessons from the Rome Conference on an International Criminal Court' in M Kamminga and S Zia-Zarifi (eds), *Liability of Multinational Corporations under International Law* (Kluwer International Law, 2000)

Collins, H, *Regulating Contracts* (Oxford University Press, 1999)

——, *The Law of Contract*, 4th edn (Cambridge University Press, 2003)

Crocker, D, 'Functioning and Capability: The Foundations of Sen's and Nussbaum's Development Ethic' (1992) 20 *Political Theory* 584–612

Crowe, J, 'Does Control Make a Difference? The Moral Foundations of Shareholder Liability for Corporate Wrongs' (2012) 75 *Modern Law Review*

Dagan, H, 'Autonomy, Pluralism and Contract Law Theory' (2013) 76 *Law and Contemporary Problems* 19–38

——, 'The Utopian Promise of Contract Law' (2016 Forthcoming) *University of Toronto Law Journal*

Davies, G, 'Process and Product Method-based Trade Restrictions in the EU' in C Barnard (ed), *Cambridge Yearbook of European Legal Studies* (Hart Publishing, 2008)

De Greiff, P and C Cronin (eds), *Global Justice and Transnational Politics: Essays on the Moral and Political Challenges of Globalization* (Studies in Contemporary German Social Thought, MIT Press, 2002)

Deakin, S, '"Capacitas": Contract Law and the Institutional Preconditions of a Market Economy' (2006) 2 *European Review of Private Law* 317–41

——, 'Contracts and Capabilities: An Evolutionary Perspective on the Autonomy-Paternalism Debate' (2010) 3 *Erasmus Law Review* 141–53

—— and A Supiot (eds), *Capacitas: Contract Law and the Institutional Preconditions of a Market Economy* (Hart Publishing, 2009)

Deneulin, S and L Shahani (eds), *An Introduction to the Human Development and Capability Approach* (Earthscan, 2009)

Du Perron, E, 'Contract and Third Parties' in A Hartkamp et al (eds), *Towards a European Civil Code*, 2nd edn (Kluwer Law International, 1998)

——, *Overeenkomst en derden* (Kluwer Rechtswetenschappelijke Publicaties, 1999)

Ehrich, KR and JR Irwin, 'Willful Ignorance in the Request for Product Attribute Information' (2005) 42 *Journal of Marketing Research* 266–77

Eijsbouts, AJAJ et al, *Maatschappelijk verantwoord ondernemen* (Handelingen Nederlandse Juristen-Vereniging, Kluwer, 2010)

Ellenberger, J, *Palandt Bürgerliches Gesetzbuch* (69. Auflage edn Verlag CH Beck, 2010)

Ercel, K, 'Orientalization of Exploitation' (2006) 18 *Rethinking Marxism: A Journal of Economics, Culture & Society* 289–306

Esbenshade, J, *Monitoring Sweatshops: Workers, Consumers, and the Global Apparel Industry* (Temple University Press, 2004)

Fabre-Magnan, M, *Droit de Obligations. 1-Contrat et engagement unilatéral* (Presses Universitaires de France, 2012)

Fenouillet, D, 'Les bonnes moeurs sont mortes! Vive l'ordre public philanthropique' in *Le droit privé francais à la fin du XXème siècle, Etudes offertes à Pierre Catala* (Litec, 2001)

Follesdal, A, 'The Distributive Justice of a Global Basic Structure: A Category Mistake?' (2011) 10 *Politics, Philosophy & Economics* 46–65

Fries, M, 'Stressforscher im Sweatshop' *Zeit Online* www.zeit.de/studium/uni-leben/2011-02/interview-bangladesch, accessed 21 September 2015

Gatto, A, *Multinational Enterprises and Human Rights* (Edward Elgar Publishing Ltd, 2011)

Ghestin, J, *Cause de l'engagement et validité du contrat* (Libraire Générale de Droit et de Jurisprudence, 2006)

Giddens, A, *The Consequences of Modernity* (Stanford University Press, 1990)

Gordley, J, *Foundations of Private Law* (Oxford University Press, 2007)

Gray, LC, 'Economic Efficiency and Competitive Advantage of Slavery under the Plantation System' (1930) 4 *Agricultural History* 31–47

Hearson, M, 'Cashing In' (Clean Clothes Campaign, 2009)

Hesselink, MW, 'The Politics of a European Civil Code' (2004) 10 *European Law Journal* 675–697

——, 'Capacity and Capability in European Contract Law' (2005) 13 *European Review of Private Law* 491–507

——, *CFR & Social Justice* (Sellier European Law Publishers, 2008)

——, 'A European Legal Method? On European Private Law and Scientific Method' (2008) 15 *European Law Journal* 20–45

——, 'The Case for a Common European Sales Law in an Age of Rising Nationalism' (2012) 3 *European Review of Contract Law*

Hiscox, MJ et al, 'Consumer Demand for Fair Trade: New Evidence from a Field Experiment Using eBay Auctions of Fresh Roasted Coffee' www.papers.ssrn.com/sol3/papers.cfm?abstract_id=1811783

Horwitz, MJ, 'The History of the Public Private Distinction' (1982) 130 *University of Pennsylvania Law Review* 1423–28

Joerges, C, 'The Impact of European Integration on Private Law: Reductionist Perceptions, True Conflicts and a New Constitutional Perspective' (1997) 3 *European Law Journal* 378–406

——, 'European Challenges to Private Law: On False Dichotomies, True Conflicts and the Need for a Constitutional Perspective' (1998) 18 *Legal Studies* 146–66

Johnston, A, 'Facing Up to Social Cost' (2011) 20 *Griffith Law Review* 221–44

Kamminga, M and S Zia-Zarifi (eds), *Liability of Multinational Corporations under International Law* (Kluwer International Law, 2000)

Katz, ML and HS Rosen, *Microeconomics*, 2nd edn (Irwin, 2009)

Katzer, M, 'The Basis of Universal Liberal Principles in Nussbaum's Political Philosophy' (2010) 2 *Public Reason* 60–75

Kennedy, D, 'Form and Substance in Private Law Adjudication' (1976) 89 *Harvard Law Review* 1685–1778

——, 'The Political Stakes in "Merely Technical" Issues of Contract Law' (2002) 10 *European Review of Private Law* 7–28

Klein, N, *No Logo* (Macmillan, 2003)

Köhler, H, *BGB Allgemeiner Teil* (33. Auflage edn Verlag CH Beck, 2009)

Kordana, KA and DH Tabachnick, 'Rawls and Contract Law' (2005) 73 *The George Washington Law Review* 598–632

Kötz, H and A Flessner, *European Contract Law. Volume One: Formation, Validity, and Content of Contracts. Contract and Third Parties* (Clarendon Press, 1997).

Kristen, FGH, 'Maatschappelijk verantwoord ondernemen en strafrecht' in AJAJ Eijsbouts et al, *Maatschappelijk verantwoord ondernemen* (Handelingen Nederlandse Juristen-Vereniging, Kluwer, 2010)

Kristof, ND, 'Where Sweatshops Are a Dream' *The New York Times Online Edition* www.nytimes.com/2009/01/15/opinion/15kristof.html

—— and S Wudunn, 'Two Cheers for Sweatshops' *The New York Times Online Edition* www.nytimes.com/2000/09/24/magazine/two-cheers-for-sweatshops.html?pagewanted=all&src=pm

Kronman, AT, 'Contract Law and Distributive Justice' (1980) 89 *The Yale Law Journal* 472–511

Krugman, P, 'In Praise of Cheap Labor' *Slate* www.slate.com/articles/business/the_dismal_science/1997/03/in_praise_of_cheap_labor.html

Kumm, M, 'The Cosmopolitan Turn in Constitutionalism: An Integrated Conception of Public Law' (2013) 20 *Indiana Journal of Global Legal Studies* 605–28

Kysar, DA, 'Preferences for Processes: The Process/Product Distinction and the Regulation of Consumer Choice' (2004) 118 *Harvard Law Review* 526–642

Lando, O and H Beale (eds), *The Principles of European Contract Law Parts I and II* (Kluwer Law International, 1999)

Lando, O et al (eds), *Principles of European Contract Law, Part III* (Kluwer Law International, 2003)

Legrand, P, 'Against a European Civil Code' (1997) 60 *The Modern Law Review* 44–63

Lipschutz, RD, 'Sweating it Out: NGO Campaigns and Trade Union Empowerment' (2004) 14 *Development in Practice* 197–209

—— and K James, *Globalization, Governmentality and Global Politics* (Routledge, 2005)

Loth, MA, *Dwingend en aanvullend recht* (Monografieën Nieuw BW A-19, Kluwer, 2009)

Mak, C, *Fundamental Rights in European Contract Law* (Private Law in European Context Series, Wolters Kluwer, 2008)

——, 'Constitutional Aspects of a European Civil Code' in AS Hartkamp et al (eds), *Towards a European Civil Code* (Kluwer Law, 2011)
——, 'Europe-Building Through Private Law: Lessons from Constitutional Theory' (2012) 8 *European Review of Contract Law* 326–41
Mattei, U, 'Hard Code Now!' (2002) 2 *Global Jurist Frontiers* 1–26
Mayer-Maly, T, 'Was Leisten die guten Sitten?' (1994) 194 *Archiv für die civilistische Praxis* 105–76
McKendrick, E, *Contract Law* (Palgrave Macmillan, 2009)
Mekki, M, *L'intérêt Général et le Contrat* (Libraire Générale de Droit et de Jurisprudence, 2004)
Meyers, C, 'Wrongful Beneficence: Exploitation and Third World Sweatshops' (2004) 35 *Journal of Social Philosophy* 319–33
——, 'Moral Duty, Individual Responsibility, and Sweatshop Exploitation' (2007) 38 *Journal of Social Philosophy* 620–26
Michaels, R, 'The Functional Method of Comparative Law' in M Reimann and R Zimmermann (eds), *The Oxford Handbook of Comparative Law* (Oxford University Press, 2006)
Micklitz, HW (ed), *The Many Concepts of Social Justice in European Private Law* (Edward Elgar Publishing Ltd, 2011)
Miller, J, 'Why Economists Are Wrong About Sweatshops and the Antisweatshop Movement' (2003) 46 *Challenge* 93–122
Murphy, L, 'Institutions and the Demands of Justice' (1999) 27 *Philosophy & Public Affairs* 251–291
Nollkaemper, A, 'Public International Law in Transnational Litigation against Multinational Corporations: Prospects and problems in the Courts of the Netherlands' in M Kamminga and S Zia-Zarifi (eds), *Liability of Multinational Corporations under International Law* (Kluwer International Law, 2000)
Nussbaum, M, 'Nature, Function and Capability' (1988) 1 *Oxford Studies on Ancient Philosophy* 145–84
——, 'Human Functioning and Social Justice: In Defence of Aristotelian Essentialism' (1992) 20 *Political Theory* 202–46
——, 'Aristotle on Human Nature and the Foundations of Ethics' in J Altham and R Harrison (eds), *World, Mind, and Ethics* (Cambridge University Press, 1995)
——, 'Capabilities and Human Rights' (1997) 66 *Fordham Law Review* 273–300
——, 'The Good as Discipline, the Good as Freedom' in DA Crocker and T Linden (eds), *Ethics of Consumption* (Rowman & Littlefield Publishers, 1998)
——, *Women and Human Development: The Capabilities Approach* (Cambridge University Press, 2000)
——, 'Aristotle, Politics, and Human Capabilities: A Response to Antony, Arneson, Charlesworth, and Mulgan' (2000) 111 *Ethics* 102–40
——, 'Capabilities as Fundamental Entitlements: Sen and Social Justice' (2003) 9 *Feminist Economics* 33–59
——, 'Women's Bodies: Violence, Security, Capabilities' (2005) 6 *Journal of Human Development and Capabilities* 167–83
——, *Frontiers of Justice* (Harvard University Press, 2006)
——, 'Reply: In Defence of Global Political Liberalism' (2006) 37 *Development and Change* 1313–28

——, 'The Supreme Court 2006 Term Foreword: Constitutions and Capabilities: "Perception" against Lofty Formalism' (2007) 121 *Harvard Law Review* 4–97

——, *Creating Capabilities* (The Belknap Press of Harvard University Press, 2011)

——, 'Perfectionist Liberalism and Political Liberalism' (2011) 39 *Philosophy and Public Affairs* 3–45

Pogge, T, *World Poverty and Human Rights* (Polity Press, 2002)

Powell, B, 'In Reply to Sweatshop Sophistries' (2006) 28 *Human Rights Quarterly* 1031–42

—— and D Skarbek, 'Sweatshops and Third World Living Standards: Are the Jobs Worth the Sweat?' (2006) XXVII *Journal of Labor Research* 263–73

—— and M Zwolinski, 'The Ethical and Economic Case Against Sweatshop Labor: A Critical Asessment' (2012) 107 *Journal of Business Ethics* 449–72

Prentice, DD, 'Illegality and Public Policy' in H Beale and AS Burrows (eds), *Chitty on Contracts Volume 1 General Principles* (Sweet & Maxwell, 2008)

Rawls, J, *A Theory of Justice* (Harvard University Press, 1971)

——, *Political Liberalism* (Columbia University Press, 1993)

——, *The Law of Peoples*, 4th edn (Harvard University Press, 2002)

Reding, V, 'The Common European Sales Law—Breaking the Mould to Help Businesses and Customers Realising the European Single Market' (Vice-President of the European Commission, EU Justice Commissioner) SPEECH/12/164 Forum Europe Brussels *Press release*

Reehuis, WHM and EE Slob, *Parlementaire Geschiedenis van het Nieuw Burgerlijk Wetboek, Invoering boeken 3,5 en 6, Boek 3, Vermogensrecht in het Algemeen* (Kluwer, 1990)

Ripstein, A, 'Private Order and Public Justice: Kant and Rawls' (2006) 92 *Virginia Law Review* 1391–1438

Robeyns, I, 'The Capability Approach: A Theoretical Survey' (2005) 6 *Journal of Human Development* 93–114

Rochefeld, J, 'A Future for la Cause? Observations of a French Jurist' in J Cartwright et al (eds), *Reforming the French Law of Obligations Comparative Reflections on the Avant-projet de réforme du droit des obligations et de la prescription* ('the Avant-projet Catala') (Hart Publishing, 2009)

Rose, N, 'Beyond the Public Private Distinction—Law, Power and the Family' (1987) 14 *Journal of Law and Society* 61–76

Rosen, EI, *Making Sweatshops: The Globalization of the U.S. Apparel Industry* (University of California Press, 2002)

Ross, RJS, *Slaves to Fashion* (University of Michigan Press, 2004)

Rothstein, R, 'Defending Sweatshops' (2005) *Dissent* 41–47

Rugman, AM, *International Business*, 3rd edn (Prentice Hall, 2003)

Rutgers, J (ed), *European Contract Law and the Welfare State* (European Studies in Private Law (4), Europa Law Publishing, 2012)

Sacco, R, 'Legal Formants: A Dynamic Approach to Comparative Law (Installment I of II)' (1991) 39 *The American Journal of Comparative Law* 343–401

Sack, R, 'Das Anstandsgefühl aller billig und gerecht Denkenden und die Moral als Bestimmungsfaktoren der guten Sitten' (1985) 14 *Neue Juristische Wochenschrift* 761–824

Sample, RJ, *Exploitation. What It Is and Why It's Wrong* (Rowman & Littlefield Publishers, 2003)

Sandel, M, 'What Money Can't Buy: The Moral Limits of Markets' (1998) *The Tanner Lectures on Human Values*

Scheffler, S, 'Distributive Justice, the Basic Structure and the Place of Private Law' (2015) *Oxford Journals of Legal Studies* 1–23

Schmid, CU, 'The Instrumentalist Conception of the Acquis Communautaire in Consumer Law and its Implications on a European Contract Law Code' (2005) 2 *European Review of Contract Law* 211–27

Schwartz, LB, 'With Gun and Camera through Darkest CLS-Land' (1984) 36 *Stanford Law Review* 413–64

Sen, A, 'Equality of What?' in McMurrin (ed), *Tanner Lectures on Human Values* (Cambridge University Press, 1982)

——, *Inequality Reexamined* (Oxford University Press, 1992)

——, *Commodities and Capabilities* (Oxford University Press, 1999)

——, *Development as Freedom* (Oxford University Press, 1999)

——, 'Capabilities, Lists, and Public Reason: Continuing the Conversation' (2004) 10 *Feminist Economics* 77–80

——, *The Idea of Justice* (Allen Lane, 2009)

Shavell, S, *Foundations of Economic Analysis of Law* (Belknap Harvard, 2004)

Shiffrin, SV, 'Paternalism, Unconscionability, and Accomodation' (2000) 29 *Philosophy and Public Affairs* 205–50

Sieburgh, C, *Tertium datur: de niet uitgesloten derde in het burgerlijk recht* (Kluwer, 2004)

Singer, P, 'Famine, Affluence, and Morality' (1972) 1 *Philosophy and Public Affairs* 229–43

Singer, JW, 'Things that We Would Like to Take for Granted: Minimum Standards for the Legal Framework of a Free and Democratic Society' (2008) 2 *Harvard Law & Policy Review* 139–59

Smith, SA, *Contract Theory* (Oxford University, 2004)

Snyder, JC, 'Needs Exploitation' (2008) 11 *Ethic Theory Moral Practice* 389–405

Study Group on a European Civil Code and Research Group on EC Private Law (ed), *Draft Common Frame of Reference* (Sellier, 2009)

Study Group on Social Justice in European Private Law, 'Social Justice in European Contract Law: A Manifesto' (2004) 10 *European Law Journal* 653–74

Terré, F, *Pour une Réforme du Droit des Contrats* (Dalloz, 2009)

—— et al, *Droit Civil: Les Obligations* (Dalloz, 2009)

Teubner, G, *Standards und Direktiven in Generalklauseln* (Athenäum Verlag, 1971)

Tjong Tjin Tai, TFE, *Over de grenzen van het privaatrecht* (Tilburg University, 2011)

Van Dam, C, *Onderneming & Mensenrechten* (Boom Juridische Uitgevers, 2008)

Van den Brink, V, *De Rechtshandeling in strijd met de goede zeden* (Boom Juridische Uitgevers, 2002)

——, 'Artikel 3:40 onder het mes?' (2012) 44 *Nederlands Tijdschrift Burgerlijk Recht*

Van Es, A, 'Gevangen tussen fabrieksmuren voor bruidsschat' *De Volkskrant, Online Edition* www.volkskrant.nl/vk/nl/2844/Archief/archief/article/detail/1020348/2010/09/04/Gevangen-tussen-fabrieksmuren-voor-bruidsschat.dhtml

Van der Hulst, A, 'Snelle mode, onveilige arbeidsomstandigheden' *Het NRC Handelsblad, Online Edition* www.nrc.nl/carriere/2013/02/08/snelle-mode-onveilige-arbeidsomst andigheden/

Van der Weele, JJ, 'When Ignorance is Innocence: On Information Avoidance in Moral Dilemmas' http://paperssrncom/sol3/paperscfm?abstract_id=1844702

Van Kooten, HJ, *Restitutierechtelijke aspecten van ongeoorloofde overeenkomsten* (Kluwer, 2002)

——, 'Burgerlijk Wetboek 3, Artikel 40' in *Groene Serie Vermogensrecht* (2012)
Van Schaick, AC, *Contractsvrijheid en Nietigheid* (WEJ Tjeenk Willink, 1994)
Van Zeben, CJ et al, *Parlementaire Geschiedenis van het Nieuw Burgerlijk Wetboek, Boek 3, Vermogensrecht in het Algemeen* (Kluwer, 1981)
Varian, HR, *Microeconomic Analysis* (WW Norton & Company, 2006)
Varley, P et al, *The Sweatshop Quandary: Corporate Responsibility on the Global Frontier* (Investor Responsibility Research Center, 1998)
Venzke, I, 'Making General Exceptions: The Spell of Precedents in Developing Article XX GATT into Standards for Domestic Regulatory Policy' (2011) 12 *German Law Journal* 1111–40
Warendorf, H et al, *The Civil Code of the Netherlands*, (Kluwer Law International, 2009)
Weinrib, EJ, *The Idea of Private Law* (Harvard University Press, 1995)
——, *Corrective Justice* (Oxford University Press, 2012)
Whittaker, S, 'Introductory' in H Beale and AS Burrows (eds), *Chitty on Contracts Volume 1 General Principles* (Sweet & Maxwell, 2008)
Wilhelmsson, T, 'Varieties of Welfarism in European Contract Law' (2004) 10 *European Law Journal* 712–33
Young, IM, 'Responsibility and Global Labor Justice' (2004) 12 *The Journal of Political Philosophy* 365–88
Zweigert, K and H Kötz, *An Introduction to Comparative Law*, 3rd revised edn (Oxford University Press, 1998)
Zwolinski, M, 'Sweatshops, Choice, and Exploitation' (2007) 17 *Business Ethics Quarterly* 689–727
——, 'Structural Exploitation' (2012) 29 *Social Philosophy and Policy* 154–79

INDEX